TEACHING VALUES IN THE LITERATURE CLASSROOM

A Debate in Print

A Public School View
by Charles Suhor

A Catholic School View
by Bernard Suhor

 Clearinghouse on Reading
and Communication Skills

 PRESS

 National Council of
Teachers of English

S0-AGT-626

A Public School View by Charles Suhor

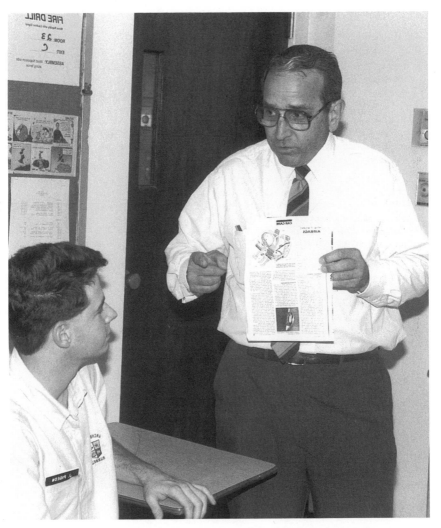

A Catholic School View by Bernard Suhor

Published 1992 by the ERIC Clearinghouse on Reading and Communication Skills, Carl B. Smith, Director; Indiana University, 2805 East 10th Street, Suite 150, Bloomington, Indiana 47408-2698 in cooperation with the EDINFO Press, Carl B. Smith, Director, and the National Council of Teachers of English, 111 Kenyon Road, Urbana, Illinois 61801.

Editor: Warren Lewis
Cover Design: Lauren Gottlieb
Design: Lauren Gottlieb
Production: Theresa Hardy, Carolyn McGowen

NCTE stock number: 52376-3050   ERIC stock number: G31

ERIC (an acronym for Educational Resources Information Center) is a national network of 16 clearinghouses, each of which is responsible for building the ERIC database by identifying and abstracting various educational resources, including research reports, curriculum guides, conference papers, journal articles, and government reports. The Clearinghouse on Reading and Communication Skills (ERIC/RCS) collects educational information specifically related to reading, English, journalism, speech, and theater at all levels. ERIC/RCS also covers interdisciplinary areas, such as media studies, reading and writing technology, mass communication, language arts, critical thinking, literature, and many aspects of literacy.

This publication was prepared with funding from the Office of Educational Research and Improvement, U.S. Department of Education, under contract no. RI88062001. Contractors undertaking such projects under government sponsorship are encouraged to express freely their judgment in professional and technical matters. Points of view or opinions, however, do not necessarily represent the official view or opinions of the Office of Educational Research and Improvement.

Library of Congress Cataloging-in-Publication Data

Suhor, Bernard.
    Teaching values in the literature classroom: a debate in print / a Catholic school view by Bernard Suhor; a public school view by Charles Suhor.
        p.   cm.
    Includes bibliographical references (p. 181).
    1. Literature—Study and teaching (Secondary)—Moral and ethical aspects.
m 2. Values in literature I.   Suhor, Charles. II. Title.
PN61.S87   1992   92-10117
807'.1'2—dc20.   CIP

ISBN 0-927516-32-2

Dedications

To my New Orleans mentors and colleagues:

Edwin Friedrich, Lou LaBrant,
Cresap Watson, and Velez Wilson

Charles Suhor

To my beloved mentors:

the Benedictine monks of St. Joseph Abbey,
especially Fr. Andrew Becnel and Fr. David Melancon

and to all colleagues, past and present:
especially the ever-devoted School Sisters of Notre Dame,
and five fabulous teaching comrades:
Jim Galendez, Skeeter Theard, Earl Mylie,
Art Schmitt, and Al Armbruster

Bernard Suhor

To our parents, Anthony B. Suhor and Marie Suhor

Bernard and Charles Suhor

Table of Contents

Religion at School:
A Word from the Moderator

Carl B. Smith

The Hot Political Climate of the Values Debate

A debate is raging in America over the values being taught in the public schools. Ought moral, ethical, social, and religious values of any kind be taught or inculcated or clarified in the public-school setting, at the taxpayer's expense, in the presence of impressionable students who are under the control of their teacher, but with whose values they and their parents may not agree? More specifically, ought the values embodied in the writings typically read in English-literature classrooms be advocated by the teachers, or ought the literary and historical discussion of meaningful texts be used by teachers as an opportunity to help students work towards clarity about their own sets of values?

Educators do not agree; parents do not agree; politicians and judges do not agree.

In 1983, Federal District Judge Thomas G. Hull ruled in favor of a group of Christian fundamentalist parents against the school authorities, that children ought not to have to read books about Cinderella, the Wizard of Oz, and the Horse God, if the parents find the books religiously objectionable. The judge ordered the school system to permit the parents to teach reading at home. His ruling was reversed, however, by the Court of Appeals for the 6th Circuit, which ruled that the children had to read whatever the school prescribed.[1]

In Alabama, Federal District Judge W. Brevard Hand ruled that "for purposes of the First Amendment, secular humanism is a religious belief system," and he ordered that 44 elementary and secondary textbooks be removed from the public schools. The Court of Appeals for the 11th Circuit, however, overturned this judicial definition of secular humanism, and no further appeal was made. "Secular humanism" had become fighting words in 1982 during the fundamentalist crusade against sex education in a Corvallis, Oregon, high school.[2] "Secular humanism" continues to be perceived as the enemy standard to be knocked down by conservative religionists,[3] and it is so targeted by one of the contestants in this debate.

Whether the issue be "secular humanism" or any number of other matters of conflict—the teaching of evolution; the use of swear words, and the mention of sex and Satan(ism) in books in the school library; and education in schools about sexuality and sexually-transmitted diseases (such as AIDS)[4]—the lines of debate are drawn, and people are taking sides. In 1974-75 in Kanawha County, West Virginia, a battle over the books escalated into a shooting war when some parents protested against their children being required to read texts that, in their opinion, "demean, encourage skepticism, or foster disbelief in the institutions of the United States of America and in western civilization."[5] Since that time, a wide range of organized groups and lobbies have arrayed themselves against one another at schools, in the streets, and especially in the courts. People for the American Way, who have taken an annual survey of the battlefield over the past decade, reported in 1990 no fewer than 244 engagements in 39 States and every region of the country.[6] Although each one of these incidents is local, none is isolated or unrelated. The all-out war over values at school is, in the final analysis, a nationwide struggle over control of the schools and their curricula, and there are more than just two sides. Some values *shall* be taught: that is unavoidable; the question is *which* values, *whose* values, and *how* they shall be taught.

A Debate between Brothers

The present debate on teaching values in the English classroom is another engagement in the ongoing struggle to shape the value structures of young Americans. This time, we forego fire-bombs and vituperation for sweetly reasonable exchanges between two brothers, Ben and Charlie Suhor. We are still very far from resolution, but the issues become clearer, here, because there is more light and less smoke, even though the fires do burn hotly.

Bernard Suhor

Ben is a devout Roman Catholic who passionately affirms the English teacher's responsibility to instruct students in Christian moral values when those values are represented in the literature being read and discussed in class. Ben takes his teaching personally and his students' moral welfare to heart. He believes that when high-school teenagers come to *you*, the English teacher, for advice on sex or God or drugs or anything else, you owe those kids a strong, clear, honest answer, and your best moral leadership. It may be more up to you than to anyone else to keep them out of trouble and set them on the high road to decency, self-discipline, a healthy life, and salvation (whether in this world or the next). To do less than that, according to Ben Suhor, is not only to betray being their friend but also to miss part of your calling as a teacher of the riches of Western, largely Christian, literature.

Ben graduated from St. Joseph Minor Seminary and Loyola University in New Orleans. He went on to get a Master of Education degree at L.S.U., and a Master of Religious Education degree at Notre Dame Seminary in New Orleans. He was a teacher of English, religion, and social studies at Redemptorist High School for over 35 years. He was assistant principal for three years, and he has been the chair both of the English and the religion departments. Ben knows the school business from many points of view. He has also been a teaching staff member of the Pontifical Institute of Catechetics and Spirituality at Notre Dame Seminary in New Orleans. He now teaches English, Latin, and French at Archbishop Rummel High School in Metairie, Louisana, a New Orleans suburb.

Although Ben's universe of discourse is thoroughly theological, he has focused his argument here in terms of its pedagogical implications. He approaches the question authentically from the viewpoint that makes the most sense to his Roman Catholic mind; had he been a Baptist or a Quaker, a Jew or a Native American, his rhetoric, his literary examples, and his heroes would have been different, but his pedagogical argument would have been just as essentially religious.

Charles Suhor

Charlie is Deputy Executive Director of the National Council of Teachers of English, an experienced high-school English teacher and teacher of English teachers. Charlie is also a distinguished semiotician, a poet, and a jazz drummer. Like Ben, he attended public elementary and secondary schools. He received the baccalaureate degree from Loyola, an M.A. from Catholic University in Washington, D.C., an Advanced Certificate from the University of Illinois, and a Ph.D. from Florida State University. Charlie is an ex-Catholic, now a Unitarian with eleven children.

Charlie took a neutralist position early in the debate; as things developed, he discovered that he disagreed with Ben more than he had thought he did. Charlie recommends self-control and reserve to teachers faced with the daunting task of refereeing an all-out class discussion of values. In a democracy like ours, fair play and respect for the sensitivities of every student and every family represented, and teaching students how to think about values—rather than teaching any specific set of values—are of the essence. With as broad an experience and awareness of public-school English teaching as anyone in America, Charlie's position might well be taken as normative pedagogy for the tax-supported public school.

Both Charlie and Ben supply abundant examples from the literature, and they engage in critical reflection on the nature of instruction in the English literature classroom. Both Ben, who is a little to the right, and Charlie, who is a little to the left, know that the implications of their pedagogical positions are as important as the positions themselves, if not more so. They would agree that their debate about teaching moral values in the classroom is no mere tempest in an inkwell. Many more, different, and other issues

are involved with political, economic, social, ideological, theological, and philosophical implications
that go on and on and on, but Ben and Charlie agreed
to stick to the pedagogy of values clarification.

The Multicultural Context of the Values Debate

This book is a two-person debate, not a sympo-
sium. Had we elected to do so, we could have included
a round-table of many voices advocating a rainbow-
range of opinion from a variety of non-believers to a
variety of true-believers, embracing the many faith
perspectives of America's patchwork quilt of cultures
and subcultures. To offer a single example, a debate
that has developed over Native American values parallels the Suhors' debate.

Ought the cultural values and traditional heritage (including religion) of the Native American community be taught to Native American students in
public schools? The theological issues implicit in this
question are different from the Suhors' debate over
Christian and "Western" values, but the pedagogical
issues remain the same. Opinion in that debate was
divided among the American Natives themselves. On
the subject of teaching the values inherent in Native
religion, as with Ben and Charlie, some of the "medicine men" thought yes, and others of the "medicine
men" thought no.

At Rough Rock Demonstration School in Rough
Rock, Arizona, "a bold experiment in Native American ownership of education" was attempted when it
became the first school to incorporate systematically
the Native language and culture into the curriculum.

*The resource center director, a medicine man, de-
veloped another bilingual curriculum based on
traditional ritual knowledge. The school board
approved this curriculum but did not require its
use; later, the board formed a bilingual-bicul-*

tural advisory committee, composed of medicine men, to work under the Resource Center director and "monitor the progress being made in attaining the objectives of [Rough Rock's] bilingual/bicultural program." Despite the advisory board's authority, this third program was difficult to implement, as teachers lacked the specialized knowledge needed to cover the material and some, including Navajos on the Resource Center staff, openly objected to the program's religious content. As a result, these Resource Center materials remained largely unused.[7]

In the spirit of this experiment, one advocate of teaching Native values exhorted his fellow teachers to "make the Native American culture a visible part of your instruction program. Give it a place of honor." He explained that "for the traditional Indian, religion, spirituality, still has a place in every act, and every decision, every day," and he warned teachers not to "underestimate the importance of the spiritual in the lives of even the most modern of Indians."[8]

The Indian culture should become an integral part of basic instruction. Bring the Indian heritage, Indian values, Indian contributions to thought and knowledge into the discussions in every subject whenever possible. Show the students that you value their heritage. Impress upon the students that they have a great heritage and that their values are important. Help them to put their values into words that they can use to defend these values.[9]

But—we ask—is public school the place, are tax dollars the funds, and is the First Amendment's free-exercise clause the right rule whereby to secure for Native Americans that which is denied to Christian or Jewish Americans, or Americans of any other religious persuasion? What about the rights of "Afrocentrists" and "African infusionists" who are using the public schools as a platform from which to inculcate the traditional values (including the spirituality) of Africa?[10] What about the rights of Buddhists (who are neither theological nor non-theological)? And women's rights and militant feminism? And witches and the wicca? And gays, lesbians, and bi-sexuals? And the American Nazi Party and the Ku Klux Klan? And the cultural rights of so many more among America's most lately arrived masses yearning to breathe free? All of these might rightly clamor for "equal time" in the classroom.

Is Invisible Religion OK in Schools?

Ben Suhor is self-evidently a Catholic content to teach at a parochial school, although he has a warning that he would like to issue to fellow teachers in all schools about the invisible religion of "secular humanism" which he sees corrupting the youth. Charlie Suhor remains almost strictly neutral, but in doing so, he affirms a morality of fair play and an ethic of tolerance for diversity. Without taking sides for or against either Ben or Charlie, we can acknowledge that an invisible religion has, in fact, been taught in America's schools since our beginning. That set of values has been variously referred to as the "American public faith" or "American civil religion."

As this book goes to press in 1992, the Supreme Court has just taken another stab at adjudicating the argument by ruling that public prayers at school-sponsored convocations and athletic contests are unconstitutional—a ruling that would have made no sense in 1892. It is a ruling—like many others since mid-century—that upholds the non-establishment clause of the First Amendment at the expense of the free-exercise clause. The Constitution has not changed, but the climate of opinion has, and inconsistency is rife. Legal judgments in the second half of the 20th century have broken with the tradition of American civil religion, tending to uphold the rights of the non-religious or the otherwise-religious, intending to keep religion far away from the schools.

In reaction to this changed situation, to a perceived loss of national morality and American spirituality thanks, in part, to the Supreme Court, a school-prayer amendment to the Constitution has been proposed; Christians and others have seceded from the public schools to establish their own "independent" schools; and increasing numbers of parents now teach their children at home, where specific values may be positivistically taught; a "voucher system" and "school choice" has been proposed by the President and the Secretary of Education; and American public education is under threat of being Balkanized in a variety of ways. This values debate between Ben and Charlie Suhor is, therefore, taking place in the context of the changed situation in American values at the end of the 20th century.

In this debate, neither Ben nor Charlie Suhor advocates classic American public faith. Ben is too Catholic to be an American civil religionist, and Charlie is too neutral. What is American civil religion? Formerly more or less the definition of American orthodoxy in values, American public faith has been the default religion of many Americans, an invisible reality in the American public mind, the political belief that God has especially blessed America. Listen to your local Rock music radio station on the 4th of July, and you'll hear the latest version of American civil religion, accompanied by guitars. Neither Christianity nor Judaism, American faith is a borrowing and recycling of Judeo-Christian beliefs. (In Christianity, Jesus of Nazareth occupies the center of focus; in Judaism, the Torah is all-important; neither is the case in American civil religion.)

According to the well-nigh universal, political faith of 18th-, 19th-, and early-20th-century Americans, just as the God of Exodus had freed the slaves and led the dispossessed out of Egyptian bondage under the pharaoh, so also New England's God brought Americans out of bondage in Europe and Great Britain under "Pharaoh" George III, led us into the New-World wilderness to engage in an experiment in democracy, and created us a nation with our own manifest destiny (with repercussions as negative for the American Native "Canaanites" as was the case when Joshua conquered the Promised Land). Thanksgiving, Memorial Day, and the Fourth of July were our high holy days; Abe Lincoln was the slain savior of our Union, and Martin Luther King, Jr., was our latest martyr.

The practice of American civil religion took place—and still does take place—in temples such as the U.S. Senate, where legislators began their political deliberations in prayer, relying on divine aid; and in the mission field, where chaplains in the Armed Forces led—and still lead—public worship to invoke the "Eternal Father, strong to save" to protect our fighting forces "making the world safe for democracy." Every President has appealed to the American deity in every Inauguration Day sermon (except one: Washington's second), and many Presidents have proclaimed national days of prayer. Every American confesses the public faith every time we pay in cash, proclaiming "In God We Trust." Every school child recites the national creed every morning by pledging allegiance to the national icon, proclaiming that America is "one nation, under God"—an act of devotion in which Jehovah's Witnesses, among others, refuse to participate, seeing the flag as a national idol of civil religion. And it used to be that reciting the Pledge was followed in many schools by a morning prayer, and then the day's announcements over the P.A. system.

Part of the values-educational issue for debate, now, becomes sharper when one juxtaposes these tenets and practices of American public faith with the implications of the "reformation" of faith and morals that has been worked by the Supreme Court in our generation. If Presidents, legislators, chaplains, armed warriors, and tax-payers may still invoke the American deity, why are school children and their teachers forbidden? If the catechism of American faith is no longer to be taught to school children in the "Sunday School" of the public-school classroom, what structure of positive values is to take its place?

The positive values of America's civil religion for public ethics and private morality has previously been understood to be essential to the long-lasting foundations of the republic, essential to the working of the democracy, and necessary, therefore, to be *inculcated* as part of the public-school curriculum. Speaking with the judicial infallibility of the High Bench in *Bethel School District No. 403 v. Fraser* [106 S. Ct. 3159 (1986)], Chief Justice Warren Berger, having intoned the sacred traditions, came to his civil moral conclusion:

> *The role and purpose of the American public school system [is to] "...prepare pupils for citizenship in the Republic. ...It must inculcate the habits and manners of civility as values in themselves conducive to happiness and as indispensable to the practice of self-government in the community and the nation." ...We [the High Court in Ambach v. Norwick (1979)] echoed the essence of this statement of the objective of public education as the "inculcation of fundamental values necessary to the maintenance of a democratic political system...."*

> *The process of educating our youth for citizenship*
> *in public schools is not confined to books, the cur-*
> *riculum, and the civics class; schools must teach*
> *by example the shared values of a civilized social*
> *order. Consciously or otherwise, teachers—and in-*
> *deed the older students—demonstrate the appro-*
> *priate form of civil discourse and political*
> *expression by their conduct and deportment in*
> *and out of class. Inescapably, like parents, they*
> *are role models. The schools, as instruments of*
> *the state, may determine... the essential lessons of*
> *civil, mature conduct....*

Since the "consciousness revolution of the Six-
ties," the dismay following Vietnam, the thorough
sensitization to multiculturalism in America, and the
decisions of a High Court expressive of this *Zeitgeist*,
everything is different now. The public faith has been
shaken, private morality has changed, and many
school teachers no longer inculcate school kids with
the specific religious and ethical values that once allowed Americans to think of themselves as "a nation
with the soul of a church."

Certainly, one might elect to disagree with Chief
Justice Berger, as, in fact, Justices Marshall and
Stevens did do. Nonetheless, instruction in public
religion and moral values had long and legally been a
part of American public-school practice, and we
might quite authentically have included the perspective of an American civil religionist in this exchange.
In any event, this is the historical and political context of this debate, and the decline of American public faith is the occasion of the multitude of energies
competing to fill the void left by its absence.

Having agreed to table most of these issues for
the sake of a focus on pedagogy, the Suhors' statements nevertheless make new again the old questions
that have never been fully answered, especially for

school teachers who sense a responsibility to engage in values clarification with their students both in the classroom and one-to-one.

On the one hand, do we want our education dollars spent to pay for moral mission work of any persuasion in public schools like that which Ben Suhor is comfortable promoting in his parochial schools?

On the other hand, can a teacher with strong convictions about morals and ethics, and with a set of particular values, function freely in a values vacuum of neutrality? Does not Charlie's idea of the teacher as a neutral referee on the playing field of values clarification constrain teachers from being true to themselves when their values differ significantly from his?

A Word from the Sponsor

In publishing Ben's and Charlie's statements, ERIC/RCS does not necessarily recommend the religious, pedagogical, or ideological viewpoints of either contestant, or of any other point of view, American civil religion included. It is ERIC's policy not to take sides in any way. ERIC/RCS's purpose was to insure a fair hearing for two, strong, articulate, well-informed, highly individual positions in a purely pedagogical debate. As the moderator of this debate, I find that, as both a Catholic Christian and an English teacher, I do not always agree either with Ben or with Charlie. In my personal judgment, a satisfactory solution to this complex of problems still lies beyond our horizon.

All publications that issue from the presses of ERIC/RCS are peer-reviewed, and this debate has been scrutinized by more than the usual number of critics. A debate like this one between the Suhors becomes an occasion—and rightly so—for each reviewer and critic to express his or her own point of view. Perhaps because the Suhors are brothers, and in fact because they agreed from the outset to focus on pedagogy, the range of play in this debate is intentionally constrained. We are well-aware, of course, that there are as many viewpoints as there are readers, so we invite you, dear reader, to join the fray.

One reviewer said that ERIC ought not to publish the Suhor debate at all because the two brothers engaged in theological discourse. Another reviewer made the opposite point: ERIC ought to publish the Suhor debate because theological issues are squarely at stake in the wrangle over the pedagogy of values clarification, and insofar as ERIC—a function of the U.S. Department of Education—is officially neutral in the matter, a debate was the proper format in which to address this legitimate matter.

Another reviewer pointed out that many Christian readers would predictably be quite dissatisfied with Ben as their champion. Certain right-wing Protestant fundamentalists, for example, would argue that Ben is a *Catholic*, not a *Christian*, and that he does not speak for them. Many liberal—or even moderate—Roman Catholics may find that Ben's intense rhetoric does not speak for them, either.

Similarly, but at an opposite extreme, radical secularists, agnostics, and atheists might argue that Charlie is far too willing to allow the inculcation of moral values of any kind at the taxpayer's expense. English teachers are not hired to be guides of the perplexed; as authority figures in the classroom, they ought not to be allowed to pass off onto the students their private morals, however benign, at the public's expense.

Yet another of our reviewers, a devoutly religious individual, made an argument identical to that of the atheists and agnostics, but for wholly other reasons: Values, ethics, morality, and religion—she said—are far too important to be entrusted into the hands of theologically untrained English teachers, or to be celebrated in the generic, and therefore meaningless, fashion that becomes the school routine when a moment of empty silence is kept in the name of an unknown god for some non-specified reason.

In the annotated bibliography at the back of this book, we present a considerable range of opinion as represented in the ERIC database. Voices speak there both for and against the tax-supported teaching of religious and moral values in the schools; atheists and Christians speak out, and so do Buddhists and Hindus and Jews, as do the advocates of multiculturalism who would like to hold it all together (or pull it all apart).

If you find that your position is not represented at all, or not well enough, take that as your cue to make a speech or write an article on the subject, and submit your contribution to ERIC for inclusion in the database. Funded by your own tax dollars through the U.S. Department of Education, ERIC and its educational information retrieval system are here to serve all Americans interested in education, whatever their convictions about values. If your effort comes up to our academic standards and passes muster with our board of peer reviewers, we will be pleased to enter what you have written into the ERIC database.

Carl B. Smith
Director
ERIC Clearinghouse on
  Reading and Communication Skills

NOTES

1. Ralph D. Mawdsley and Alice S. Mawdsley, "Diminished Status of Religious Liberty in Public Education: Interpreting Mozert and Smith," *West's Education Law Reporter 46* (July 21, 1988): 897-912. Hugh J. Breyer, "Cinderella, the Horse God and the Wizard of Oz: Mozert *v.* Hawkins County Public Schools," *Journal of Law and Education 20* (Winter 1991): 63-93; Gail P. Sorenson, "'Mozert and Smith': Implications for Curriculum Policy," *West's Education Law Reporter 42* (January 7 1988): 693-703.

2. Franklin Parker and Betty Parker, "Behind Textbook Censorship," speech given before the Northern Arizona University Chapter of Phi Delta Kappa (Flagstaff, Arizona, July 30, 1987). [ED 286 798]

3. Richard Baer, "Commentary: Fighting the Wrong Battle in Public School Censorship Disputes," *Social Education* 50, 3 (March 1986): 164-65.

4. *Attacks on the Freedom To Learn: People for the American Way 1989-1990 Report.* (Washington, D.C.: People for the American Way, 1990.) [ED 329 475]; and see *Attacks on the Freedom To Learn. 1986-1987 Report.* (Washington, D.C.People for the American Way, 1988.) [ED 290 144] Defending their middle ground against extremists, People for the American Way published a guide to censorship resistance, including an "Overview of Censorship," that is an introduction to the several groups whose Right-wing ideology they oppose: Barbara Parker and Stefanie Weiss, *Protecting the Freedom to Learn: A Citizen's Guide.* (Washington, D.C.: People for the American Way, 1983.) [ED 240 345]

5. James Moffett, *Storm in the Mountains: A Case Study of Censorship, Conflict, and Consciousness.* Carbondale and Edwardsville: Southern Illinois University Press, 1988: 15.

6. *Attacks on the Freedom to Learn: People for the American Way 1989-1990 Report.* (Washington, D.C.: People for the American Way, 1990.) [ED 329 475]

7. T. L. McCarty, "School as Community: The Rough Rock Demonstration," *Harvard Educational Review* 59/4 (November 1989), pp. 497-498.

8. Hap Gilliland, with John Reyhner and others, *Teaching the Native American.* (Dubuque, Iowa: Kendall/Hunt, 1988.): 30-31.

9. *Ibid.*, p. 224.

10. Bob Honeman, "Rationale and Suggestions for Emphasizing Afrocentricity in the Public Schools," paper presented at the Conference on Rhetoric and the Teaching of Writing (Indiana, Pennsylvania, July 10-11, 1990): 17 pp. [ED 321 268]; David L. Kirp, "Textbooks and Tribalism," *Public Interest* 104 (Summer 1991): 20-36.

Values in the Teaching of Literature—A Public School View

Charles Suhor

Over the years I have thought a great deal about the question of values in the teaching of literature in elementary and secondary schools. Values was an important question in my daily classes during eight years of public school teaching, and it was important during my nine years as a K-12 supervisor in a public school district. The matter is of continuing interest in my work with the National Council of Teachers of English. The Council's members include public, religious, and private school teachers who have the privilege of teaching literature and the task of answering to their constituencies about how values are taught in their classrooms.

Public school views on values in literature instruction vary widely, so I do not claim to represent anyone but myself in this exchange of ideas. In fact, I will try to avoid two all-too-common stances. The first is virtucratic posturing—issuing a brave call for tolerance because, after all, we educators in the public sector have a keener vision than one will find among those who conform to dogmas. I believe that anyone who really endorses pluralism must acknowledge that absolutist belief systems have a legitimate place in open discussion in public school classrooms, so long as the teacher remains publicly neutral, and the absolutists do not suppress other viewpoints.

Another unbecoming stance is liberal grandstanding—shaking one's fist at right-wing Christian fundamentalists, and suggesting that deep down, they are all fascists. When I criticize radical religious activists as enemies of public education, I will back up my claims with data, including some of their own truly fascinating words.

I also want to state up front my belief that moderate groups like the Interfaith Consortium for Pluralism (IFCP), the National Council on Religion and Public Education (NCRPE), and the First Liberty Institute, not radical right or radical left polemicists, represent the dominant views of the proper relation between religion and public education in the United States. An Interfaith Consortium brochure describes IFCP as follows:

> ...conservatives, moderates, and liberals who cherish our right to practice our religion freely, who value the separation of church and state, and who do not want the terms of religion or political patriotism to be coopted by a vocal minority which purports to speak in the name of all religion.... We are religious people who affirm religious tolerance. (p.1)

The group criticizes religious extremists' efforts "to 'Christianize' our society. This effort not only excludes persons of other religious faiths, but it also utilizes a very limited interpretation of the word Christian." (p.1)

The NCRPE, publishers of the journal *Religion in Public Education*, believe in the "academic study of religion in public education," including "study of comparative religion as part of the secular program of education." The group also aims to "increase the awareness on the part of both educational and religious groups of the limitations of such study as well as its permissibility and desirability." (n.p.) Unfortunately, moderate groups like IFCP and NCRPE exert little political influence, so the public debate tends to pit ideologues from the left against ideologues from the right.

My main claim is this: *Most public school English teachers can and do teach values in their literature programs while remaining publicly neutral with regard to religious and philosophical belief systems. When they stray markedly and persistently from the neutral position to urge that students adopt particular religious or anti-religious views, they are acting against the interests both of their students and of public education as an institution; they should be fired.*

To explain this position, I will deal first with some widely publicized aspects of the issue, such as secular humanism, and then with more teacherly matters, such as students' values and response to literature.

The "Attack on Values" in Public Schools

The most bizarre idea in the current debate is the claim that traditional values are under serious attack in public school classrooms. In recent years we have seen some worrisome headlines in the education press. One story told of efforts to "establish" in the schools a "common core of values," among them honesty, human dignity and worth, justice, self-respect and fairness.[1] But is there any evidence that teachers of literature or any other subject are endorsing dishonesty, the worthlessness of the human person, injustice, self-contempt, and unfairness?

There was the yarn (used in the highly political context of the 1988 Presidential elections) about a guidance counselor who refused to discipline a student for stealing because the counselor presumably did not want to impose his own value system on others. But occasional horror stories do not demonstrate that large numbers of school personnel are out to undermine common decency. If we are to spend time, money, and energy on repelling an attack on values in our public schools, those who want to prepare a counterattack have the burden of demonstrating that a genuine attack exists.

To some, the attackers on traditional values are indeed organized, and they even have a name—they are called "secular humanists." I acknowledge that there are people who can be called by that name, and that a duly constituted group called the American Humanist Association exists. They have issued two "Humanist Manifestos," and they publish a magazine called *The Humanist*. The manifestos contain clear philosophical statements favoring atheism over religion. A negative view of organized religion permeates the association's statements about moral values, social action, and political institutions.

Insofar as the manifestos clearly articulate an antireligious stance, they compete with articulated religious stances and are in no sense neutral. Any public school teacher who urges students to subscribe to the ideas in Humanist Manifesto I or II is in the same business of indoctrination as a public school English teacher who preaches the New Testament in the classroom.

Even the U.S. Supreme Court has stated (albeit ambiguously) that secular humanism is a religion. A footnote in a 1961 decision (*Torcaso v. Watkins*), which involved a specific secular humanist congregation in California, acknowledged the existence of secular humanism as a religion as well as a philosophic persuasion.[2] For purposes of this discussion, however, the issue is not whether secular humanists are a congregation of kindred believers, but whether or not one is paranoid to imagine that secular humanists are taking over the public schools. As Robert Primack and David Aspy noted, polls have shown that public school teachers are mostly theists from Judeo-Christian backgrounds. By contrast, secular humanists in America, denominational and otherwise, can be liberally estimated at a maximum of about 300,000 citizens.

"If God decided to strike every secular humanist dead, He would pass over almost the entire population of public school teachers. Every serious survey we have done of strong beliefs held indicates that the people associated with education—school board members, administrators, teachers—are all quite conservative in most matters and particularly religious matters. Secular humanists have a miniscule membership among public school personnel."[3]

These data are consistent with my experience. The English and humanities teachers I have met are often humanists from the tradition of Christian humanism represented by Erasmus, Thomas More, John Donne, Cardinal Newman, Gerard Manley Hopkins, Teilhard de Chardin, Harvey Cox, and others. The agnostic and atheist teachers I have known seldom seem interested in conquering either the teachers' lounge or the classroom, let alone the church and the world.

I suspect that many who warn us about secular humanism are more crafty than paranoid. They seldom make distinctions between secular humanism, broader humanist philosophies, and the interrelated fields known as the humanities. They offer little solid data, but they produce reams of inferences about an underlying anti-American intent of literary works. They ask: "How can we stop secular humanism from poisoning our public schools?" They answer: "We can prescribe a dose of Christian fundamentalist beliefs as an antidote."

I am not creating paper tigers here. This very solution to the imagined rampage of secular humanism was advanced by parents in the 1987 Mobile, Alabama, public schools case. U.S. District Court Judge W. Brevard Hand, ruling in favor of the parents who wanted textbooks that champion Christian belief, offered greater cause for concern among Americans than do the secular humanists when he said that the Constitution "does not prohibit the state from establishing a religion." As for those who might not share the religious beliefs of the Christian majority, Hand said that "a member of a religious minority will have to develop a thicker skin if state establishment offends him."[4] The history of state-sanctioned religions suggests that the thicker skin might also need to be supplemented by an asbestos suit, bulletproof windshield, and places to hide.

Fortunately, the decision of Judge Hand (punningly called the unLearned Hand) was appealed and subsequently overruled, but the aggressively sectarian actions of the parents, and the responses of a district judge, disturb me. I think those things should disturb anyone who believes that public education ought to be free from religious (or anti-religious) indoctrination.

In the more recent tirades of the religious Right, atheists are not the only ones running roughshod over public school curriculum; oddly, an unseemly group of theists—the New Age religionists—are also threatening our schools.

I risk the appearance of presenting a parody by citing the actual words of warning on Texe Marrs' book, *Dark Secrets of the New Age*. Marrs' subheadings give you an idea of where he is going—"The Underhanded, Deceitful Tactics of New Age Educators"; "Books Written in Hell"; and "Are Public Schools the Devil's Playhouse?" Go to the text and you will find, of course, that the answer to the last question is "yes." "Atheism and secular humanism, though extremely successful, were only crude first attempts by the Devil. In the New Age movement and religion, Satan has latched onto something far more effective and more direct."[5]

I am familiar with the literature of many groups that are described, too broadly, as advocates of "New Age beliefs." The fact is, there is no such body of belief. Groups labeled as New Age are extremely varied in creed. Their common denominator is interest in Eastern (and sometimes Native American) forms of religious expression. Despite highly publicized exceptions like the defunct Rajneesh community in Oregon, those who are called New Age believers are among the least programmatic and evangelistic people I've known.

I cannot tell whether ignorance or misguided zeal prompts an ultra-Fundamentalist to yoke a Satanic cult with Buddhist belief and Maria Montessori, and label them all as part of a New Age "movement," a movement that Marrs says has "cast its rotten net in a bold quest to destroy an entire generation" in order to "wipe out all vestiges of Christianity and the Bible from our schools and our culture."[6] One could, with equal illogic, link traditional Mormonism with the murderous Ohio cult that misnamed itself the Reorganized Church of the Latter Day Saints, or yoke all Fundamentalist Christians with the outlandish No-Name Fellowship in Illinois.[7]

Among the educational programs attacked for alleged New Age philosophy are the materials from the Association for Supervision and Curriculum Development, *Tactics for Thinking* by Robert Marzano and Daisy Arredondo. Marzano, the chief architect of the program, is a mainstream language-arts educator who has published, among other things, a book on vocabulary for the International Reading Association. In one *Tactics* exercise, the authors present an activity intended to help students focus their attention. A protest group in Indianapolis blasted this exercise as an attempt to induce a trance, similar in intent to brainwashing, hypnosis, and New Age meditation.

Protests like these are an exercise of the Constitutional right of free speech, but they are not conducive to freedom of expression in public education. When they succeed, they can and should be brought to court by groups like People for the American Way and the American Civil Liberties Union. These watchdog groups should be joined by NCTE, IRA, ASCD, and the American Library Association, lest we all have fundamentalist ideologies shoved down our throats.

Sins of Omission: Ignoring Values

Some critics claim that basic values are not directly attacked in public schools but are undermined, nonetheless, because they are ignored. Can these critics possibly be observing public school literature programs? I agree with Sue Howell, a teacher at Carbondale Community High School in Illinois, who says that English teachers are constantly asking students to "make ethical as well as aesthetic judgments" during the study of literature.[8]

Surely moral insight and moral conflict are at the heart of most good literature—and even inferior literature. Ludicrous as it may seem, works as varied in quality as Hawthorne's *The Scarlet Letter*, Bret Harte's "The Luck of Roaring Camp," Alice Walker's *The Color Purple*, and the Sweet Valley High teen romance series, have one thing in common—a concern with moral reality. The question for public school English teachers, then, is not "Should values be a part of literature instruction?" but "What is the role of the teacher in dealing with the moral elements in works under study?"

Curiously, those who claim that English teachers give inadequate attention to values in literature instruction are a few decades late. When New Criticism was most in vogue (roughly, from the 1930s through the 1960s), teachers were encouraged to focus exclusively on analysis of form—counting off iambs in sonnets, talking about setting and plot development in short stories, hunting down symbols in novels, and the like.

As a classroom teacher, I was strongly influenced by New Criticism, but I shared with most of my colleagues a belief that formal analysis alone is little more than literary autopsy. It does not capture the excitement of literature, nor does it respect the complex thoughts and feelings of students as they respond to the works they are reading.

The shift to response-based teaching in recent years is a further acknowledgement by teachers and scholars that literature is first and foremost a way of imagining human experience. The reader's imaginative entry into the text is, after all, what makes literature most vital and appealing. Robert Probst's description of response instruction explicitly places the students' experiences, and implicitly their values, as central elements in literary study:

> *Students are encouraged to respect and examine their responses—emotions, associations, memories, images, ideas. Out of those elements they will create their understandings of the text. Teaching guided by this theory becomes a matter of encouraging students to articulate responses, examine their origins in the text and in other experiences, reflect upon them, and analyze them in the light of other readings—those of other students and critics—and of other information about literature.*[9]

Classroom teachers know that they cannot engage students in penetrating literary analysis, even a New Critical analysis, without being led to a discussion of values. For example, students learn that there is a "turn of thought" in the ninth line of many Petrarchan sonnets. So in Wordsworth's "The World Is Too Much with Us" we find in the ninth line, ". . . Great God! I'd rather be / A pagan suckled in a creed outworn." Now what is the nature of that form-related change in thought, and what is Wordsworth daring to say about humanity, nature, and religion here?

Similarly, students discuss the development of Iago's manipulation of Othello, as Iago casts Desdemona in an increasingly suspicious light. Only a vegetable, a computer, or a very frightened formalist could avoid asking value-related questions about these relationships. Why is Iago so damned hateful? Is Othello a fool, or what? Scratch the surface of form and you find content, replete with questions that call for an exploration of values.

Sins of Commission: Cheerleading and Deck-Stacking

There are at least two ways in which public school English teachers in elementary and secondary schools might violate the trust placed in them. One is by cheerleading—using classroom discussion of values as a vehicle to win the class over to their own personal religious and philosophical belief systems. The public school classroom is no place for the English teacher who cheerleads the anti-clericalism of Marlow's *Faustus*, or for the teacher who roundly condemns it, or for the teacher who force-feeds the message of Donne's "Death Be Not Proud" to students while ridiculing the implied pantheism of Bryant's "Thanatopsis," or for the teacher who does the reverse.

Over the years I have met numerous religious evangelists and militant agnostics and atheists who peddled their personal beliefs in public school classrooms. As a young teacher in New Orleans, I had colleagues who openly preached racism in English and social studies classes. (Until 1961, they were protected by state law in doing so.) As a K-12 supervisor between 1967 and 1977, I had to confer with a self-appointed village atheist about his blatant ridicule of religious beliefs in the English classes he taught. In 1989, I heard an English teacher at an official school function in a small Texas town quoting the Bible incessantly as he told graduating seniors that the scriptures are the sole guide for living, and that Jesus is the Way, the only way.

In cases such as these, there is no need to infer underlying intentions, or to talk about the subtle effects of the teachers' actions or the hidden implications of what they are saying. The intentions, messages, and effects are clear and can be dealt with in a forthright manner. That is, the teachers can and should be warned, in accordance with the particular school district's procedures for dealing with unacceptable professional conduct, about using the classroom as a bully pulpit for particular religious or secular values. Then, if the teachers don't heed the warnings, they should be fired.

Some forms of evangelizing are subtler than the overt intellectual and emotional intimidation of students described above. Teachers in public schools can also err by stacking the curriculum deck—overloading their programs with works that reflect a particular philosophical or religious view. Of course, I am referring here to literature selected for general English programs and not to specialized courses such as "The Bible as Literature" and "Literature of the East"—a legitimate kind of program advocated by groups like the National Council on Religion and Public Education. Works selected for study over a semester or a year in regular K-12 English programs should reflect a wide range of values and beliefs.

In retrospect, it appears that conscious or unconscious deck-stacking of materials was a real problem in the notorious Kanawha County, West Virginia case in the mid-seventies. It is true that the local protestors raised the conventional idea of American Civil Religion—a belief in patriotism, the Bible, and social activism—to a deafening amperage. But there was more to it than that.

George Hillocks of the University of Chicago, no Bible-thumper, studied the textbooks in use during the controversy. His research revealed that the parents were accurate in claiming that the literature textbooks were highly loaded in favor of pessimistic world views and that the books contained "deprecations of Christian belief." According to Hillocks:

> *It is clear that some of the protestors' objections—*
> *that is, what they say appears in the textbooks—*
> *does appear. . . . They are angered that the*
> *successful completion of a high school course re-*
> *quires the reading, and they assume, the learn-*
> *ing, of such materials—especially when there is*
> *little or no material showing the other side, the*
> *Christian side that conserves the fundamental be-*
> *liefs.*

In the aforementioned Mobile, Alabama case, the school board admitted that certain textbooks were underplaying the importance of Christianity in American history.

Whether the curriculum deck is stacked by design or neglect, the problem is relatively simple to resolve. The individual teacher, the English department, or the school district can act with good will to show the other side, i.e., to broaden the available materials so that a better balance is struck within the total array of student readings.

In short, the problem of deck-stacking does not require panicky responses like censorship, litigation, or legislation. As columnist George Will, no bleeding-heart liberal, pointed out in a discussion of the Mobile case, a few flawed textbooks don't constitute abridgment of parents' religious rights, nor are they evidence that a pernicious anti-religious plot is afoot. The U.S. Constitution does not carry "a commitment to protect parents and children from influences that might complicate the transmission of sectarian beliefs." No doubt some textbooks are tilted away from religion, "but imagine a ruling that the use of such texts abridges parents' 'free-exercise' right, or 'establishes' the 'religion' of 'secular humanism.'" That way, Will said, lies chaos.[10]

I leave it to English teachers and school officials in private and religious schools to develop their positions on cheerleading and deck-stacking in relation to the teaching of literature. I recognize that their problems will be complex within a different dimension. Because they are often committed to communicating a particular belief system, it is within their Constitutional right and in their denominational interest to look at literature through their own Christian lens, Jewish lens, Mormon lens, or whatever.

But I do believe that religious education is more robust and serviceable when students read broadly and are encouraged to do multiple perspective-taking during a discussion of values in the English class. When they read a Sartre play, a Rand novel, or excerpts from scriptures other than their own, they are expanding their knowledge of our cultural heritage and laying the groundwork for lifelong communication.

Throughout their adult lives, students from sectarian schools will meet and interact with innumerable people who hold views different from their own, so it makes sense to help them to define points of overlap and contrast among philosophies. In non-school situations, they will inevitably confront the reality of pluralism; their teachers ought to cultivate perspective- taking ability in them as a valuable intellectual and social skill.

I hasten to add that research on works studied in public schools does not show that public school teachers have rushed to incorporate more varied viewpoints into the literary canon.[11] The most frequently required books and authors are almost identical in public, Catholic, and private schools. A few of the books that are read in a variety of settings are controversial (e.g., *Huckleberry Finn, Lord of the Flies*), but most are not. It is as if the most-often-taught works embody a safe range of values exploration, beyond which only the more adventurous teachers will move. Wholesome expansion is evident, though, in the occasional inclusion of works like *The Autobiography of Malcolm X*, Chaim Potok's *The Chosen*, and Sylvia Plath's *The Bell Jar*.

In fairness to teachers in all kinds of schools, I must reiterate that the efforts of censors have a chilling effect on both selection of works and discussion of values. An attack—a well-documented attack—is being launched on the teaching of values, but it is not led by secular humanists or new-age religionists. It is the assualt by ultraconservative individuals and groups who are challenging the democratic practice of providing wide access to books and ideas.[12] The teacher who assiduously avoids deck-stacking and cheerleading is subject to these attacks because censors want to stack the literature program with works that are consistent with their private visions of the world, and they want the teacher to be an advocate of their belief system.

Doing the Right Thing: A Public School Stance

What is an appropriately neutral stance for a public school teacher in dealing with works that touch on religious, philosophical, and political issues? In my own teaching, and that of many other teachers I have met, the neutral approach was like the audio-visual equipment—it worked most of the time if you handled it carefully.

I always thought it was my job to help students critically analyze the values reflected in the literature under study, rather than to advocate this or that moral position. The only advocacy I indulged in was *playing* the Devil's (or Angel's) advocate when the discussion became too one-sided.

I felt it was my responsibility to ask about other ways of looking at things. For example, in considering the end of Steinbeck's *Of Mice and Men*, I might ask, "If Steinbeck had chosen not to have George shoot Lenny but to show them making a getaway, or maybe dying together in some sort of accident, how would that have changed the view of the world that Steinbeck presents in the novel?"

Sometimes I would gather different commentaries on the same subject—such as speeches on the American Dream by James Baldwin, William Buckley, Martin Luther King, and Malcolm X—and ask students to compare and contrast the views, drawing their own conclusions. Once I developed a unit on religion that included passages from the *Bible*, the *Bhagavad-Gita*, Jonathan Edwards' "Sinners in the Hands of an Angry God," Gwendolyn Brooks' "The Preacher Ruminates behind the Sermon," Carl Sandberg's "To a Contemporary Bunkshooter," and several musical selections.

The flaw in any attempt to provide multiple viewpoints, of course, is that few of us are always resolute against ourselves. Consciously or unconsciously, we might choose more or better material that favors our view of the world, and ask more penetrating questions about the philosophies that we do not personally hold. For my part, I am still not absolutely sure of my honest answers to questions like these: During my eight years as a public school teacher—during which I was a devout Catholic—did I really give attention to Donne's conversion from wasted youth to esteemed cleric and poet because I like metaphysical poetry (which I do), or because I approved of the conversion? Did I encourage discussion of the ridiculous aspects of "Thanatopsis" because it is a silly and overrated poem (which I believe it is), or because of its pantheistic overtones? If you are a public school teacher, asking such introspective questions is central to your professional integrity, whether you love Donne, hate Bryant, love or hate both of them, or something inbetween in your heart of hearts.

Some English teachers find the posture of public neutrality unbecoming. They believe that it is much better for the class to know, up front, where the teacher stands in a discussion. They claim that their academic freedom—a concept with little definition at either the elementary or the secondary level—would be violated if they were unable to state their religious and philosophical beliefs in the classroom.

Some teachers do seem to work best that way, either giving the students an advance notice about the teacher's biases or concluding a discussion by revealing their own viewpoints. Furlong and Carroll paint an appealing picture of the teacher who states a position, yet does not indoctrinate:

> *...we see no violation of neutrality in honestly telling students where you stand and why, as long as you offer this as a reasoned option with which other reasonable people may disagree. There is no reason why your advocacy should cut off the reasoning processes of students.* [13]

This position has a fine, rational ring to it, but I have known many up-front, values-committed teachers who in fact managed to intimidate the class into taking their viewpoints on genuinely arguable questions. Students who are impressionable or frightened would rather keep the peace and give the teacher what they perceive the teacher to want. Why challenge the teacher's ideas about Jonathan Edwards' theology? About Mencken's merciless debunking? About the relative merits of Martin Luther King's and Malcolm X's beliefs? Why run the risk of alienating the teacher and getting a bad grade to boot? The punch line, the well-reasoned option, the datum to be noted for the test—in short, the teacher's opinion—will arrive on schedule, so there is no need to toss an adventurous idea across the room like an audacious spitball.

In the long run, students can probably tag our most fundamental beliefs, whether we advertise them or strive for neutrality and a balanced presentation of ideas. After all, external evidence is available in many situations, as it was in my own years as a public school teacher. I taught Sunday School for several years, was conversant with Biblical allusions, had a brother who taught at Redemptorist High School, and seemed to come up with a new baby (on one occasion, twins) every year or so. If they did not know that their teacher was a Catholic, they probably did not care to know.

Sometimes students found my lack of clear preference during heated class discussions galling; sometimes they seemed comfortable with it; sometimes they pointed out that my beliefs were coming through when I thought I was acting as an unbiased referee in the discussion. They never mistook my stance, though, for indoctrination on one hand or for lack of passion about moral issues on the other. My goal was to involve students in absorbing discussions of thematic and aesthetic issues—to provide models of enjoyable, literate, tolerant talk about the literature they read, so they would want to read more and talk more outside of class. I knew I was achieving this goal when the air in the classroom was charged with that fine communal feeling that comes with a probing exchange of ideas.

There are no standardized tests to measure that marvelous feeling, but every good English teacher knows what it is. It's the spell that is suddenly broken when the bell rings, and no one can believe that they have been talking for fifty minutes about a young girl who hid in a narrow attic in Amsterdam for two years during World War II. It's the pleasure of watching students leave the classroom, still challenging each other's ideas about Crane's anger with God in "The Open Boat." It's noticing that they have checked out Cormier's *Eight Plus One* short-story collection from the library after reading and discussing one of the stories in class.

This intellectual joy is not peculiar to public school classrooms, of course. It is a professional grace shared by English teachers in vastly different settings, and it spans the generations as well. I experienced it as a student in Edwin Friedrich's class at Nicholls High School, as a teacher during my years in the classroom, and as an observer in other teachers' classrooms when I was an English supervisor. My own children often came home from school and talked enthusiastically about their English classes after they had been talking, at length and with passion in their English classes.

Approaches to Class Discussion: Beyond Socrates

We now have an excellent theory and research base to support the idea that purposeful classroom discussion, including small-group discussion, is a key to effective teaching and learning. Classroom talk is part of every model of writing process instruction, and research has shown that thoughtful discussion improves writing performance.[14] The exchange of ideas in a classroom, whether in public or private or religious schools, permits students to give shape to barely formed impressions, undefined feelings, and unexamined ideas and experiences. Promoting and monitoring the language-making process is, like the love of literature, one of the great shared pleasures among English teachers everywhere.

Techniques of classroom discussion have expanded, and solid research supports several methods. In elementary schools reciprocal teaching places students in the role of question-makers and hypothesizers. The students are not mere respondents to teacher-made questions.[15] "Scaffolding," a concept suggested by Jerome Bruner, involves a gradual withdrawal of teacher prompts so that students learn to carry forth purposeful discussion on their own.[16] Cooperative learning (in its less regimented formats) uses classroom dialogue as a way of helping students to formulate and vocalize their ideas, "to make overt the implicit reasoning processes"[17] —in plain English, to clarify and express their values in intelligent conversation with others.

Social and moral benefits flow directly from well-wrought classroom discussion. Philosopher Richard Paul cites numerous socially valuable and personally edifying results of classroom dialogue, among them fairmindedness, empathy, tolerance of views other than one's own, and an understanding of reasoned dissent.[18] An open discussion, in which the teacher does not have a covert or overt authoritarian objective, is a model of the democratic process. A public school teacher in our country is educating students explicitly for participation in that process.

Discussion methods that support democratic goals go beyond traditional Socratic teaching—a fact that has eye-opening implications for the teaching of values. In the Socratic method, the teacher characteristically sets the agenda by posing questions—*leading* questions, as they are aptly called. The students are taken through a line of reasoning, often an admirably subtle and challenging line, as they answer questions that close in on vital ideas and themes—e.g., the interpretation of a fascinating short story like Doris Lessing's "Through the Tunnel" or a poem like Stephen Crane's ironic gem, "War is Kind." The journey can be a thrilling one, but the limitation is that there is only one Socrates in a Socratic discussion—the teacher. The direction of the dialogue—and commonly the range of values that the students must converge upon—is pre-set by the teacher-Socrates.

I am not arguing here against Socratic discussion. I believe that it is an essential part of every English teacher's repertoire. But the Socratic approach does tend to discourage divergent thinking and the broad exploration of values. Unlike approaches such as reciprocal teaching and scaffolding, the Socratic method allows students to *witness* the art of question-making without encouraging them to *formulate* thoughtful questions of their own. Even Plato implicitly admitted this. Menon says to Socrates, "You seem to argue well, Socrates. *I don't know how you do it.*" (Emphasis added)

If I were to return to public school teaching today, I would use a better mix of Socratic questioning and other classroom dialogue techniques. But I would not abandon my neutral stance in class discussion or make radical shifts in the content of my literature program based on changes in my personal philosophy. I used to be a Catholic; now I'm a Unitarian. This change would neither keep me from teaching—with delight—Gerard Manley Hopkins' poems, nor cause me to give greater attention to Thomas Paine's essay on deism. Some very important things have not changed. I still value literature as vicarious experience, and I still enjoy talking about it, even though I now connect it to my system of belief in different ways.

Jewish, Catholic, Protestant, Unitarian, Mormon, Buddhist, agnostic, atheist—you name it, public school English teachers of all persuasions have essentially the same mission in the teaching of literature: to help students grow in the understanding and love of literature in its many forms. This understanding and loving includes a critical interaction with texts—including the moral values stated or implied in the texts—in ways that sharpen students' responses to an ever-expanding range of literary experiences.

Student Response and the Author's Values

I believe that recent theoretical emphases have moved literature instruction too far away from examination of the *author's* values. I am not resurrecting the "intentional fallacy" here. Clearly, there is a wide range of reasonable inferences about the themes, values, and world views embedded in a work; and it seems to me that misapplications of reader-response theory needlessly draw attention away from the philosophical rumblings within a rich text. Robert Scholes, a major voice in contemporary criticism and pedagogy, states that authorial intention, though not "a key that unlocks valid meanings," is "a requirement of reading and therefore a partial goal of interpretation."[19]

Reader-response theorists correctly stress that the reader does not merely grasp the given content of a text, but interacts with it. The reader's experiences and values are involved in a transaction with the text and the author, so that the reader is a co-creator of meaning, not merely a recipient of the author's ideas or an interpreter of literary forms.[20] But when this psychological principle is translated into practice, the text need not be reduced to a blunt vehicle for the exchange of personal beliefs among classmates.

Although author-centered study and New Critical analysis are at worst sterile exercises, those approaches do acknowledge that a skilled author's ideas are ambiguously embedded in the structure of a work. To discover several plausible interpretations of Fitzgerald's world view in his brilliantly crafted *The Great Gatsby*, perhaps rejecting some implausible interpretations, is to set an appropriately high intellectual standard for the students' discussion of their own ideas about themes interwoven in the novel—ambition, romantic love, the American Dream, personal dedication to causes.

The flaw in historical/biographical and New Critical instruction was that we ran the risk of murdering literature to dissect it, purposely suppressing students' personal responses. With reader-response instruction, we run the risk of a literary lobotomy, treating literature as a quick prompt to self-indulgent spouting of substantially unexamined ideas. Reader-based interaction with a text can be essentially egocentric, resembling what Piaget called "collective monologue" in his observations of small children. Concerned mainly with their own responses, the children would "soliloquize before others," simply stating their own perspectives without considering others' views. A well-crafted literary text, by contrast, provides an invitation to experiment with perspective-taking, a more advanced stage of development.

We do not have to talk about analysis of authors and texts *versus* personal response; we can have it both ways, I think. As noted earlier, traditional study of a Wordsworth sonnet or a Shakespearean tragedy can lead directly and simultaneously to discussion of the author's implicit, and the students' explicit, values. Furthermore, response-based prereading activities such as opinionnaires, case studies, scenarios, and role-playing as described by Peter Smagorinsky[21] are compatible with discussions of authorial intent and literary form during and after reading. Another integrated approach involves students in recording their personal reactions in journals before entering into class discussion about the author's world view or about literary structures.

We need to explore styles of discussing literature that integrate response-based instruction with various other approaches, including even "old fashioned" ones.

Robert Probst was on target in stating that response instruction "does not deny the valuing of other approaches to literature. Historical, biographical, and cultural perspectives may all yield insight into literature. But it does assert that the fundamental literary experience is the encounter of a reader, a unique individual, with a text."[22] In the appendix, I include several lively examples of response-based instruction that I believe are appropriate for public school classrooms (see below, pp. 28-41).

Operational Pluralism and Commitment to Discourse

Does a neutral but exploratory stance necessarily convey the message that one set of beliefs is, ontologically, as good as any other? Asked another way, does a teacher's public and professional neutrality inherently erode traditional beliefs, merely by suggesting that there are alternative ways to see the world? Certainly not.

Surely, the teacher in a public school classroom can be *operationally* pluralistic without enforcing an official philosophy of relativism. Yes, the teacher's role is functionally neutral. From that, it does not necessarily follow that competing philosophies discussed in the classroom are equally reasonable or equally humane. Those who draw a frame around operational pluralism and give it names like "secular humanism" or "godless education" are not describing what goes on in public schools. They are seeking victory through wordplay. Let us not allow a facile act of labeling to distort the intent and the genius of public education—namely, *the cultivation of independent thinkers in a setting that nurtures the process of moral exploration, a process that provides balance and boundaries without enforcing an official doctrine.*

Conservative educators have little to fear from the public school teacher's official stance of neutrality. The fact is that traditional values normally have a clear edge in the real world of the public school classroom. Most students bring a version of their parents' traditional values to the study of a literary work. Insofar as a modern classic like *Lord of the Flies* or a gripping film like *Dead Poets Society* challenges their values, students are likely to pick up the scent and articulate their beliefs in open discussion. Insofar as the work supports the students' values, their belief systems will be reinforced during the class discussion.

And as noted earlier, a conservative population of teachers is selecting the works to be studied. As for basal literature anthologies, such textbooks are published by market-responsive companies, who strive to offend no one, liberal or conservative.[23] These look-alike textbooks are typically chosen for district use by committees of teachers, parents, and administrators. None of this is a formula for a literature program tilted towards wild-eyed radicalism.

Nevertheless, teenagers do often bring to discussions of values a disposition towards rebellion, sometimes towards uncritical rebellion for its own sake. Furthermore, many literary traditions are heavily iconoclastic. Historically (and perhaps structurally) the novel is a genre that leans strongly towards a critique of social values. Novels read by young adults, from Dalton Trumbo's 1939 anti-war novel *Johnny Got His Gun* to Walter Dean Myers' 1989 Vietnam saga *Fallen Angels*, continue that tradition. Consequently, feisty discussions of traditional values are virtually guaranteed some time during the course of literary study, even when the program is jam-packed with upbeat, star-spangled selections bearing the Archbishop's imprimatur and the Eagle Forum seal of approval.

Those discussions are a sign that we are winning, not losing, the battle for good public education. The critique of tradition is itself a part of the American tradition. Questioning the wisdom of the past is a risky business, but such questioning is essential in a democratic society. In a discussion of values education at a 1990 meeting of the Champaign, Illinois, Board of Education, Board President Richard Zollinger said it proudly and outright: "We take risks."

I have not always been personally happy with the direction that every discussion has taken in my classrooms or in the classrooms that I have observed. Nor am I pleased with all of the changes wrought through open discussion in American society. But the critique of traditional values has effectively destroyed or diminished many traditions that I personally consider obscene, from slavery to disenfranchisement of the poor, minorities, and women, to violations of the separation of church and state.

I suspect that all thoughtful Americans have their own personal lists of productive changes brought about at least partly through this democratic tradition of critical analysis of social institutions. The proper role of public school teachers of literature, it seems to me, is consistent with that tradition. Our calling is to develop skill in, and disposition *towards*, this kind of critical analysis in the study of literature. My democratic faith is that worthwhile institutions, ideas, and values are ultimately upheld by such analysis. Yet we must not—I use the imperative form intentionally—use the literature program for a tendentious analysis that promotes our personal ideas about religion, philosophy, or politics, whether those ideas be Christ-centered, Marx-centered, agnostic, or whatever.

Pluralism in the public school classroom does not imply either values-bashing or agnosticism. Neutrality is not vapid middle-of-the-roadism. Rather, pluralism and neutrality undergird a passionate belief in lively discourse—discourse about ideas that are absolutist or relativistic, ideas that are actually Christian or Jewish or Buddhist or only apparently so, ideas that support or attack social institutions. This huge and marvelous array of ideas makes a well-conducted public school English class one of the most exciting environments on earth.

Appendix: Specific Approaches to Teaching Values in the Literature Program

In seeking out examples of approaches to teaching values in relation to literature, I discovered three things. First, I had no trouble finding several kinds of models. Second, there is no single "values-oriented approach" to the teaching of literature. Selecting from materials that I have developed over three decades, and from ideas formulated by teachers from various regions and teaching levels, I was struck by the variety of approaches to infusing values into discussions of literary works. Third, I was happy to find that English teachers do not treat exploration of values in discrete units but feel quite comfortable integrating discussion of the authors' values and their students' values into larger contexts of literary study.

There are limitations, though, that the examples below have in common with all published "how to" materials. Even the best study guides cannot apply equally well to all student populations. They cannot predict fruitful digressions or even simulate the fluidity of good interaction. But they can be provocative, consistent with sound teaching theory, and flexible enough to invite adaptation by teachers and open response from students.

The following, then, is a potpourri of stimulating examples and models, loosely linked by my analytical comments. Another observer might have selected other examples and tasks, taking a different cut on the analysis, a possibility that testifies to the richness of the materials and to the inventiveness of the teachers who are writing about their classroom experiences. I will begin with a short theme-setting commentary by Jane Ann Zaharias. She compares response-based questions about a Frost poem to more traditional questions.

☞ ☞ ☞ ☞ ☞

Questions calling for answers that can be located directly in the text, hence requiring only recitation, should be abandoned in favor of items that require students' use of both the text and their prior knowledge in the formulation of a response. Especially important...are questions which elicit ideas, attitudes, and beliefs that are related to a given work but derived principally from the reader's experiential background. Two such items, based on Robert Frost's "The Road Not Taken," follow. Both are taken from the ninth-grade edition of a Canadian anthology.

1. Discuss some of the important choices that you have had to make. Does the poem express any of your feelings about the decisions you made? You may wish to write a paragraph describing an important decision, your reasons for choosing as you did, and the feelings that you now have about your decision.

2. What do you think is the most important choice or decision you will ever have to make? Why? What things should you consider in making your choice? After doing some research, write a list of directions entitled "How to Choose a _____." (Ireland 1983, Level C, 251)

Although the two items given above explicitly lead the students to conclude that Frost's poem is about making choices, and this approach may, as a result, prematurely thwart interpretation, these items are more likely to lead to an enhanced appreciation of the poem than do the following questions taken from a tenth-grade U.S. anthology:

1. How does the speaker decide which of the two roads to take?

2. Explain lines 13-15.
   (Miller, McDonnell, and Hogan 1985, Traditions in Literature, vol. 5 of *America Reads*, 228)

Questions like those contained in the U.S. text have as their basis the formalistic approach to the study of literature espoused by the New Critics. They inappropriately suggest that the "real meaning" of a literary work resides in the text rather than in the re-creation of the text by the reader.[24]

Here is a more elaborated example of post-reading discussion. The questions follow a reading of Benjamin Franklin's "Plan for Moral Perfection" from his *Autobiography*. I prepared these questions for a 1973 text in Alan Purves' *Responding* series, which attempted to give students a more personal and active role in discussing literary works.[25]

You'll recall that Franklin listed several virtues (e.g., Sincerity, Silence, Industry, etc.), providing epigrammatic advice on each and resolving to pursue moral perfection by cultivating the virtues. (e.g. "Temperance—Eat not to dullness; drink not to elevation.")

- Do you think that Franklin's system for arriving at moral perfection is a workable idea? Why?

- Picture a person who has completely mastered all of the virtues on Franklin's list. What kind of individual do you think he or she would be—interesting or dull? light-hearted or grave? popular or unpopular?

- What virtues—if any—do you think Franklin might have added to his list? Which virtues—if any—on his list strike you as unnecessary? as repetitive?

- Which particular virtue or virtues seem to reflect traditional Christian ideals? Which seem to deviate from Christian ideals?

The suggestion that follows can be handled effectively as a topic for (1) individual *ex tempore* talks, (2) class discussion, or (3) a short writing assignment.

- Complete the following sentence, supplying the name of one of Franklin's thirteen virtues, and tell why you chose the particular virtue named: *What the world needs now is a lot more ____.*

Writing Assignments

Students might select and complete one of the following suggested writing activities....

- The old writing game called "Happiness Is..." consists of a series of statements like these:

"Happiness is a canceled test."

"Happiness is a driver's license—and a car to go with it."

Substituting one or more of Franklin's virtues for *Happiness*, play the game by devising a series of original statements beginning with "Sincerity is...," "Cleanliness is...," "Order is...," and so on.

Activities

- Let two students improvise a TV talk-show interview of an imaginary character who has achieved absolute perfection according to Ben Franklin's plan. Students might well make up names for the character and the TV host-interviewer. If possible, have them tape the interview or put it on videotape for presentation to other classes.

The pages of NCTE's popular publication *Notes Plus* include numerous examples of literature instruction that invite students to discuss values. Rhoda Maxwell's post-study questions for a young adult novel, *All Together Now* by Sue Ellen Bridgers, demonstrate that good, values-oriented instruction is not limited to a study of the classics.[26] You do not have to know the plot of the novel to understand Rhoda Maxwell's approach. I will cite some of her prefatory comments because they are highly insightful; then I will point to some particularly appealing aspects of her approach.

> *It's not surprising that young adult novels can sometimes prompt a stronger response from students than do time-honored classics of literature. The characters and plots in young-adult novels generally parallel people and events in students' own lives; the emotional crises and struggles faced by the protagonists tend to be ones that all adolescents face. Because of students' heightened interest and the degree to which they relate to the characters, young-adult novels provide a natural background against which to explore literary concepts such as character development, motivation, and point of view.*

Sue Ellen Bridgers' novel *All Together Now* (Knopf, 1979) is a good choice for class reading and closer examination. As in Bridgers' other young-adult novels, *Home before Dark* (Bantam, 1985), and *Notes for Another Life* (Knopf, 1981), the characters in *All Together Now* are finely and realistically drawn, the settings are of historical importance, and the plot combines external action with interior, emotional events. The reading level for Bridgers' novels is designated as upper-elementary, but, depending on students' ability, the characterization and plot development might be better appreciated by readers in grades eight through ten....

1. After you have read the description of Hazard in chapter 2, explain your impression of him. Do you think you will like him? Is he similar to anyone you know? What does Jane think of him?

2. In chapter 2, what is Casey's motivation for letting Dwayne believe she is a boy? Sometimes lies such as this one are called "white lies." Write about a time when you told a white lie. Then assume that you were caught in the lie, and write a persuasive letter explaining your rationale for the lie.

3. Using the first person, tell the story of Hazard's life up to where the novel begins, from his point of view. Invent details as necessary.

4. In chapter 8, Dwayne's gift to Casey means a lot to her. Explain why it is so significant. Then write about a time when you received a gift that was of equal importance to you.

5. Pansy and Hazard's honeymoon, described in chapter 10, is a disaster. Could you have predicted that it would be? Contrast their values and expectations, using evidence from the text.

6. In chapter 11, Marge blows up at Dwayne. Describe Dwayne's mood and what he is thinking about before, during, and after this scene. What words, phrases, and images are used to convey Dwayne's feelings? Write about a per-

sonal experience when you felt the same way Dwayne did after his encounter with Marge.

7. Describe the impression that you have of Gwen when you first meet her in chapter 6. Trace the development of her character in chapters 7, 8, 11, 14, and 15. Is your overall view of Gwen any different by the end of the book? If so, explain what particular details or events alter your first impression of her. Describe what you predict Gwen's future with Taylor will be like.

8. Casey believes the adults have let her down because Dwayne has to spend the night in jail. Write about a time when you, too, had the sense of being let down. Could the situation have been changed? Is there a time when you felt you let someone else down?

9. How do different characters in the novel view Casey? How does Taylor's view of Casey change over the course of the novel? Use passages from the novel to support your opinion.

10. Descriptions of one's own family members, including oneself, would change depending on the point of view. Write a description of yourself or someone else you know very well—a close friend, a brother or sister, or even a pet—from your own viewpoint. Then write a detailed description of the same individual, seen through someone else's eyes.

11. After reading the description of the car race in chapter 6, write about a similar event or activity that you have been part of or have witnessed. Choose your verbs and adjectives carefully to give your description a sense of movement and excitement.

12. By the conclusion of the novel, Casey feels that she has learned much about responsibility and love. Describe the changes she has gone through and the results of those changes. Find specific passages that illustrate what, in your opinion, are significant learning experiences for Casey.

In the materials above, Rhoda Maxwell couples questions about the student's impression of the novel with an invitation to draw parallels to their lives. She also deals with literary concerns such as predictability of the plot (e.g., question 5), asking students to cite textual evidence. Question 7 is well-handled in terms of probing Gwen's character development; then it is amplified by an invitation for students to call on their previous understandings of the text in order to predict a probable future for Gwen and Taylor.

In many cases, a single question—e.g., the one about "white lies" or the one about being "let down"—will in all likelihood lead to an extended class discussion of ethical issues. This, of course, is an important quality of response-based instruction. Because the question deals with interestingly ambiguous material, extensive and authentic discussion rather than recitation is encouraged, and students learn the give-and-take of good conversation that is so useful in a democratic society.

So far, the examples have focused on students' discussions *during* or *after* reading part or all of a selection. But many of the best values-oriented materials in recent years have focused on *pre-reading* activities. In pre-reading, the idea is to develop a personal framework—a "schema"—for the study of a complex literary work. Students explore their own beliefs about an important moral issue before reading, and thereby establish a personal frame of reference as they read and discuss the work.

Values can be embedded in pre-reading activities in many ways. Students can do a dramatic improvisation in which a moral dilemma is dramatized. The teacher can present a real or hypothetical case study that sets up the conflict in a mini-narrative, asking the students to react. Class discussion of a current political situation, of a school or community event, or of other real-life moral issues can be introduced before reading one or more works that explore the same issue.

Smagorinsky, *et al.* suggest that an opinionnaire be circulated among the students for their initial response.[27] Students exchange ideas about their first reactions, developing their opinions on the issues that will later be explored in literary works. The opinionnaire below deals with the issues of the individual in relation to governments and other sources of authority. Smagorinsky notes that this pre-reading discussion is useful before studying works like Thoreau's "Civil Disobedience," Orwell's *1984* or *Animal Farm*, or Kesey's *One Flew over the Cuckoo's Nest.* I would feel comfortable using the opinionnaire before other works, too, like Melville's *Billy Budd* or Wouk's *The Caine Mutiny Court Martial.* The opinionnaire can be adapted for use with many literary works.

> *Below is a series of statements. Circle the response which most closely indicates how you feel about the statement.*

> 1. Most governments genuinely do have the interests of the people at heart.
>
>   Strongly   Agree   Not Sure   Disagree   Strongly
>   Agree   Disagree

> 2. If the people feel that a government is not working fairly for them, they have the right to

start a revolution to overthrow that government.

Strongly   Agre   Not Sure   Disagree   Strongly
Agree   Disagree

3. A citizen of legal age has the right to do anything he or she wants to do as long as it does not directly harm another human being.

Strongly   Agree   Not Sure   Disagree   Strongly
Agree   Disagree

4. Governments are interested only in keeping themselves in power.

Strongly   Agree   Not Sure   Disagree   Strongly
Agree   Disagree

5. The best government is the one that governs *least*.

Strongly   Agree   Not Sure   Disagree   Strongly
Agree   Disagree

6. You should always complain when things aren't going the way you want them to go.

Strongly   Agree   Not Sure   Disagree   Strongly
Agree   Disagree

7. A person should be loyal to his or her government first, and to his or her own interests second.

Strongly   Agree   Not Sure   Disagree   Strongly
Agree   Disagree

8. When you want society to change, you should do it through your vote, not by protesting.

Strongly   Agree   Not Sure   Disagree   Strongly
Agree   Agree

9. We should never question the decisions of people who are placed in administrative positions,

because they are doing what they feel is best
for everyone.

Strongly   Agree   Not Sure   Disagree   Strongly
Agree   Disagree

10. Most people are too meek to stand up for what
they believe in.

Strongly   Agree   Not Sure   Disagree   Strongly
Agree   Disagree

11. I always make my opinions known when I disagree with the way things are being run.

Strongly   Agree   Not Sure   Disagree   Strongly
Agree   Disagree

I conclude with a values-oriented approach that
deals with more intensive study of a work. Sally
Reisinger's method in teaching the popular novel by
Harper Lee, *To Kill a Mockingbird*, makes use of a brief
list of hypotheticals for pre-reading discussion, followed by a focus on attitudes of characters in the novel
(in the "core-reading activity," conducted when the students are midway through the book). The post-reading
activity is cleverly cast not as an abstract essay but as
teen-related advice on tolerance and respect for others,
realized in an imaginary dialogue between a senior and
an incoming freshman.[28]

> *Empathy is an ingredient essential to maturity. But*
> *until we accept the fact that we are all individuals*
> *with our own personal weaknesses, our subjectivity*
> *can make it difficult for us to empathize with oth-*
> *ers and to understand their actions. A worthy goal,*
> *then, is to engage students in activities that will*
> *open their eyes to individual differences and give*

them an occasion to develop compassionate discernment.

To Kill a Mockingbird *is one appropriate vehicle for teaching individuality. I use pre-reading, core-reading, and post-reading activities. Activity I (pre-reading) employs "sentence stubs" to jolt students into recognition of the various opinions and attitudes toward given situations. The "sentence stubs" or incomplete sentences can be written on the board or overhead for students to complete according to their personal experiences or preferences.*

Some possible sentence provokers are listed below. These sentences address some of the issues found in To Kill a Mockingbird, *and the responses will provide students with some insights into their own belief systems.*

Activity 1

1. If my best friend began socializing with a social outcast, I would...

2. If I lived next door to someone who others thought was violent, I would....

3. If my friend used poor table manners while eating at my home, I would feel....

4. If my parent(s) were older than my friends' parents, I would feel....

5. If someone I care for were trying to conquer an addiction (e.g., food, alcohol, tobacco, drugs), I would feel....

After students have completed Activity 1, they share their responses and note the varying viewpoints that emerged. By giving special attention to those attitudes nurtured by society, I try to help students to see how environment shapes our conceptions of others. With this new understanding, students begin to read the novel.

*Midway through the reading, I use Activity 2. In
this core-reading activity, each student selects a situation in the novel that reveals varying attitudes or
beliefs concerning others. Students are asked to
compose a brief paragraph in which they reflect on
a particular character's motivation in a given situation.*

*For example, Atticus's decision to stay outside of
Tom Robinson's cell in order to protect his client
from a lynch mob is motivated by his sense of justice and a wish to ease Tom's fear of violence. A student selecting this situation might briefly discuss
what part society has played in the formation of
Atticus's attitude. Another typical student paragraph might focus on Atticus's conversation with
Scout concerning Scout's conflicts with her teacher
and another student; the student author might explore the motivations behind Atticus's strong sense
of fair play.*

*At the completion of Activity 2, students locate their
"core sentence" or "center-of-gravity" sentence, using
the technique described in* Writing, *by Elizabeth
and Gregory Cowan (Scott, Foresman, 1980). To do
this, each student examines his or her paragraph
and locates a sentence that pinpoints the external
or internal influences that prompt the character's
behavior. For instance, the author of the second student paragraph mentioned above would be looking
for a sentence that helps to explain why Atticus dis-
courages Scout from prejudging people. In this
case, the sentence selected as a "core sentence"
might be one stating that Atticus's personal belief
in human rights and his experience as an attorney
have motivated him to advise Scout to refrain from
judgmental arrogance when she has not been "inside the skin of another."*

*This activity reinforces the connection between the
causes and effects of individual actions, allowing
students to comprehend the complexities behind a*

person's actions and appreciate the significance of incentive.

A valuable side effect of this exercise is students' realization that although many outside sources may affect our volition, each individual alone must face the consequences of his or her decisions. To Kill a Mockingbird *reinforces this principle elegantly.*

At the completion of the novel, Activity 3 (post-reading) focuses on the understandings and sensitivities cultivated by the students during this study. Students are assigned to write a dialogue between a senior and an incoming freshman in which the older student imparts advice about how one should respond to, and coexist with, peers, parents, and teachers during the next four years. The insight students have gained can then be passed on to the freshman English teachers to be shared the following year. What better way for students to learn tolerance and respect for others than through the encouragement of their peers?

NOTES

1. "Values Education Belongs in the Schools," *Education USA* 29 (27): 199.

2. Robert T. Rhode, "Legal Discussion and Censorship: A Game of Chance," in *Dealing with Censorship,* James E. Davis, ed. Urbana, Illinois: National Council of Teachers of English, 1979.

3. Robert Primack and David Aspey, "The Roots of Humanism," *Educational Leadership 38* (December 1980): 226.

4. Stuart Taylor, "Judge a Hero of Right Wing," *News Gazette* (Champaign-Urbana, Illinois, March 8, 1987): D-1.

5. Texe Marrs, *Dark Secrets of the New Age: Satan's Plan for a One World Religion* (Westchester, Illinois: Crossways Books, 1988): 230.

6. *Loc. cit.*

7. For a readable and sensible perspective on Eastern-based religions in America, from looney cults to creative adaptations of Buddhist and Hindu practices, see Dick Anthony and Bruce Ecker, *Spiritual Choices* (New York: Paragon House, 1987).

8. Sue Howell, "On Values Education," *IATE Newsletter* 23 (Fall, 1987): 5.

9. Robert E. Probst, *Transactional Theory in the Teaching of Literature.* ERIC Digest. Urbana, Illinois: ERIC Clearinghouse on Reading and Communication Skills, 1987, n.p.

10. George Will, "Conservative Court Action Has Its Dangers," *News Gazette* (Champaign-Urbana, Illinois, November 9, 1986): A-4.

11. Arthur Applebee, *A Study of Book-Length Works Taught in High School English Courses* (Albany,

N.Y.: Center for the Learning and Teaching of Literature, 1989).

12. National Coalition against Censorship, *Books on Trial: A Survey of Recent Cases* (New York: National Coalition against Censorship, 1987).

13. John Furlong and William Carroll, "Teacher Neutrality and Teaching of Ethical Issues," *Educational Forum 54* (Winter 1990): 162.

14. George Hillocks, *Research on Written Composition* (Urbana, Illinois: ERIC Clearinghouse on Reading and Communication Skills and National Conference on Research in English, 1986).

15. A.S. Palincsar and A.L. Brown, "Reciprocal Teaching: Activities to Promote Reading with Your Mind," in *Reading, Thinking, and Concept Development: Strategies for the Classroom,* T.L. Harris and E.J. Cogen, eds. (New York: The College Board, 1985).

16. Jerome Bruner, "The Role of Dialogue in Language Acquisition," in *The Child's Conception of Language,* A. Sinclair, *et al.*, eds. (New York: Springer-Verlag, 1978).

17. David Johnson, *et al., Circles of Learning: Cooperation in the Classroom* (Alexandria, Virginia: Association for Supervision and Curriculum Development, 1984).

18. Richard Paul, "Critical Thinking, Moral Integrity, and Citizenship: Teaching for the Intellectual Virtues." Paper distributed at Association for Supervision and Curriculum Development Conference at Wingspread (Racine, Wisconsin, 1986).

19. Robert Scholes, *Textual Power: Literary Theory and the Teaching of English* (New Haven, Connecticut: Yale University Press, 1985): 49-50.

20. Louise Rosenblatt, "The Literary Transaction: Evocation and Response," *Theory into Practice 21* (1982): 268-277.

21. Peter Smagorinsky, *et al., Explorations: Introductory Activities for Literature and Composition, 7-12.* (Urbana, Illinois: NCTE and ERIC/RCS, 1987).

22. Robert E. Probst, *op. cit.*

23. Bruce Appleby, *et al.*, "A Hefty New Literature Series: Something for Everyone?" *English Journal 78* (October 1989): 77-80.

24. Jane Ann Zaharias, "Literature Anthologies in the U.S.: Impediments to Good Teaching Practice," *English Journal 78* (October 1989): 22-27.

25. Charles Suhor, *American Dream,* Teachers' Edition (Boston: Ginn, 1973): T17-18.

26. Rhoda Maxwell, "Exploring Characters in *All Together Now,"* *Notes Plus* (Urbana, Illinois: NCTE, January 1989): 7-8.

27. Peter Smagorinsky, *et al. Explorations: Introductory Activities for Literature and Composition, 7-12.* (Urbana, Illinois: NCTE and ERIC/RCS, 1987).

28. Sally Reisinger, "Developing Maturity through Responding to Literature," *Notes Plus* (Urbana, Illinois: NCTE, April 1990): 10-11.

REFERENCES

Anthony, Dick, and Bruce Ecker. "The Anthology Typology: A Framework for Assessing Spiritual and Consciousness Groups," in *Spiritual Choices*, D. Anthony, B. Ecker, and K. Wilber, eds. New York: Paragon House, 1987.

Applebee, Arthur. *A Study of Book-Length Works Taught in High School English Courses.* Albany, N.Y.: Center for the Learning and Teaching of Literature, 1989.

Appleby, Bruce, *et al.* "A Hefty New Literature Series: Something for Everyone?" *English Journal 78* (October 1989): 77-80.

Bruner, Jerome. "The Role of Dialogue in Language Acquisition," in *The Child's Conception of Language*, A. Sinclair, *et al.* eds. New York: Springer-Verlag, 1978.

Furlong, John and William Carroll, "Teacher Neutrality and Teaching of Ethical Issues," *Educational Forum 54* (winter 1990): 157-168.

Hillocks, George. "The Kanawha County Textbook War: Ideological Confict or Censorship?" NCTE audio cassette. Address at NCTE Annual Convention, Chicago, November, 1976.

Hillocks, George. *Research on Written Composition.* Urbana, Illinois: ERIC Clearinghouse on Reading and Communication Skills and National Conference on Research in English, 1986.

Howell, Sue. "On Values Education," *IATE Newsletter 23* (fall 1987): 50.

"Interfaith Consortium for Pluralism in American Life (IFCP)." Brochure distributed by IFCP/NCJJ, 940 Logan Street, Denver, Colorado 80203, n.d.

Johnson, David, *et al. Circles of Learning: Cooperation in the Classroom*. Alexandria, Virginia: Association for Supervision and Curriculum Development, 1984.

Marrs, Texe. *Dark Secrets of the New Age: Satan's Plan for a One World Religion*. Westchester, Illinois: Crossways Books, 1988.

Marzano, Robert and Daisy Arredondo. *Tactics for Thinking—Teacher's Manual*. Alexandria, Virginia: ASCD, 1986.

Maxwell, Rhoda, "Exploring Characters in 'All Together Now'," *Notes Plus* (Urbana, Illinois: NCTE January 1989): 7-8.

National Coalition against Censorship. *Books on Trial: A Survey of Recent Cases*. New York: National Coalition against Censorship, 1987.

"National Council on Religion and Public Education." Brochure distributed by NCRPE, 1300 Oread Avenue, Lawrence, Kansas 66045 n.d.

Palincsar, A.S. and A.L. Brown. "Reciprocal Teaching: Activities to Promote Reading with Your Mind," in *Reading, Thinking, and Concept Development: Strategies for the Classroom*, T.L. Harris and E.J. Cogen, eds. New York: The College Board, 1985.

Paul, Richard. "Critical Thinking, Moral Integrity, and Citizenship: Teaching for the Intellectual Virtues." Paper distributed at Association for Supervision and Curriculum Development Conference at Wingspread. Racine, Wisconsin, 1986.

Primack, Robert and David Aspey, "The Roots of Humanism," *Educational Leadership* (December 1980): 224-226.

Probst, Robert E. "Transactional Theory in the Teaching of Literature." ERIC Digest. Urbana, Illinois: ERIC Clearinghouse on Reading and Communication Skills, 1987.

Reisinger, Sally. "Developing Maturity through Responding to Literature," *Notes Plus* (Urbana, Illinois: NCTE April 1990), 10-11.

Rhode, Robert T. "Legal Discussion and Censorship: A Game of Chance," in *Dealing with Censorship*, James E. Davis, ed. Urbana, Illinois: NCTE, 1979.

Rosenblatt, Louise. "The Literary Transaction: Evocation and Response," *Theory into Practice 21* (1982): 268-277.

Scholes, Robert. *Textual Power: Literary Theory and the Teaching of English*. New Haven, Connecticut: Yale University Press, 1985.

Smagorinsky, Peter, *et al. Explorations: Introductory Activities for Literature and Composition, 7-12.* Urbana, Illinois: NCTE and ERIC/RCS, 1987.

Suhor, Charles. *American Dream.* Boston: Ginn, 1973.

"Values Education Belongs in Schools," *Education USA 29* (March 2, 1987): 197.

Will, George. "Conservative Court Action Has Its Dangers," Champaign-Urbana *News Gazette* (November 9, 1986, A-4.

Zaharias, Jane Ann. "Literature Anthologies in the U.S.: Impediments to Good Teaching Practice," *English Journal 78* (October 1989): 22-27.

Values in the Teaching of Literature—A Catholic-School View

Bernard Suhor

"The world is charged with the grandeur of God."[1]

So sang Jesuit poet Gerard Manley Hopkins a century ago. So sing I today in a world that is far sadder and madder than Hopkins' ever was. Yet the grandeur of God that Hopkins saw and sang then appears the more glorious now by contrast with the growing darkness that is itself doomed to disappear. From my own Judaeo-Christian perspective, God and His grandeur will surely win.

Part of my joyful burden as an English teacher is to help unfold to my students, and ponder with them, values in literature that are both secular and sacred. If literature is a mirror held up to nature, then literature too is charged with the reflection of a grandeur that is God. Whether authors intend it or not, their characters are all in some way God-geared, as Hopkins might have put it. Macbeth and Gatsby, Anna Karenina and Hester Prynne, Holden Caulfield and David Copperfield: You are all creations of your authors. Some of you are heaven-hounded, and too precious few of you are heaven-hounding, but all of you—along with your creators—are ultimately the marvelous makings of the Master Builder who is God the Father.

As an English teacher, I mine the sometime hidden veins of God's gold in literature. I can bring that gold to the light of day and then just let it dazzle or glow for its own sake, like Hopkins' "shook foil." At the secular level of my teaching vocation, I agree to be what has been redoubtably called a "facilitator of learning." So be it. At a higher level, I want to be a facilitator of sanctification. So may it be. Wisdom shall enter into my students' minds and hearts, not just knowledge. From values literary I can strike sparks in my students' awareness that rise to values that are supernatural. The medieval scholastics called this process *contemplata aliis tradere*, handing over the fruits of our own contemplation to others.

Do I intend to make much of an explicit dichotomy between the secular and the sacred in my teaching of literature? I hope not, unless perhaps I am teaching the medieval morality play *Everyman*. Yet I also hope that I may never, like some of my fellow Catholics, say with misbegotten raptures, "But the sacred and the secular are really identical! To be holy is to be whole and holistic!" No, Christians are not caterpillars-turned-butterflies. We have been neither metamorphosed nor colorized. We have been baptized. "If anyone is in Christ, he is a new creation," sang Paul to the Corinthians two millennia ago, that "in him we might become the very holiness of God."[2] God's grace always builds on nature, but it is certainly not to be identified with fallen human nature. Aye, and there's the rub.

Before giving examples of what I would do with specific literary works in a classroom situation, let me further state "where I am coming from," or perhaps better, "whereon I stand." This is my *apologia* without any intention of being an apology. Moreover, it is *a* Catholic viewpoint about the teaching of values through literature, but not an attempt to speak for *all* Catholic teachers. However, it is only fair to warn that I have every intention of proselytizing. As a Christian Humanist, I have every right to be as missionary-minded as the most ardent Secular Humanists teaching in America today.

Whereon I Stand: The Source of Values

Although with some anonymous modern poet, I have "a lover's quarrel with the world," I do not believe that the secular order *per se* is necessarily opposed to the sacred. Neither did St. Augustine, as he stated in his *City of God* (19:17):

> *The Celestial City...in this mortal life...does not hesitate to obey the laws of this earthly city;... Since this mortal life is common to both, a harmony may be preserved between both cities concerning things belonging to it.*[3]

In our own time, the Second Vatican Council stated the following:

> *The way in which the earthly and the heavenly city inter-penetrate each other can be recognized only by faith.... The Church believes that she can make a great contribution, through individual members and the community as a whole, toward bringing a greater humanity to the family of man and its history.*[4]

Now *that* is truly the work of Christian Humanism. These statements should both defuse and diffuse any expectations that I, as a Catholic teacher, must necessarily presuppose a conflict between secular education and religious education. *In no way do I equate secular education with Secular Humanism.* All I want to do, as Vatican II says that faith only can do, is to "make a great contribution toward bringing a greater humanity" to my students through the teaching of literature. Because, moreover, my students are made in the image and likeness of God, I can best humanize them by helping to divinize them.

Like any other American teacher in a church-affiliated school, I have the civil right to communicate religious values in my classroom. This right I share with every other sectarian school teacher—Lutheran, Episcopalian, Jewish, Amish, Mormon, Baptist, Assembly of God. Each of us has the right in our private schools to be as public as we choose in the indoctrination of our students. This is one of the few points on which I am in major agreement with the American Civil Liberties Union.

We Catholics have schools, as that passage from Vatican II goes on to say, to advance "the coming of God's Kingdom and the salvation of the whole human race." I do that in my literature classroom by helping the kingdom of God enter into the minds and hearts of my students by helping them understand the values represented in literature. Catholic schools are not secular schools with the added subject of religion. Our first objective is to inform our students about Jesus Christ and then help to form them into his greater image and likeness. What begins at Baptism, increases at Confirmation, and we then nurture and advance through Catholic education, but not in religion class only. Unfortunately, not all Catholic parents, nor even teachers, see this deep religious growth as the primary value, the *sine qua non,* of Catholic schooling. Secular values have clouded our vision and distorted our priorities.

As a Catholic teacher, I am first and always a learner, a disciple of the perfect teacher, Jesus Christ. Regardless of what subject I am teaching, I must strive "to teach as Jesus did," or to teach as he would if he were in my classroom. I can never for one moment forget that the school I teach in is his school, not mine; that the students I teach are his students, not mine.

My own formation into Jesus is a never-ending adventure. I first met him personally as the Way, Truth, and Life, through the loving catechesis of my parents. That was the beginning of an ongoing journey into the mind and heart of God, an arduous journey, but one of endless fascinations. Jesus revealed himself through Matthew, Mark, Luke, John, and Paul. He continues to reveal himself to me in the power of the Holy Spirit, through his Church, One, Holy, Universal, Apostolic, and through the lively teaching office of Peter and his successors, whom Jesus himself established as his representatives. Let me pray:

> *Thank you, Lord, a million times over for the gift of these supreme shepherds. Some have been holy; some have been horrible; and some, by the mysteriously weird wedding of the secular and the sacred, have managed to be both holy and horrible. But without these men and the keys and the shepherd's crooks you have placed in their hands to guide the likes of "infallible" little creatures like me, there is no telling into what dangerous pastures and irrelevant fast lanes I might have strayed, seeking pseudokingdoms and following the creeds and commandments of secular messiahs. Amen.*

During my life as both a student and teacher, I have learned so much also from reading the lives and writings of the Saints. They are the living

proof of the validity of the Gospel message. But I
need not, as did poor Miniver Cheevy in E.A.
Robinson's poem, yearn to have lived in a romantic
and spiritual past. These men and women *made* the
past spiritual. By eagerly allowing themselves to be
transformed into Christ, they transformed, to some
degree, their own times. They tell me to stay in my
own century and in my own school, and do Christ's
thing in the here and now.

This is what I want to do as a Catholic Humanist
teacher of literature. I begin my classroom day by
reflecting on the gift of my vocation as a Catholic
teacher in the words of Daniel 12:3: "The wise shall
shine brightly like the splendor of the firmament,
and those who lead the many to justice shall be like
the stars forever."

To summarize whereon I stand: Created in the
image and likeness of God; baptized into the life,
death, and resurrection of Jesus Christ; filled with
the Holy Spirit; incorporated into the Body of Christ
which is the Church; lovingly and solicitously
watched over by Mary, the angels, and the cloud of
witnesses that we call the Saints, I find myself called
to be, by God's mercy, an English teacher in a Catholic high school. (Reading the Gospel according to St.
John the Evangelist and *The Spiritual Canticle* of St.
John of the Cross, as well, does not excuse me from
reading *The English Journal.*) For me, *contemplata
aliis tradere* means sharing with my students the
fruits of years of study and reflection on the treasures of literature, both sacred and profane.

The What: Some Values in Literature to Which I Call My Students' Attention

While I do not equate the secular with the sacred,
I revel in agreement with Gerard Manley Hopkins'
line: "The world is charged with grandeur of God." In

the same way, a situation in literature, whether casual or cataclysmic, may be charged with a meaning that transcends the here-and-now.

To call attention to these transcending values, I set questions before my students. The following baker's double dozen of literary masterworks poses a range of values to be clarified. Some of these values are specifically Christian, some are Roman Catholic, and all of them are controversial:

1. In Nathaniel Hawthorne's "The Minister's Black Veil," would the Puritan minister still have felt the need to wear that symbolic veil of guilt, if he and his congregation had known the release available in the Sacrament of Reconciliation?

2. In Arthur Miller's play *The Crucible*, several people are accused of trafficking with Satan. Do you believe that the Devil is real, and that there are other evil spirits as well? Did Jesus believe that evil spirits exist?

3. Reading Mark Twain's novel *Huckleberry Finn*, suppose that you were a priest, and Huck confessed to you that he had done two very bad things: He had helped a runaway slave escape from his rightful owner, and he had then defiantly expressed a willingness to go to hell for the wrongdoing he had committed. What would you, the priest, representing Jesus Christ, tell Huck?

4. In John Steinbeck's novel *Of Mice and Men*, do you think George was right to shoot Lennie in order to save him from being jailed or put into an asylum? Is your judging of George's *act* the same thing as your judging

George's personal guilt or innocence before God?

5. William Cullen Bryant wrote his poem "Thanatopsis," which means "a view of death," while he was a teenager, when he thought he was dying. If you were dying, would you find your chief consolation, as Bryant did, in the thought that you were returning to "nature," going where all living things before you had preceded you?

6. In Shakespeare's tragedy *Hamlet*, young Laertes curses the priest who refuses to bury Laertes' sister Ophelia in hallowed ground because she has committed suicide. Why do you think the Church refused Christian burial to suicides? Does the Church have the same attitude today?

7. Emily Dickinson, in her poem "Some Keep the Sabbath," made a case for a Sunday morning liturgy with Nature in her own back yard, in preference to going to church for worship. How would you respond to Emily? How do you think St. Francis of Assisi might respond to her, loving God and Nature (and the Mass) as he did?

8. In Jack Schaefer's novel *Shane*, in what ways might the hero be considered a Christ-figure? If Jesus had lived in the American West at the time of Shane, do you think he would have carried and used a gun to keep the peace, the way Shane did?

9. In *West Side Story*, two Catholic teenagers, Maria and Tony, suddenly fall deeply in love and go through a mock wedding ceremony the day after they meet, only then to become

embroiled in some senseless gang warfare, during which Tony kills Maria's brother. In desperation, they plan to run away together. Having thus become "engaged," they apparently spend an amorous night in Maria's bedroom. All things considered, were they morally justified in spending the night together as husband and wife?

10. In Edgar Allan Poe's short story "The Black Cat," the narrator admits that some of the cruel things he had done were done out of a spirit of perverseness, and for no other reason. What do you recall from your religion studies about the distinction between sins of weakness and sins of malice? What do you believe about Original Sin and the human inclination to evil?

11. In Homer's *Iliad* and *Odyssey*, we read much about the Greek gods and goddesses. How is Zeus like and unlike God the Father, as revealed in the New Testament by Jesus Christ, and in songs like Carey Landry's "Abba, Father"? How close do any of the other Greek gods come to resembling Jesus Christ in his attitude towards mankind?

12. At the end of W.S. Maugham's novel *The Razor's Edge*, Larry has rejected the materialistic values of the West; he embraces a life of simplicity and self-renunciation that he had learned from a guru in the East. Do you think that people can find as much salvation and happiness in Eastern religions as they can in Christianity? Would Jesus agree with your answer?

13. In Clarence Day's *Life with Father*, consider the relationship between Mr. and Mrs. Day.

Was this the kind of relationship St. Paul had in mind when he wrote in Ephesians 5:22, 25: "Wives should be submissive to their husbands as unto the Lord...Husbands love your wives, as Christ loved the Church"? If not, what do you think St. Paul did have in mind? Read the whole section, 5:22-30, before answering.

14. In Charlotte Bronte's novel *Jane Eyre*, do you think a good case could have been made for having Rochester's first marriage annulled, considering his wife's duplicity at the time of their marriage? What is the difference between an annulment and a divorce?

Also in *Jane Eyre*, Rochester pleads with Jane to live with him in an adulterous union, after the fact of his first marriage is revealed. Jane is torn between her love for Rochester and her sense of values. Read her response to Rochester, and then answer the questions that follow:

> *I will keep the law given by God; sanctioned by man....Laws and principles are not for the times when there is no temptation: they are for such moments as this, when body and soul rise in mutiny against their rigor....If at my individual convenience I might break them, what would be their worth?*[5]

How do you think Jane Eyre would have responded to Rochester's invitation if they were a typical couple in a daytime TV soap opera? Do you think that Jane, in her response in the novel, is speaking like a "liberated woman"? How would you define a "liberated woman"?

15. In Stone and Edwards' *1776*, serious questions are raised about the right to revolt against England. Do you think that conditions justifying a revolution were present in the American situation? Christian moral theologians have said that these conditions are as follows: 1) The government in power is exercising intolerable tyranny. 2) All diplomatic and peaceful means have been tried, but to no avail. 3) There is a genuine possibility of the revolution's being successful.

16. In Stein, Bock, and Harnick's *Fiddler on the Roof*, Tevye the Jew disowns his daughter for marrying a Gentile. Can you make a case at all in defense of a parent's doing such a thing, regardless of what religions are involved? How do you think Tevye would answer the question, "Why did you do it, Tevye, loving father that you are?"

17. In Graham Greene's novel *The Power and the Glory*, a priest who seems to be "living in sin" can be read as becoming a Christ-figure as the novel progresses. Do you agree? Why or why not? Which is the more credible to you as a Christ-figure: Graham Greene's priest or Herman Melville's Billy Budd? Why?

18. In Hawthorne's "Dr. Heidegger's Experiment," the question arises whether we would be better humans if we were given "a second time around." What do you believe about reincarnation? What do Scripture and the Church say about reincarnation?

19. How can Macbeth and Lady Macbeth be seen as counterparts to Adam and Eve? What does Jesus' statement in Matthew 16:26 about a

man gaining everything, but losing his soul, have to say about Macbeth's situation?

Macbeth consulted three witches to find out about the future. In the Scriptures, God has forbidden consulting fortune tellers (Deuteronomy 18:9-14, Revelation 21:8). Do you think Jesus approves of Christians reading their horoscopes or going to palmists or tarot-card readers? What reading might Jesus recommend for people who are concerned about their futures?

20. In Hart and Kaufman's play *You Can't Take It With You*, Grandpa communicates his image of God. Jonathan Edwards communicates a different picture of God in his sermon "Sinners in the Hands of an Angry God." What, if anything, do you find unsatisfactory in the two images?

21. In Muriel Spark's *The Prime of Miss Jean Brodie*, Miss Brodie is accused by one of her former high-school students of having been a truly bad influence on her pupils. Do you think that Jesus' statement in Matthew 18:6 about the millstone and evil teachers is applicable here? Why was Jesus so tough on this issue? Does Miss Brodie's passionate sincerity make everything all right? Do you think there should be a Nobel Prize for sincerity? Why or why not?

22. In Hawthorne's *The Scarlet Letter*, he not even once refers to the how, when, or where of the sin between Hester and Arthur. How is this different from modern portrayals of infidelity? Why did Hawthorne not give us the details? Was he being prudish?

Reflect further: Why do you think erotic movies and television shows hardly, if ever, focus on love scenes between husbands and wives? Why do they focus so much on premarital and extramarital sex? What does this say about script writers? About advertisers? About TV executives? About viewers?

23. Agree or disagree with the following statement, and give your reasons:

    In Stephen Crane's *The Red Badge of Courage*, it is strange that the youth, a sensitive young man from rural New England, not once thinks of turning to God in prayer for counsel or courage to face his overwhelming dilemmas.

24. Read the dying speech of Cyrano de Bergerac to Roxanne. Make a list of those values that Cyrano held dearest all his life. Make another list of the things that Cyrano despised all his life. Which of his values reflect your own? Which of his values reflect the values of Jesus Christ?

25. In Robert Louis Stevenson's *Dr. Jekyll and Mr. Hyde*, how does Dr. Jekyll's desire to segregate (and in a sense liberate) the evil side of his human nature from the good side compare with what St. Paul said on the very same subject in Romans 7:13-25?

26. In Lorraine Hansberry's powerful drama *A Raisin in the Sun*, Mrs. Lena Younger, the matriarch of a black family, slaps her nineteen-year-old daughter in the face for speaking disrespectfully of God. Did Mrs. Younger have the right to do that? Why or why not?

a. When the Younger family gets ready to move into an all-white neighborhood, a representative from the neighborhood requests that they reconsider and not break the color barrier. What do you think Jesus would have said to this white man and the people he represented?

b. Now suppose that you and your family are living in that now well-integrated neighborhood next door to the Younger family. You and your family hear that your bishop is about to buy several houses across the street from your property, where he intends to settle some ignorant, destitute, unskilled Mexican immigrant families. What would your reaction be? Why? How would Jesus respond to your reaction?

c. On another page in Hansberry's *A Raisin in the Sun*, Ruth is depressed and is considering having an abortion. Her mother-in-law, Mrs. Lena Younger, says to her son, "We a people who gives children life, not who destroy them."[6]

Given that scene, imagine that you are a serious science-fiction writer like Ray Bradbury. You place a spokeswoman from the National Organization of Women (NOW) in a time machine and transport her back to the scene in the play. The lady says to Mrs. Younger:

"No, Lena dear, your daughter-in-law is not really carrying a baby, only a fetus. A fetus is not fully human."

How would Mrs. Younger respond to the NOW lady?

d. The same NOW lady gets back into the time-machine and travels almost 2,000 years into the past to Galilee in Palestine. She tells a pregnant teenaged girl named Mary that the way the Gospel writers will record her pregnancy is erroneous. The NOW lady speaks:

> *No, Mary dear, Matthew and Luke (both of them males, as you might expect) will say that you were "found with child through the power of the Holy Spirit." But they are wrong. You are only carrying a fetus at this point.*

> *You see, what later generations of male theologians will call the Incarnation has not taken place in your womb. The incarnation will take place later, dear, when you bring your pregnancy to full term, at the nativity. Only then will it really be a baby, you see.*

> *Now, don't you understand that I have brought you true wisdom and some really good news?*

How does Mary respond to the NOW lady?

e. Undaunted, the NOW lady tarries in Galilee and follows Mary to the home of her older cousin Elizabeth, also pregnant. After listening to Mary greet her older cousin, the NOW lady hears Elizabeth say to Mary, "The baby leapt in my womb for joy." Then the NOW lady speaks to Elizabeth:

> *Now, dear, you are carrying a fetus—not a human being, just a fetus. A fetus is a living thing, yes, of course, but not a*

baby, for heaven's sake! A thing does not leap for joy, now does it?

I come as the bearer of good news from a distant, much more enlightened future. I want to liberate women in all periods of history with a truth that will make you free. No, you are not carrying a child in your womb. See here? I have it in writing on the highest conceivable authority: the United States Supreme Court, Roe v. Wade, 1973. What higher authority could you ask than that, dear?

How do you think Elizabeth and Mary might respond to the NOW lady?

The How: Clarifying Values through Discussing Literature

These are the guidelines I follow in an informal way when discussing values with my students:

1. The primary value of literature is art for its own sake, not as a vehicle for teaching Christian values.

2. In some cases, when a moral point treated by an author touches explicitly on values, then a discussion of morals becomes central to understanding the writing. For instance, the whole point of Emily Dickinson's poem about the sabbath has to do with how Christians express their values through worship. If I fail to discuss the moral frame of reference in this poem, including the Catholic perspective, I am not doing my full duty either as a teacher or as a Catholic.

3. Many literary works do not lend themselves to discussion of values at all. It is enough that I affirm the value of everything we do in

class by beginning each class with an informal prayer; there is no need to attach moral tags to "The Secret Life of Walter Mitty" or "Shall I compare thee to a summer day?"

4. I approach moral questions in terms of my assessment of where the class as a whole is in relation to Jesus Christ and his values. Are my students indifferent? Are they hostile to religion? Are they ignorant? Are they open? (Are they awake?) The answers to these questions determine my approach. I do not introduce moral considerations by saying bluntly, "Now let's see what the Catholic Church says about this!"

5. Many of the moral questions that I raise, and observations about values that I make in my Catholic school classroom, could be raised in broader ethical terms in a public school classroom. Values like honesty, integrity, generosity, forgiveness, and self-sacrifice are not exclusively Christian virtues; however, in a Catholic setting, my approach most often needs to be not only specifically Christian but also specifically Roman Catholic. I ask my students to think: "How would Jesus deal with this?"

6. Overall, I judge that the "What do you think?" approach is the best way to introduce a discussion of values. I encourage my students to begin without any initial comment from me. I like to see them react to one another's views in a free flow of opinions. I sometimes play the devil's advocate, the better to achieve the much-touted "values clarification." St. Thomas Aquinas used this technique throughout his great *Summa The-*

ologica, arguing as forcefully as he could for all sides of an issue, and then only at the end presenting his own considered viewpoint by stating, "I answer that..." As an authentic part of this dynamic, and at the appropriate point, I do not hesitate to state openly, simply, with charity, and—if necessary—due boldness, what I perceive to be *the* correct doctrine of the Catholic Church and thus of Jesus Christ.

7. When there is no explicit Christian or Catholic teaching on the subject being discussed, I acknowledge the silence of tradition. I must resist the temptation to present my private viewpoint as the "official" one of the Church. On the other hand, concerning those values that do have a sanction in revelation and the teaching of the Church, my job is to hand on this tradition—with kindness and gusto.

The truth that continues to set me and my students free is one that circumscribes us within its absolute, no-nonsense limits. We are often pinched and pained in the process, but we are also protected and preserved. I do not wait eagerly for some new-truth season to see how the hemlines of truth may rise or fall, which colors of transcendent value are now passé or outré. I do not fawn over the moral couturiers and their exciting new collections of the ethics of the hour. I have no desire to line up with the theological faddists for tickets to this year's fashion shows from the Houses of Hefner, Landers, Maclaine, Westheimer, or Smeal; nor, for that matter, from the Houses of Küng, Curran, Fox, or Ruether, unless they conform their patterns to the changeless and seamless standards of the House of Peter.

The Why: The Ethics of Teaching Values in Literature

Why do I want my students to learn Christian values not only in their religion classes but also in their English literature classes? Because in literature, they see these values incarnate, enfleshed in real-life situations. Or, as in *Macbeth* and *West Side Story* and *The Prime of Miss Jean Brodie*, they see these values ignored or violated with the horrendous consequences that follow.

If, because I am an English teacher, I am supposed to keep values secret from my students, then I am like that faithless steward in the parable who buried his talent and did nothing with it. My educational "Miss Jean Brodie" colleagues are doing their libertarian thing all over the place, but I must do Jesus' thing—teaching what he taught, bringing the kingdom of God into the world, making the secular sacred; rendering to Caesar (and the State Board of Education) what is Caesar's, but unto God what is God's. Part of my job as a literature teacher is to sow the wheat of commitment and contemplation, in season and out of season, in adolescent hearts and minds that have already been sown with the tares of confusion and corruption.

Having lighted my small candle, I must now also curse the darkness a little: I take aim at three major false gospels that are scattering evil seed unto a frightful harvest in my students' lives: Sub-Humanism, Secular Humanism, and Pseudo-Christian Humanism. Each of them offers a spurious salvation and empty fulfillment. Each of them can be counteracted effectively by the Gospel of Christian Humanism, which I am called to preach as a Catholic teacher of literature, both by word and existential example.

The Gospel of Sub-Humanism

This gospel is celebrated in much of today's Rock culture. Its message? "Have fun! Rebel! Do your own thing! It if feels good, do it! The only commitment you have is to your glands and your guts. You're Number One, and in a way the Only One. Screw everything else!" It is the old *carpe diem* theme of the Cavaliers, but the 17th-century fops lacked the demonic insistence of a Heavy Metal beat.

The Sub-Human gospel to adolescents these days is revealed in the doctrinaire lyrics of any number of popular Rock albums. Hear a few snatched from random interviews with Rock performers quoted in Rock magazines:

The stage is the last place where you can get away with flashing. In rock and roll there are no rules. Anything goes.

Isn't sex what rock and roll is all about?

Songs like ours have an unquestionable rebelliousness about them. They all say that we and our fans are going to do what we want, so leave us alone.

Turn on MTV. Look at the teen audiences attending Rock concerts. See their mesmerized faces, their arms flailing in a pseudo-liturgy celebrating self and rebellion. Sub-Humanism preaches self-gratification—the opposite of the self-mortification of the Christian Gospel. Jesus said: "Unless the grain of wheat falls to the earth and dies, it remains just a grain of wheat. But if it dies, it produces much fruit." (John 12:24) The Sub-Human gospel of death sometimes parodies this Christian self-sacrifice by preaching self-destruction. Instead of saying, "Sacrifice yourself in the interests of God and others," it says, "Kill yourself to satisfy your own interests." The driving beat of Rock culture peters out into a threnody of self-pity, and its song saddens into a melancholy of self-annihilation.

The missionary names of some groups who proclaim the Sub-Human gospel enshrine their message: Forbidden, Old Skull, Judas Priest, Black Sabbath, Poison, Bad Company, Whitesnake, Megadeth, Violence, Death Angel, Grim Reaper, and yes, even Bad English.

Are these just bad-boy, essentially innocent, adolescent inventions? The titles of some of their songs and albums proclaim otherwise: "The Ultimate Sin," "Sex Drive," "Love Hunter," "Slide It In," and "Hot Spot." The captions emblazoned on the T-shirts of the Sub-Human counterculture—"See You In Hell," "I Kill For Thrills," "Metal Up Your Ass," and "Get Off My Dick"—are the inverse of Jesus' words: "You must be made as perfect as your heavenly Father is perfect," (Matthew 5:48) and of St. Paul's words: "The temple of God is holy, and you are that temple." (1 Corinthians 3:17)

Sometimes the bad news of the Sub-Human gospel comes through in "cute" packages. In movies like *Porky's*, sexuality is trivialized into a toy that adolescents (like adults) are now old enough to play with. The "loss" (or rather, the throw-away) of one's virginity becomes a consummation devoutly to be wished. One of the wisest things I ever heard a teenage boy say was this: "Too many adults are nothing more than children old enough to do what they want." The gospel of Sub-Humanism is evangelizing our young people for citizenship neither in the City of God nor in the City of Man. It is preparing them for a city charged not with the grandeur of God, but with what St. Paul catalogued as anti-values in Galatians 5:19: "...lewd conduct, impurity, licentiousness, idolatry, sorcery, hostilities, bickering, jealousy, outbursts of rage, selfish rivalries, orgies, and the like." I am not smiling when I say that the arch-heresy of Sub-Humanism is indoctrinating my students for citizenship in a glitzy, hellish wasteland that is tantalizingly portrayed in the soap operas and some talk shows of American commercial television.

The Gospel of Secular Humanism

More subtle than Sub-Humanism, the false gospel of Secular Humanism subjects my students to the culturally pervasive idea of "humanity's independence from God." Asserting that human freedom shapes our future, this seductive philosophy has quietly insinuated itself into the fabric of our daily lives, whispering that "no deity will save us; we must save ourselves."[7] More and more, Secular Humanism is becoming America's "Established Religion," and is being convincingly taught at the Day Schools of Secular Academe. Ongoing declarations of independence, most eloquently and effectively trumpeted by the American Civil Liberties Union, are making us into a nation that needs no deity other than the goddess Liberty.

Secular Humanism dates its organizational impact on America from 1933, when the *Humanist Manifesto* was promulgated by the American Humanist Association in Yellow Springs, Ohio, affirming the self-existence of the universe and proposing the replacement of worship and prayer by "a heightened sense of personal life and in a cooperative effort to promote social well being."[8] Forty years later, a second *Humanist Manifesto* was published. Among the signers of this latter document were such notables as Sidney Hook, John Ciardi, Paul Blanshard, B.F. Skinner, Isaac Asimov, and Betty Friedan.[9] Although not every signer agreed with every article of faith in the secular credo, here are some of the articles:

We can discover no divine purpose of providence for the human species.

Traditional dogmatic religions that place...God...above human experience do a disservice to the human species....No deity will save us; we must save ourselves.

Ethics is autonomous and situational, needing no theological or ideological sanction.[10]

Even the most committed card-carrying Secular Humanist will tell you that the urge to worship is instinctive; hence it is good to worship. This weaning away from God-worship to self-worship—how eerily reminiscent it is of what happens in the third chapter of Genesis! We hear the great-great-great-granddaddy of Secular Humanism telling a young couple who felt themselves coming of age: "You certainly will not die! God knows well that the moment you eat of the fruit your eyes will be opened, and you will be like gods."

Then, a few thousand years later, another preacher of Secular Humanism, Ralph Waldo Emerson was offering the same poison fruit:

Nothing is at last sacred but the integrity of your own mind. On my saying, "What have I to do with the sacredness of traditions, if I live wholly from within?" my friend suggested: "But these impulses may be from below, not from above."

I replied, "They do not seem to me to be such. But if I am the Devil's child, I will live then from the Devil....No law can be sacred to me but that of my nature....The only right is what is after my constitution; the only wrong what is against it."[11]

Our natures, said Emerson, are healthy, not damaged; our integrity is intrinsic to our natural being and needs only to be coaxed out and nurtured into magnificent growth. We are our own gods, informed by something big and tame, Romantic and innocuous, the impersonal Oversoul. (I imagine a Peanuts cartoon: Lucy says to Charlie Brown, "The Oversoul in me says that the Oversoul in you is a nitwit, Charlie Brown!" To which the only answer that Charlie Brown can make— and we with him—is: "Good grief.")

In 20th-century pop-psych lingo, Emerson is saying, "I'm O.K. You're O.K. So who needs to hear about something as outdated as Original Sin and the need for something called Salvation?"

If Emerson were alive now, he would be a member of the A.C.L.U. and this gospel of Secular Humanism would have the popular ring of the Bill of Rights and its First Amendment defense of freedom of thought and liberty of expression. Censorship is among the deadliest sins condemned in the Secular Catechism.

Does this mean that I am an advocate of public censorship? By no means. And I especially want to distance myself from the censorship that some of the extreme fundamentalist groups would like to introduce. On the other hand, my school and my whole private school system do have the right to screen what is taught, to judge what books and magazines are not appropriate to a Catholic high school milieu. We hire and fire based on norms of the Gospel of Jesus Christ and the State Board of Education.

But we "narrowminded" Catholics are not the only ones who engage in censorship. The censurers of censorship do a bit of censoring all their own. Paul Vitz, Professor of Psychology at New York University, in his muckraking account of *Censorship: Evidence of Bias in Our Children's Textbooks*, systematically reviewed 90 widely used elementary-school readers and social-studies texts, and high school history texts, and found that, "Religion, family values, and certain

political and economic positions have been systematically omitted from textbooks."[12] In place of these standard American values, Vitz discovered a bias in favor
of doctrinaire liberalism and "a feminist emphasis,
even projected anachronistically into the distant
past....Anne Hutchinson is almost always misrepre-
sented in a way that is protofeminist. Joan of Arc's
story is told without any reference at all to God, to
religion, or to her being a saint."[13] About family life
and women's roles in the family, Vitz wrote:

> *There is not one text reference to marriage as the*
> *foundation of the family. Indeed not even the*
> *word "marriage" occurs once in the forty books [re-*
> *viewed].... There is not one citation indicating*
> *that the occupation of a mother or housewife rep-*
> *resents an important job, one with integrity, one*
> *that provides real satisfaction.*[14]

Whose influence is at work in at least some of
this? Vitz concluded:

> *There can be no doubt that the NEA has a secular*
> *and liberal political philosophy and that it has in-*
> *creasingly come to control education. Indeed the*
> *biased content of the textbooks described...is con-*
> *gruent with the politics of the NEA....An organiza-*
> *tion with a very particular or partisan political*
> *involvement is also controlling our schools. Conse-*
> *quently, it would be naive to expect what is*
> *taught in the public schools to contradict the bias*
> *of the NEA. The people who write, select, and im-*
> *plement the textbooks are opposed to the values,*
> *beliefs, and politics that are missing from these*
> *books.*[15]

If the liberal program of Secular Humanism
comes through efficiently as a philosophy, it roars
through triumphantly as a psychology. In his *Psy-*
chology as Religion: The Cult of Self-Worship, Vitz
traces much of today's secular thinking back to Lud-

wig Feuerbach's *The Essence of Christianity*, published in 1841 (the same year as Emerson's "Self-Reliance"—the Oversoul was working overtime that year). Feuerbach said that "God is...in truth and reality something second, for God is merely the projected essence of Man."[16] Over comments like these, Friedrich Engels went into an existential tizzy, rhapsodizing that "Enthusiasm was general; we all at once became Feuerbachians." Marx, Freud, and Dewey, along with Engels, also came under Feuerbach's spell; and from Dewey, of course, Secular Humanism has flowed naturally into the mainstream of American public education.

Citing the psychologist Carl Rogers, Vitz summarized the value-free, "uncensored," secular, humanistic, American educational agenda:

> *The intelligent believer will sooner or later rebel from the faith...[and]the abandonment of one's "religious background" is reliably assumed to be a rational consequence of getting an education, particularly in graduate school.*[17]

Knock out "the God professed by Christian theology...an illusion" (Erich Fromm, *The Art of Loving*) and you are left with "unconditional self-regard" (Carl Rogers). Knock out the unconditional love of God, and you are left with, as Vitz says, "a full-fledged self-devotion." Follow the program of Secular Humanism to its intended conclusion, and you knock out the doctrinal basis of Christianity, and you knock out as well the moral theology that is based upon it. You are left not with Commandments from Mt. Sinai or the Mount from which Jesus preached the Beatitudes, but the crumbly pinnacle of what Emerson called "the sacred integrity of your own mind." Exit the Decalogue, and enter the Dialogue-with-Myself. Enter also situation ethics, moral relativism, and rampant personal subjectivism as the only Code of Canon Law in the Church of Secular Humanism.

Emerson is no longer with us, but his Oversoul seems to have reincarnated itself this time as Shirley MacLaine, New Age evangelist. Although Secular Humanism may be doctrine without religion, New Age does not exactly appear to be religion without doctrine. Theologian MacLain promulgates her doctrine in accents that would do most Secular Humanists proud: "Each soul is its own God. You must never worship anyone or anything other than self. For *you* are God. To love self is to love God."[18]

That citation, Charlie, is used in an important book by an ex-occultist, now a Jesuit priest, who has documented the infiltration of Catholic educators by New Age ideas, and the infiltration of Catholic schools by New Age instruction. Fr. Mitch Pacwa, S.J., presents the evidence of a campus chaplain at a Catholic university who recommends crystals, the energy source of Atlantis, for personal help; and of a Catholic women's college that offers workshops in Wicca and "the goddess within." Parishes and convents are doing it, too. Professional astrologers and spiritualists make the rounds, telling parishioners how to make contact with deceased loved ones, and how to derive guidance from the stars.[19] Little wonder, then, that New Age values have become the values of some Catholic educators, passing on to eager adolescents this worship of the creature in place of the Creator.

I do not deny that Secular Humanists have made their useful contributions to the City of this Earth, but it is the harm they have done and continue to do, especially to my students, that concerns me. I cannot dismiss as irrelevant what some might call the *small* percentage of their erroneous teachings.

Analogy: Do you want to teach in a school where only 5% of the food served in the cafeteria is contaminated? Do you want to teach in a room where only 5% of the class suffers from contamination from only 5% of the fixtures containing asbestos, lead, or mercury? Percent me no percentages! My quarrel is not with the (less than) 95% that is all "sweetness and light" in Secular Humanism; it is with the lethal, virulent (more than) 5% with which I am at metaphysical and moral odds.

The world and its secularism are evangelizing my students and their friends in public school under the protection of the Bill of Rights. Why may I not teach them the values of their Judeo-Christian heritage with equal protection? The *philosophes* of this age are as condescending to us Christians today as were their French forebears two centuries ago during the so-called Enlightenment, or their philosophic ancestors in Athens when St. Paul preached the Gospel of the resurrection in the Areopagus. Referring to the Secular Humanists of his day, St. Paul said that in their eyes, the Gospel was "complete absurdity." "But," he added wryly a few verses later: "God's folly is wiser than men."[20] Amen, Brother Paul.

The Gospel of Pseudo-Christian Humanism

My student's most blatant enemy is Sub-Humanism.

Their most sophisticated enemy is Secular Humanism.

Their most subtle enemy is Pseudo-Christian Humanism.

We in Catholic education are engaged in an identity crisis that holds implications for other educators and schools as well, both religiously affiliated and public tax-supported alike. To be or not to be more secular than we already are—that is the question.

How this question is being resolved—and it is a question of quintessential moral values—is inexorably affecting the values of our students throughout the curriculum. The teaching of religion is the biggest battleground, but this affects only sectarian schools. The teaching of values in literature is the second-biggest field of battle, and that is a war being waged both in Catholic and other religious schools and in public schools as well.

The Pseudo-Christian counterfeit of true Christian Humanism had found its way into our schools two decades ago, as Bishop Fulton Sheen realized in 1972: "I tell my friends and relatives with college age children to send them to secular colleges where they will have to fight for their faith, rather than to those Catholic colleges where it will be taken from them."[21]

Since Vatican II, muddled Catholics have been trying to synthesize, or rather to *syncretize*, the values of Christianity with some of the values of Secular Humanism. The hybrid offspring may look and sound Catholic, but it is instead a mutation. The genes have been tampered with. We confront Pseudo-Christian Humanism, a mutant little monster who is anything but mute.

Gerard Morrissey (pseudonym for a Catholic priest) in his *The Crisis of Dissent* dedicated a chapter to "The Effect of Dissent on Young Catholics." He had made a study showing how pre-Vatican II Catholic schools were remarkably successful in promoting Catholic doctrine. But fifteen years after the Council, another study showed these results:

1. Eighty percent of young Catholics rejected the teaching of the Church on sexual matters.

2. Almost as many rejected the infallibility of the Pope.

3. Only 37% of the young attended Mass weekly.

4. Catholic education itself was no guarantee of full acceptance by its students of Catholic doctrine.[22]

The statistic about young Catholics rejecting the Church's teaching on sexual matters is disappointing but not surprising. For two decades or so, many young Catholics have been sadly deprived of Jesus Christ's teaching on human sexuality. But happily, the Vatican published in 1975 its *Declaration on Certain Questions Concerning Sexual Ethics*[23] It was lucid, concise, authoritative, and eminently benign and pastoral. The only surprise I had in reading it was that there were no surprises at all. So the Catholic Church had *not* changed its teachings on human sexuality after all. The document was, and is, an excellent re-presentation of the Church's traditional teaching on sex. It systematically shows that Christian marriage is the only situation in which the gift of erotic sensuality may legitimately be employed and enjoyed.

The limits defined, broadly speaking, by this important little document can be very helpful to an English teacher in dealing with the subject of sexuality in literature, particularly in works like *The Scarlet Letter*, *West Side Story*, *The Sun Also Rises*, *The Great Gatsby*, *A Tree Grows in Brooklyn*, *The Catcher in the Rye*, *A Bell for Adano*, and *The Prime of Miss Jean Brodie*.

For two examples, recall the final scaffold scene of *The Scarlet Letter*. When Hester Prynne tries to rationalize that what she and Arthur Dimmesdale have done was something sacred and beautiful, Arthur will have none of it. Adultery is always ugly and sinful. Also, in *A Tree Grows in Brooklyn*, the kind of "Do what your heart tells you" advice that Francie's mother gives her concerning her boyfriend, needs to be examined in the light of Christian sexual ethics.

Secular Humanism has long legitimized things that Catholic students—because of their teachers and parents—formerly considered intrinsically immoral acts: masturbation, fornication, adultery, artificial birth control, homosexual activity, abortion, occultism, to say nothing of the "trust your feelings" mandate that pervades all of the above. Yet, I love to recall what a teenage girl told me some ten years ago: "The next time some adult tells me he wants to put me in touch with my feelings, I'm gonna scream!"

Take a poll in Harvey Cox's Secular City, and my guess is that you will find a steadily increasing percentage of teens who are sexually active. No wonder. They want to become "adult" like their secular role models. (One of the best-selling magazines in a Capitol Hill concession shop is *Penthouse*.) No wonder, either, that the values of my own Catholic teenage students are often not very different from those of their peers in secular schools. They, too, watch MTV.

A New Age syncretism is being attempted, a forced miscegenation of Secular Humanism and Christianity: the Beast is trying to ravish the Beauty, and a monstrous procreation is being brought forth.

Pseudo-Christian Humanists complain that the rest of us Christians are not sufficiently in love with *the grandeur of the world*, that we are insufficiently incarnational. To the contrary, I believe that they

have confused "incarnational" with "secular." Their
scrambled values have scrambled their perspectives.
They are the Roman Catholic version of Muriel Spark's
devilishly fascinating Miss Jean Brodie. They are oh-
so-eager to bring their own revised and updated version of the Gospel to our Catholic youth in our Catholic
classrooms, like Miss Brodie, who tried to make her
hand-picked student protégés both converts and apos-
tles of her 1930's version of liberation, or libertarian,
philosophy.

These Pseudo-Christian Humanists can still be
found diligently trying to evangelize and liberate
Catholic youth from "outdated values" in seminaries,
universities, and high schools. They are also trying,
with less success, to evangelize, catechize, and theol-
ogize the Pope and the magisterium [teaching author-
ity] of the Catholic Church. Perhaps taking a cue
from their adolescent students, they complain that
those in authority "aren't listening" to them or are
"misinformed" about their positions. "The Holy Father doesn't understand our American tradition of
freedom of expression." Pseudo-Christian Humanists
are a determined and quasi-infallible breed. Very
vocal about their own right to dissent, they become
even more vocal when other Catholics try to dissent
with them. They are knee-jerk quick to cry out
"Witch-hunt! Censorship!"

When I taught values through literature during
the first ten years or so of my career in a Catholic
high school, I had no reason to doubt that those values would be upheld and fostered in literally every
classroom in school. However, from 1965 to the present, I have noticed a gradual incursion of Pseudo-
Christian values into my school, introduced often
enough unwittingly by students and even teachers,
but introduced nonetheless.

To Catholic-school teachers I put the question: Do you think that everything being taught in your religion and liberal-arts and sciences classes would be approved by your bishop, the Pope, and Jesus Christ himself? (And I would like to put a similar question to my colleagues teaching in schools of other religious denominations.) Now, a Pseudo-Christian Humanist teaching in a Catholic school would probably answer thus: "I'm sure I'm teaching the values that Jesus Christ would approve of, so I don't really care whether my bishop or the Pope approves or not." Thus answer the Catholic Jean Brodies in Catholic schools.

Any wonder that in my desire to teach values through literature I should be most dismayed and challenged by the sincere Pseudo-Christian Humanists in our system? As I try to communicate traditional Christian values through the teaching of literature, I am saying to my students with Paul in Galatians 4:19: "You are my children, and you put me back in labor pains until Christ is formed in you." Now note carefully: That is a declaration that no Sub-Humanist or Secular Humanist would ever desire to make to my students, but it is exactly what a Pseudo-Christian Humanist would say to them in utter conviction and sincerity. Christian Humanists and Pseudo-Christian Humanists are thus saying the same thing but doing quite different things in Catholic classrooms. I am certain that those whom I label as Pseudo-Christian would deny the epithet and hurl it right back at me.

I have seen what the siren-summons of Pseudo-Christian Humanism has done to Catholic teachers and students with whom I have worked over the past 35 years. Indeed, I have felt its own deleterious effects in my own being. Most of all, I despise it for trying to convince the Church, which Paul calls the faithful bride of Christ (Ephesians 5:25-32), that it is perfectly all right to exchange her immaculate wedding garment for something more modern, colorful, cute, and bold; and that it is possible to remain faithful to Christ while harmlessly entertaining whatever "gentlemen callers" ask admittance to her chambers, where they can purvey their alien creeds. All of this in the name of "ecumenism," no less.

Let me summarize what each of these three archheresies of our time is trying to do in the lives of my students:

1. Sub-Humanism wants to replace the grandeur of God with the grimy grandeur of glands and guts. There is a whole "literature" of magazines and movies and videos that is propagating this easy-to-sell Gospel to my students.

2. Secular Humanism wants to replace the grandeur of God with the grandeur of man, proclaiming that human grandeur should not be extrapolated to some external deity. It loves to twist the meaning of Alexander Pope's couplet:

   Presume not the illimitable to scan.
   The proper study of mankind is man.

3. Pseudo-Christian Humanism wants to return God's incarnational favor of charging the world with His grandeur, by trying to charge God's grandeur with the redoubtable grandeur of the world. Truly an experiment perilous.

The Gospel of Christian Humanism

Will a true Christian Humanist please stand up?

Thomas Aquinas? Teresa of Avila? Cardinal Newman? Jacques Maritain? Let us hear from the Flemish Jesuit priest, Peter Fransen:

> *Christian humanism...should take pride in the*
> *profound and religious vocation received in and*
> *through grace. God's word makes the world trans-*
> *parent, turns it into a shrine and tabernacle of*
> *the divine, living presence....We are God's fellow*
> *workers. The world is to us a divine milieu in*
> *which our earthly life achieves its fullest mean-*
> *ing, thanks to God's love.*[24]

"In the world, but not of the world," the Church
prays the prayer of the Christian Humanist beauti-
fully and succinctly in the *Liturgy of the Hours*:

> *Lord, remember your Pilgrim Church.... Do not*
> *let us be drawn into the current of the passing*
> *world, but free us from every evil and raise our*
> *thoughts to the heavenly Jerusalem.*[25]

The inspiration comes from St. Augustine, and
before him from Hebrews 12:14: "Here we have no
lasting city; we are seeking one which is to come."
But even while seeking the city to come, we have a
mandate to work and serve one another in the city of
this life. Consequently, I apologize to no one for guiding my students away from Ayn Rand's fountainhead
of sophisticated selfishness, to choose instead the
living waters that flow from the utterly selfless heart
of the Savior, pierced with a lance. As a Christian
Humanist, I smile at the arch wisdom of my confrere
in the Spirit, C.S. Lewis, who encouraged a kind of
crafty metaphysical economy: "Aim at heaven and
you will get earth 'thrown in': aim at earth and you
will get neither."[26]

As a Christian Humanist teaching in a Catholic
high school, I want my students to know that the
Catholic colleges and universities they will be attending are unabashedly Christian and explicitly Catholic. I want them to grow and deepen in the love of
values that I have tried to communicate through the
teaching of literature. The Catholic school at any

level must not become a theological flea market, sec-
ond-handing on everyone else's ideological trash and
supposed spiritual treasures. This again is Pseudo-
Ecumenism, syncretism at its worst.

As a Christian Humanist, I ask myself this question: *How is what I am doing, as a teacher of literature in my Catholic high school, any different from
what I would be doing if I were teaching the same
literature in a public school?*

If I answer that there is no difference, I hear
Someone asking me an embarrassing question: *Then
what are you doing teaching in a Catholic school at
all?* The question that Jesus asked in Luke 18:8,
translates in pedagogical terms to me: "When the Son
of Man comes *to your English class,* will he find any
faith?"

My students should not have to make an act of
faith in my invisible faith: It must be manifest, not
hidden under a secular bushel.

As a Catholic educator, I must not be like the
young Jewish males in I Maccabees 1:15. During
the time of the Greek domination of Israel, young
Jewish athletes in the new secular Hellenistic milieu
were ashamed of their circumcised flesh, in the presence of their uncircumcised Greek friends at the gym-
nasium. So they "covered the mark of their
circumcision and abandoned the holy covenant; they
allied themselves with the gentiles." Catholic educators must not, likewise, cover their unique and sacred
identity, must not allow Christian education more
and more to resemble secular education, must not
abandon the sacred for the secular—the ultimate cop-
out.

As a Catholic Humanist, wanting to prepare my
students for citizenship in both the Earthly City and

the City of God, I do not *preoccupy* myself with secular priorities, or measure academic achievement exclusively by secular standards. Certainly, it is also my duty to help prepare my junior and senior students annually for the SAT and ACT test, diligently working with them through the English sections in their practice manuals. But that is only the lesser half of my job. God will grant me spiritual merit pay based not on how many National Merit Scholarship students I have successfully helped to prepare and process but rather on how well I as a good English teacher have helped to form *all* my students into good citizens of *both* Cities.

Summary

As a Christian Humanist, I am called by God to be a professional English teacher in this Earthly City. I must teach good English usage, composition, critical thinking, vocabulary, and literature. And I really ought to read the *English Journal*. (When I die, I do not want to be asked, after all, to remain just outside Heaven in a special detention room for English teachers who are required to catch up on the professional literature that they should already have read on earth.) All these things constitute my being a good *professional*; but then, I am also called to a Catholic *profession* of the faith, teaching openly the values of Jesus Christ, and the value that *is* Jesus Christ.

I began this highly personal presentation by quoting the beautiful line of Gerard Manley Hopkins: "The world is charged with the grandeur of God." As a Christian Humanist English teacher, I get to be an integral part of that charging dynamic when I teach literature. But first, I myself must become charged with the very grandeur of God's grace, "by Love possessed." Some anonymous medieval scholastic once sagely observed that "we cannot give what we do not have." Lacking that touch of God's grandeur myself, how could I hope to awaken my students fully to a sense of the sacred, so pitifully lacking in their lives, and to its obverse, a sense of sin, both in literature and in the life it reflects?

The teaching of values through literature to my students is essentially the work of the Holy Spirit. Any genuine grandeur this world holds, its literature can be an endeavor to reveal—and how glorious much there is!—but it is not autonomous. It is at once both merely and magnificently the reflection of the grandeur of God. Its revelation must be a Pentecost in my English class. Pope John XXIII prayed at the beginning of the Second Vatican Council to the Holy Spirit for a "new Pentecost," both for the City of God and the City of Man.[27] After him, Pope Paul VI said, "The Church needs a perennial Pentecost; she needs fire in the heart, words on the lips."[28]

Surely this is what Hopkins was talking about as he looked out on the sickly world of his day, bent out of shape by the Sub-Humanism and the rapidly rising Secular Humanism of a century ago. Hopkins' paean to "God's Grandeur" concludes with this symbol of the "perennial Pentecost":

> *The Holy Ghost over the bent*
> *World broods with warm breast and ah! bright*
> *wings.*

To which I can only respond:

> *Come, then, Holy Spirit. Hover, hallow, holily*
> *haunt all halls and classrooms, secular and sacred,*
> *on the face of the earth. Begin Your perennial Pente-*
> *cost in my classroom. Today. Please. Thank You.*
> *Amen.*

Jesus Christ, who with the Father sends the Holy Spirit, thrice asked Peter a question at the end of

John's Gospel.[29] He poses a similar question, I think, to all English teachers today, perennially inviting us to the fullness of our secular vocations in the City of Man and simultaneously inviting us to the holiness of our sacred vocations in the City of God:

"My beloved English teachers, do you love me?"

"Yes, Lord, you know we love you."

"Feed my sheep."

NOTES

1. Gerard Manley Hopkins, S.J., "God's Grandeur," in *The Liturgy of the Hours, IV* (New York: Catholic Book Publishing Company, 1975): 1, 997.

2. 2 Corinthians 5:17, 20. *The New American Bible* (New York: J. Kenedy and Sons, 1970).

3. Augustine of Hippo, *Selected Writings*, Mary T. Clark, tr. (New York: Paulist Press, 1984): 462, 463.

4. Vatican Council II, "Pastoral Constitution on the Church in the Modern World," IV: 40.

5. Charlotte Brontë, *Jane Eyre* (New York: Dodd, Mead, 1941): 329.

6. Lorraine Hansberry, *A Raisin in the Sun* (Signet, 1966): 65.

7. James Hitchcock, *What Is Secular Humanism?* (Ann Arbor: Servant Books: 1982): back cover.

8. *Ibid.*, p. 11.

9. *Ibid.*, pp. 14, 15.

10. *Ibid.*, pp. 13, 14.

11. Ralph Waldo Emerson, "Self-Reliance," in *Major Writer of America*, Perry Miller, ed. (New York: Harcourt, 1962): I, 511.

12. Paul Vitz, *Censorship: Evidence of Bias in Our Children's Textbooks* (Ann Arbor: Servant Books, 1986): back cover.

13. *Ibid.*, p. 36.

14. *Ibid.*, p. 38.

15. *Ibid.*, p. 88.

16. Paul Vitz, *Psychology As Religion: The Cult of Self-Worship* (Grand Rapids: Eerdman's, 1980): 68.

17. *Ibid.*, p. 77.

18. Shirley MacLaine, *Dancing in the Light* (Toronto: Bantam Books, 1985): 343.

19. Mitch Pacwa, *Catholics and the New Age* (Ann Arbor: Servant Publications, 1992), introduction.

20. 1 Corinthians 1:18, 25.

21. Quoted by Msgr. George A. Kelly in *The Crisis of Authority: John Paul II and the American Bishops* (Chicago: Regnery, 1982): 98.

22. Gerard Morrissey, *The Crisis of Dissent* (Front Royal, Virginia: Christendom Publications, 1985): 19.

23. Sacred Congregation for the Doctrine of the Faith, Declaration on Certain Questions Concerning Sexual Ethics (Boston: Daughters of St. Paul, 1975).

24. Peter Fransen, S.J., *The New Life of Grace*, G. Duoont, tr. (Belgium: Desclee, 1969): 344.

25. The Liturgy of the Hours, III, p. 1182.

26. C.S. Lewis, *Mere Christianity* (New York: Macmillan, 1960).

27. Walter M. Abbott, S.J., ed. *The Documents of Vatican II* (New York Guild Press, 1966): 709.)

28. Pope Paul VI in general audience, November 29, 1972, translated from *Osservatore Romano*, December 7, 1972.

29 John 21:15-17.

REFERENCES

Augustine of Hippo, Selected Writings, translated by Mary T. Clark. New York: Paulist Press, 1984.

Bonhoeffer, Dietrich. *The Cost of Discipleship*. New York: Macmillan, 1976.

Bronte, Charlotte. *Jane Eyre*. New York: Dodd, Mead, 1941.

Chesterton, G.K. *Orthodoxy*. Garden City: Image, 1959.

The Documents of Vatican II, Walter M. Abbott, S.J., ed. New York: Guild Press, 1966.

Emerson, Ralph Waldo. "Self-Reliance," in *Major Writers of America*, Perry Miller, ed. New York: Harcourt, 1962.

Fransen, Peter, S.J. *The New Life of Grace*, translated by G. Dupont, S.J. Belgium: Desclee, 1969.

Groeschel, Benedict J. *The Courage to Be Chaste*. Paulist Press, 1985.

Hansberry, Lorraine. *A Raisin in the Sun*. Signet, 1966.

Hitchcock, James. *The New Enthusiasts and What They Are Doing to the Catholic Church*. Chicago: Thomas More Press, 1982.

_____. *What is Secular Humanism?* Ann Arbor: Servant Books, 1982.

Hopkins, Gerard Manley, S.J. "God's Grandeur" in *The Liturgy of the Hours*, four volumes. New York: Catholic Book Publishing Company, 1975.

Kelly, Msgr. George A. *The Crisis of Authority: John Paul II and the American Bishops*. Chicago: Regnery, 1982.

Kilpatrick, William Kirk. *Psychological Seduction: The Failure of Modern Psychology*. Nashville: Nelson, 1983.

Lewis, C.S. *Mere Christianity*. New York: Macmillan, 1960.

MacLaine, Shirley. *Dancing in the Light*. Toronto: Bantam Books, 1985.

Martin, Ralph. *A Crisis of Truth: The Attack on Faith, Morality and Mission in the Catholic Church*. Ann Arbor: Servant Books, 1982.

Menninger, Karl, M.D. *Whatever Became of Sin?* New York: Hawthorn, 1973.

Morrissey, Gerard. *The Crisis of Dissent*. Front Royal: Christendom Publications, 1985.

The New American Bible. New York: J. Kenedy and Sons, 1970.

Pacwa, Mitch. *Catholics and the New Age*. Ann Arbor: Servant Publications, 1992.

Paul VI in general audience, November 29, 1972, translated from *Osservatore Romano*, December 7, 1972.

The Sacred Congregation for the Doctrine of the Faith, "Declaration on Certain Questions Concerning Sexual Ethics." Boston: Daughters of St. Paul, 1975.

Sheed, Frank. *Theology and Sanity*. New York: Sheed and Ward, 1946.

Vitz, Paul. *Censorship: Evidence of Bias in Our Children's Textbooks*. Ann Arbor: Servant Books, 1986.

_____. *Psychology as Religion: The Cult of Self-Worship*. Grand Rapids: Eerdman's, 1980.

Response to Bernard Suhor's *Values in the Teaching of Literature—A Catholic School View*

Charles Suhor

The late Jean Sulivan wrote: "A divided family is hell. But there's something worse—a united family."[1] That is a fascinating idea, and a handy one for talking about Ben's viewpoints and mine, and about the ways that our views relate to larger families of believers.

Sulivan was talking about how families can be insular, clannish, and suffocating when unity is sought at the expense of individual growth. I agree with him, so I feel good about the fundamental differences between my brother's viewpoints and mine. If there is a unity, it is derived from an earnestness in seeking, each within our own realms, rather than from similarity of belief systems.

To begin on a positive note, I was happy to find some areas of clear agreement. I think that Ben implicitly acknowledges that the public school classroom is not without values, virtues, and ethics when he says that "values like honesty, integrity, generosity, forgiveness, and self-sacrifice are not exclusively Christian virtues," and that "the moral questions that I raise, and observations about values that I make, in my Catholic school classroom could be raised in broader ethical terms in a public school classroom."

I am certainly in agreement with Ben concerning the Constitutional rights of teachers in religious and private schools to teach values through literature in accordance with their particular beliefs.[2] Ben and I both celebrate a society in which Catholic or Hebrew or Amish or Hindu schools can freely teach literature from a particular doctrinal perspective. A private school, of course, enjoys the same freedom. For example, the Urban Day school in Milwaukee looks at literature from an Afrocentric view and in light of a code of values called "Nguzo Saba"—the Seven Principles of Blackness.[3]

I must raise questions about whether Ben's particular approaches to "unabashedly Christian and specifically Catholic" instruction are as cautiously balanced with literary concerns as he suggests. His pedagogy seems so heaven-bent as to compromise the literary experience in terms of the student, the author, and the text. But that critique in no way alters my belief that parents and teachers and administrators outside the public sector have a Constitutional right to present a doctrinalized view of literature, even if the view strikes me as absolutist or intolerant.

I will go a step further and say that even those who are doctrinal absolutists (as I believe Ben is, within the larger Catholic community) have two important contributions to make. First, within their own families of believers, they represent an option that merits attention. This is especially true when their arguments are sophisticated and energetic ones (like Ben's) that touch on central issues in their shared faith. I will not go so far as to take sides on Ben's "Psuedo-Christian Humanities" arguments. I cannot tell Catholics that the Ben Suhors and Joseph Ratzingers within their flock are wrong, and that the Matthew Foxes and Rosemary Reuthers are right, or vice versa. I do believe, though, that it is extremely illiberal to dismiss conservative religious views simply because they are out of step with recent thinking in liberal theology.

English teachers working within any given religious education setting would do well, I believe, to ask themselves some version of Ben's hard questions:

"How is what I am doing, as a teacher of literature in my... [denomination's] high school, any different from what I would be doing if I were teaching the same literature in a public school? If I answer that there is no difference, I hear Someone asking me an embarrassing question: *Then what are you doing teaching in a... [denominational] school at all?"* (emphasis in original)

Second, even within a public school setting, *students* who hold absolutist beliefs have as much right as anyone else to discuss their values in relation to literary works. It is enrichment, not encroachment, if an Orthodox Jewish student at a public high school criticizes Philip Roth's treatment of the rabbi and other traditional believers in *Conversion of the Jews*, or if an atheist student claims that T.S. Eliot's *Ash Wednesday* is a sad regression to primitive belief. The important thing is that the teacher assures that other perspectives are represented in the discussion as well.

In my lexicon, "absolutism" isn't a dirty word, but "intolerance" and "exclusion" are. Who has the right to say that absolutist views should be banned from discussion in a genuinely pluralistic public school classroom? I see Ben's traditional theology as a species of belief that doctrinaire liberals, in the public sector and elsewhere, have sometimes intolerantly sought to suppress. It has been my experience that doctrinal liberals on one hand cannot abide doctrinal conservatism, and on the other they are often too smug to perceive their own beliefs as an orthodoxy.

I saw in Ben's text several other points of apparent agreement, although some of those points might be clarified. For example, Ben explicitly distances himself from "extreme fundamentalist groups" who would be "public censors"—presumably, groups such as the ones I criticize in my essay. I also welcome Ben's clear statement: *"In no way do I equate secular education with Secular Humanism."* (Emphasis in original) But he goes on to say that "this seductive philosophy [secular humanism] has quietly insinuated itself into the fabric of our daily lives" and that "secular humanism is becoming America's 'Established Religion,' and is being convincingly taught at the Day School of Secular Academe."

Ben seems to agree with Protestant Fundamentalists on at least one point—*viz.*, that Secular Humanism is damn near everywhere. In light of the strong survey evidence that I cited, indicating that public school teachers and the citizenry at large do not hold to tenets like those Ben lists from the *Humanist Manifesto*, I see some scapegoating here.

I should add that I do not see in Ben's essay a subtle argument for a secular humanist witchhunt. But I do see prodigious exaggeration, in common with the radical religious right, of the organizational moxy and actual effectiveness of the secular humanist movement. If there is a Satan, and if such a force is wreaking havoc in our culture, the secular humanists have proved to be a weak phalanx.

Let me move now from philosophical and sociopolitical issues to questions of pedagogy. I appreciate Ben's general declarations about the "how" of his teaching of values in relation to literature. He does not see literature merely "as a vehicle for teaching Christian values"; nor does he "introduce moral considerations by saying bluntly, 'Now let's see what the Catholic Church says about this.'" Ben goes on to say, "I must resist the temptation to present my private viewpoint as the 'official' one of the Church"—having earlier asserted that his is "*a* Catholic viewpoint, not one that speaks for all Catholics." (emphasis in original)

As a public school educator, I would be pleased to adopt Ben's words as a strong statement of reader-response-based teaching:

> *Overall I judge that the 'What do you think?' approach is the best way to introduce a discussion of values. I encourage my students to begin without any initial comment from me. I like to see them react to one another's views in a free flow of opinions.*

What troubles me is not those broad statements of principle but the thrust of many of the specific illustrative questions and comments that follow. I am troubled by the gap between Ben's guidelines and the implications of many of his examples of pedagogy.

Assuming a Catholic school setting, I do feel comfortable with many of Ben's 26 questions. For instance, numbers 3, 4, 8, 15, and 22 get at discussion of values without a blatant nudge towards the teacher's preferred response, but other questions strike me as loaded and heavy-handed, at best. They seem geared towards making the literature under study "safe for theology" (to use a phrase invoked in criticism of Hopkins) and not towards generating an open discussion of values, either the author's or the students' values.

Granted, Ben has consciously pulled his examples from their total teaching context, so I assume that the questions would be less directive in actual practice, but I also assume that he conceived the questions as true exemplars, and that their structure reflects core pedagogical assumptions and intent. So I cannot help but be disturbed about tendentious and answer-begging items such as these:

- With regard to Emily Dickinson's "Some Keep the Sabbath": Dickinson "made a case for a Sunday morning liturgy with Nature in her own back yard, in preference to going to church for worship. How would you respond to Emily? How do you think St. Francis of Assisi might respond to her, loving God and Nature (and the Mass) as he did?"

The issue here, as in so many of Ben's questions, is clearly theological. That is all right, of course; but notice that the item as structured implicitly calls for a viewpoint that opposes Emily Dickinson's. She "made a case," as if in a legal argument, and the student should "respond." In genuine reader-response instruction, the student is not gently elbowed towards an adversarial response. The clincher question about St. Francis of Assisi contains a not-so-thinly veiled criticism of both Dickinson and those who would support her "case." Since St. Francis is characterized as "loving God and Nature (and the Mass)," one puts oneself at considerable risk in testifying for Emily.

- With regard to W. S. Maugham's *The Razor's Edge*: "Do you think that people can find as much salvation and happiness in Eastern religions as they can in Christianity? Would Jesus agree with your answer?"

Given the amount and quality of exposure to "Eastern religions" that Catholic school students will have had in reading *The Razor's Edge* and in their previous experiences, I find this question a bit oversized. A starting point proportionate to the apparent context—I assume that the kids did not also read Lao-Tse or Krishnamurti—might be to compare *what they know* about *Eastern concepts* of salvation and happiness to similar concepts in Christian belief. Authentic valuing is possible only if some information, good information, fair information, is on hand.

- With regard to Hawthorne's "Dr. Heidegger's Experiment": "What do you believe about reincarnation? What do Scripture and the Church say about reincarnation?"

Hawthorne's story is an extremely poor vehicle for a discussion of reincarnation, dealing as it does with an elixir that restores youth. So I would have to ask here whether the students have been given any basis for assessing reincarnation beyond the zany portrayals in popular culture (e.g., "Switch," "Defending Your Life") that Ben typically mistrusts. Have they looked at any Hindu or Buddhist texts? Have they read Plato's stunning metaphor of the winged steeds in *Phaedrus?* Have they discussed the claims of psychical researchers and the rebuttals in the scientific community? Have they heard about disputes over reincarnation in the early Church? If the issue is raised via a phrase from Hawthorne's story, neither students nor the topic are dignified by an approach that pools the ignorance of the class and then appeals to the school's official belief system as the richer viewpoint.

- With regard to Shakespeare's *Macbeth*: "Macbeth consulted three witches to find out about the future. In the Scriptures, God has forbidden consulting fortune tellers. Do you think Jesus approves of Christians reading their horoscopes or going to palmists or tarot card readers?"

There is no subtlety here—only the most transparent loading of a question. Since the students have already been told that God has forbidden going to fortune tellers, how many will be so bold as to take a stand in favor of horoscopes, palmists, and tarot cards?

Here, as in many of Ben's questions, the item begins "Do you think...." but the phrase seems phatic, a mere linguistic courtesy. The desired response is often built into the substance and rhetoric of the question itself, and the question seems to have little to do with what is actually resonating in the student's mind and feelings.

Ben's treatment of Lorraine Hansberry's *A Raisin in the Sun* gets truly quirky with the series of unabashed, no, bashing questions related to abortion. Raising the abortion issue in studying this play is fair game, of course. But again, the questions as posed in Ben's sequence are bullishly loaded towards eliciting responses consistent with conservative Catholic moral theology. Additionally, the questions are flawed in their logic, and the strategy of the item is ham-fisted.

Whether abortion is absolutely wrong or is morally permissible in certain circumstances, the matter has nothing to do with speculation about how St.

Elizabeth and the Virgin Mary might have answered a biological query about whether they considered themselves to be carrying fetuses or real persons. The rhetorical effect of posing the question as a biblicized hypothetical is to place before the student the intimidating notion that Elizabeth and Mary, under the influence of a wicked and smarmy "NOW lady," might have voluntarily aborted St. John the Baptist and Jesus.

The questions in this contrived scenario are neither literary nor logical, nor even philosophical in the sense of Scholastic natural law argumentation. They are psychologically daunting, rather like asking the class how they would have liked it if their own mothers had considered them to be mere disposable fetuses.

There are a few other points in Ben's essay that lead me to wonder whether or not literature is, at times at least, an underemployed handmaiden of theology. Given Ben's passionate critique of Emerson (who is identified with the A.C.L.U. and Secular Humanism, which in turn is linked with the serpent in the Garden of Eden), is Emerson likely to get a decent shake as an essayist, let alone as a thinker, in Ben's classroom? And what of Ayn Rand? I am not enamored either of Rand's ideas or her prose, but will she get a fair hearing in a program devoted without apology to "guiding my students away from Ayn's fountainhead of sophisticated selfishness?"

I looked back at my own text and re-analyzed the classroom examples (which were drawn from a variety of sources). I invite Ben and you, reader, to challenge my conclusions, but I believe that I saw a far more participatory and invitational spirit in the examples that I cited. Students were genuinely encouraged to reflect on their experiences, personal and vicarious; to exchange ideas with others; to define, to refine, and—if they wished—to modify their values.

I have granted that Ben's hyper-Catholic stance—if you're a Catholic English teacher in a Catholic school, *be* one—is legitimate and principled. But I question whether such a pedagogy really requires all of those subtle and blatant doctrinal buffers, and I wonder whether Ben would think that the student-centered qualities of, say, Rhoda Maxwell's approach to *All Together Now* (pp. 31-34) or Sally Reisinger's treatment of *To Kill a Mockingbird* (pp. 37-40) could be usefully emulated in a sectarian classroom.

Standing back for a larger view, I find Ben's text disturbing not because it is absolutist, Christian, and aglow with real belief, but because it too often falls prey to the generic hazards of zealotry—*viz.*, an overweening certitude and an insensitivity to nonbelievers.

Ironically, I have run into true believers most frequently in Academe in recent years. David Dillon, former editor of *Language Arts*, aptly called it "hardening of the ideologies."[4] Zealotry runs rampant, if not cloven-footed, among certain champions of cultural literacy, deconstruction, feminism, Marxism, classical literature, phonics, whole language, and what have you.

It makes no difference if the particular set of beliefs is absolutist, as Ben's is, or agnostic at the core, as deconstruction theory is. The generic flaw is that the beliefs are *held* absolutely and advanced with a crusading fervor that polarizes instead of encouraging dialogue. In Ben's text in particular, I found myself looking for fewer well-turned phrases in criticism of the unredeemed world and more attempts at helping students to probe the galling ambiguities of that world and their ambivalent responses to it. I, for one, am more persuaded by moral and aesthetic analyses in the manner of Gary Wills and John Leo (in their early writings) and the late Jacques Maritain. All wrote from a distinctively Catholic perspective without overloading their arguments with evangelical energy.[5] Interestingly, Maritain's sign theory and aesthetics have been taken up by semiotics theorists in recent years.

I am being no tougher here on my brother and other sectarian teachers than I was on myself and other public school educators. I said earlier that we are seldom resolute against ourselves. In the public sector, this means that English teachers must constantly ask whether they have sufficiently guarded against promoting their personal belief systems, however subtly, through their selection of literary works and their approaches to class discussion. I ask here only that Ben and other English teachers in sectarian schools constantly examine whether or not their legitimate devotion to religious perspectives works against a fair exploration of the author's values and an unbribed articulation of students' values in the study of literature and life.

I am tempted to deviate from my primary focus on values in the teaching of literature and to address directly several of the philosophical and sociopolitical issues raised by Ben. He saw, as part of his compositional mission, a need to comment on various aspects of contemporary life that must be countered in a school that properly calls itself religious. His targets were many—homosexuality, feminism, MTV, rock culture, abortion, premarital sex, masturbation, and others. I have oodles of differences with Ben on those particular matters, and I would find it stimulating to explore those differences here in terms of the larger context of my personal beliefs.

But I won't. In discussing pluralism as the pubic school English teacher's basic stance, I did not see that my compositional mission included cataloging contemporary social problems and ethical conundrums. I did treat some pertinent contextual issues, such as the alleged effects of secular humanism and new-age religion in our schools, but I felt that the roles of English teachers in public schools and in other educational settings could be discussed without regard to my personal beliefs about, say, TV violence, suicide, or reincarnation.

I hope I have been clear about my personal beliefs that *do* relate to this discussion—belief in public schools free from control by zealots and censors; in religious and private schools free to nurture their own philosophies; in student access to a variety of texts and ideas; in the efficacy of open discussion in the classroom; in literature as aesthetic experience and as personal and communal exploration; in modeling democratic interaction and communicating basic civic and personal values through the way we teach literature; in the practice of pluralism without endorsement of relativism in public education.

Of course, I have discussed my beliefs on the widest range of topics over the years with my siblings and parents and children, and with extended families of friends and colleagues. Jean Sulivan would be pleased. There has been a great deal of disunity in these families, but the differences have usually been expressed in a spirit of love and earnest inquiry. To apply in a new context Denise Levertov's wonderfully free-floating clauses:

That our love for each other give us love for
each other's work.

That our love for each other's work give us
love for one another.

*That our love for each other's work give us love
for one another.*

*That our love for each other give us love for
each other's work.*[6]

NOTES

1. Jean Sulivan, *Morning Light—The Spiritual Journal of Jean Sulivan*, Joseph Cunneen and Patrick Gormally, tr. (New York: Paulist Press, 1988): 62.

2. I hasten to add that the American taxpayer should not be called on to pay for schools that engage in religious advocacy, a point that is peripheral to our debate but nonetheless important.

3. "Experiment in Choice Puts Milwaukee in Spotlight," *News-Gazette* (Champaign-Urbana, Illinois, January 31, 1991): B-1, 5.

4. David Dillon, "Dear Readers" (Editor's Page), *Language Arts 62* (October 1985): 585-86.

5. Wills' and Leo's columns during the early and mid-1960s in *National Catholic Reporter* were exemplary in this respect. For Maritain, see *Creative Intuition in Art and Poetry.* (Princeton: Princeton University Press, 1952) and Jacques Maritain and Jean Cocteau, *Art and Faith: Letters between Jacques Maritain and Jean Cocteau.* (New York: Philosophical Library, 1948).

6. Denise Levertov, "Prayer for Revolutionary Love," in *Cries of the Spirit: A Celebration of Women's Spirituality,* Marilyn Sewell, ed. (Boston: Beacon Press, 1991): 41.

REFERENCES

Creative Intuition in Art and Poetry. Princeton: Princeton University Press, 1952.

Dillon, David. "Dear Readers" (Editor's Page), *Language Arts 62* (October 1985): 585-586.

"Experiment in Choice Puts Milwaukee in Sportlight," Champaign-Urbana *News Gazette*, (January 31, 1991): B, 1, 5.

Levertov, Denise. "Prayer for Revolutionary Love," in *Cries of the Spirit: A Celebration of Women's Spirituality*, Marilyn Sewell, ed. Boston: Beacon Press, 1991.

Maritain, Jacques and Jean Cocteau. *Art and Faith: Letters between Jacques Maritain and Jean Cocteau*. New York: Philosophical Library, 1948.

Sulivan, Jean. *Morning Light—The Spiritual Journal of Jean Sullivan*, Joseph Cunneen and Patrick Gormally, trans. New York: Paulist Press, 1988.

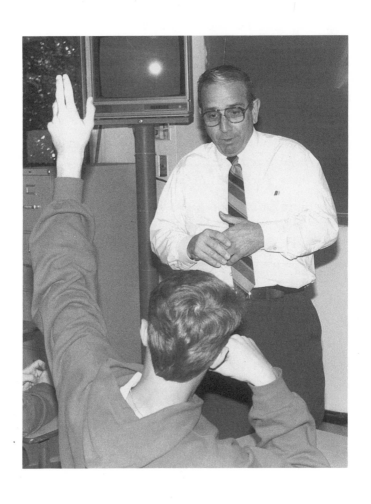

Response to Charles Suhor's *Values in the Teaching of Literature—A Public School View*

Bernard Suhor

I have chosen to respond to my brother Charlie's presentation in the style of a casual letter. I believe that this kind of response will be less labored, more genuine, and a bit more honest than if I were writing to a nameless and faceless audience.

After reading your paper, Charlie, I frankly believe that this is more a discussion than a debate. I address my comments to two of the points you make. The first is the one about how much religious talk is tolerable in a public school setting. You indicated that a teacher who proselytizes, especially after repeated warnings from school authorities, should be fired.

I think that before I were to do any firing, even in a public school setting, I would ask who was being offended by the religious talk. If that address you referred to were in a locale where virtually everyone present—students, parents, teacher—found the religious exhortations not only inoffensive but also entirely appropriate, why would I complain? I imagine a similar situation in a public school, say, in New York City, where the assembly might be almost completely Jewish. Should I complain if the guest speaker makes reference not only to the Torah but also to the Talmud? Imagining other settings, I ask whether in a Muslim setting I should object to someone's quoting from the Qur'an, or to quotes from the Book of Mormon in a public school setting in Utah. Who would be offended in these situations, except someone who is more in love with legalisms than with legalities?

Such a conscientious objector I immediately identify with Robert Frost's neighbor in "Mending Wall." Here was a man who feared goodness-knows-what calamities if the stones separating the two properties were not all balanced in their proper places, doing their work of separating. I confess to feeling more than Frost's impishness when I confront someone, anyone, who is continually wanting to "mend walls" in schoolhouses that separate Church and State. It is far better to have these barriers ill-defined and even movable than rocky and solid. Shall we rule out any kind of invocation at the beginning of every kind of public school convocation, from assembly hall to the football stadium? Shall we erase "In God We Trust" off the cash? If American lawmakers can live with a chaplain's daily opening of the U.S. Senate with a prayer, we can do more than abide a bit of religious reference and even exhortation on given occasions in public schools where our job is to teach about the broad range of human experience, including the spiritual.

People who would gag English teachers by curtailing or completely prohibiting any partisan religious reference are like the objector whose letter to the editor was published in the New Orleans *Times-Picayune* on February 12, 1991.

> *How ironic that the president, who is sworn to up-hold the Constitution, would declare a national day of prayer!*
>
> *One would expect the chief executive to be mindful of the Jeffersonian concept of separation of church and state. Sometimes I wonder if the man has ever bothered to read the First Amendment.*

The problem is not with George Bush's not having read the First Amendment. It is rather with people like that writer's having read entirely too much into it in order to canonize their own ideological (religious) biases, and gag everyone else. This man has the right to complain and even to bring suit against the President, if he chooses, but many others of us—including many an atheist, I'll wager—believe that where no harm in being religious in public is either done or intended, stacking up those stones to separate Church and State does not make for good neighbors. In Frost's words, "Something there is that doesn't love a wall," whether between farms or between Church and State. That "something," says Frost, "Sends the frozen-ground-swell under it...and makes gaps even two can pass abreast." That "something" tore down the wall between East and West Berlin. Would that the ground swell of public opinion would allow gaps large enough for the Sacred and the Secular to pass in and out without any danger to either.

Charlie, let me cite two specific instances when two public school teachers "violated" the letter of the law and "talked religion." In those days back at our own F. T. Nicholls (public) High School, we didn't know it was wrong to talk about God in the classroom, that crèches set up by Miss McVey's art classes in front of the school on St. Claude Ave. were taboo, or that learning and singing Christmas carols in a public school was a sin against the First Commandment (make that "First Amendment").

The first infraction occurred when I was a freshman (which was eighth grade during those World War II years). My algebra and science teacher, a marvel of a woman named Mrs. Mary Murtagh, told me one fine day to report after school. I did so, with four other boys. We all sat in the same desk in her classroom during different periods of the day. Some crude pornographic art had been etched into the desk, and Mrs. Murtagh expressed her extreme disappointment. We all denied having done it. She asked why we hadn't at least reported it to her. I responded, "I was too embarrassed." The other boys chorused their "Me too's." She then said that she believed it had been done by a student no longer in school, perhaps letting us gently off the hook. Then she proceeded to give us a sermonette about how God had given us our bodies, which were very good, and that he intended them and all their parts for very specific purposes, and that it was wrong for anyone to use or represent the human body or its parts for purposes that God hadn't intended. I wonder what the A.C.L.U. would have thought about this sort of classroom religious moralizing in the name of a specific deity.

Then in my junior year, the best English teacher I have ever had, Miss Amy Taggart, one day asked the class during a discussion of some topic in American literature, "Class, what is it we are all striving for ultimately?" No answers. She repeated the question. I was fifteen years old, and I knew what *my* answer was, and I was itching to say it: *God!* Having my reputation to consider, however, I kept silence. Disappointedly, Miss Taggart had to answer her own question: "Why, God, of course!"

This lady, who was not a Catholic, later assigned me two books to read in those pre-paperback days when each student had to read his own books and write those much-hated *book reports*. One book she assigned was *Man of Molakai*, a biography of Father Damien, the Belgian priest who contracted leprosy while serving the lepers in a colony of the Hawaiian Islands during the 19th century. The other book Miss Taggart assigned was Willa Cather's *Death Comes for the Archbishop*, which I thought was going to be a kind of Agatha Christie whodunnit. At any rate, I suppose somebody could make a case against this lady for steering the class— and me in particular—into "religious" avenues of thought contrary to the First Amendment.

God bless you, Mary Murtagh and Amy Taggart, wherever you are! Though what you did required little courage then because no one would have ever dreamed of objecting, the memory of what you did might inspire some of us to unscramble our priorities and reaffirm the value systems that were accepted in America before radical changes somewhere in the 1960s sent us on a frenetic pursuit of the American Mirage. More on this later.

This brings me to the second, and much longer, response that I want to make, Charlie. You imply that the influence of Secular Humanism has been minimal. If you are talking about direct influence, I would agree; however, I believe that indirectly Secular Humanism is largely responsible for much of the chaos in our public schools today.

Listen to the end of that letter from the man who faulted George Bush for declaring a national day of prayer:

> *As far as the war is concerned, prayer won't affect*
> *its outcome one iota. Men, not gods, wage war, and*
> *there's no Superman in the sky to bail us out. We'll*
> *have to do this ourselves. As Robert Ingersoll said,*
> *"Hands that help are better than lips that pray."*

How similar that sounds to one of the sacred tenets of Secular Humanism I cited earlier, that no deity is going to save us; we must save ourselves. Quite to the contrary, however, during the war with Iraq, the outpouring of the general American public's belief in prayer to a listening and merciful God was everywhere manifestly visible. I submit that despite our numerous shortcomings as a people, our public religious values in the 1990s are essentially the same as those of United States citizens of the 1890s and 1790s. Unfortunately, it is only in times of national peril that many Americans dust off those values, examine them, ponder them, and put them into practice. Why is it, Charlie, that what the generality of Americans can shamelessly do in public, you argue that teachers ought not to do in public schools?

Because of watchdog agencies like the A.C.L.U., teachers like Mary Murtagh and Amy Taggart would have to hold their tongues today, if they wanted to hold onto their jobs. When in 1955 I chose to teach in a Catholic school, I did so not because I feared prosecution if I taught religious values in a broad way in a public school. Rather it was because I wanted the larger freedom *explicitly* to teach and discuss the religious values that had won me over so completely. Since 1955, freedom to discuss religious values in public schools has diminished even more, due largely to a misdirected passion on the part of civil libertarians to protect the civil rights of American youth. But no one's rights are being violated when someone else speaks of their own religious values; in the free-for-all marketplace of ideas in the public school classroom, everyone is free to speak. It is the Secular Humanists and their disciples, in fact, who are denying others their rights by insisting that only the no-god, no-religion values of the Secular Humanists themselves shall be upheld, forcing all others into silence.

The libertarian movement has gone so far as to make students believe that their own civil rights make them, each one, a sovereign entity, the epicenter of a whole microcosm. You point out correctly, Charlie, that in public education in the South during the 1960s, racist statements made flagrantly by some teachers went uncontested then. Truly there was a need for civil-rights legislation and implementation. But somewhere along the way in the civil process of rights implementation, anarchy slid in. In practical terms, these civil, or inalienable, rights, as many students tend to interpret them, have placed the student as the creator of his or her own personal value system. That is the "religious" prerogative of the offspring as a sovereign-self of the "me-generation." This is also what has made it difficult for English teachers to make much of an impression, much less an impact, on students' values systems. A corollary of the gospel of Secular Humanism tells the student: "You have a sacred mission to discipline American society into acknowledging, respecting, and even championing your right to be as *un*disciplined as you want." "Freedom fighters" in too many classrooms today in America battle to cast off any restraint that they find unpleasant; they seek not so much life, liberty, and the pursuit of happiness as easy living, libertinism, and the pursuit of pleasure.

The English teacher's primary job is not to teach ethics as such; nevertheless, I submit that an overall malaise affects American education today primarily because it has become increasingly difficult to teach not only ethics but also *any* subject to classrooms full of students who lack the internal discipline that ethics-from-without would have taught them. Students find it more tempting and rewarding to pay homage to their own sovereignty and to obey their own self-indulgent promptings than to obey some external authority.

Charlie, if I were in today's public school system, I doubt I could go as far as Miss Taggart or Mrs. Murtagh did without being called on the carpet by somebody. I would be told, I fear, that the only values I can teach categorically, without violating my students' sovereign civil rights, are those values which are scientific, mathematical, or democratic (the latter as re-defined by the chief high priests of libertarian casuistry, the *canon lawyers* of the A.C.L.U.).

These libertarian vigilantees seem to be saying that I, as an English teacher, may function only as a resourceful midwife attending the students' bringing forth of their *own* values. The English teacher as values instructor may, at most, take students on field trips through literature and history—as through a museum or laboratory—and invite students to observe: "Thus did Macbeth. How did his values affect himself and others? Thus did Romeo. Thus did Tony in *West Side Story*. Thus did Dr. Jekyll, and thus Cyrano, and Huckleberry Finn, and Hester Prynne." Should the students ask what the teacher thinks, the teacher is forbidden to reply. Because my values have been conditioned by my belief in revealed religion of which I must not speak, I would be required by the A.C.L.U.'s interpretation of the Constitution to remain dumb about my own values.

For years, I have been disappointed, but not surprised, when former students told me about the way some university professors make disparaging remarks in classroom lectures about belief in God, Christianity, and Christian ethics. Now it is precisely here, Charlie, where the principle of selective outrage on the part of

civil libertarians is at its most outrageous self, another
version of the old double standard at its hypocritical
worst. These agnostic or atheistic or just plain bigoted
professors—in publicly funded universities, mind you—
openly mock those religions and religious values that
they dislike, and they do it, of course, in the name of
academic freedom! But just let anyone, especially an
undergraduate student, so much as dare to say anything that could be construed as in the least disparaging about some group or value that the professor
considers sacrosanct, and you will hear tenured wails
of "Bias! Discrimination!"

Charlie, I would like to see someone like Neil
Simon write a play, assuredly a tragicomedy, in which
some college students file a class action through the
A.C.L.U. (ha!) against professors who have been using
the State College classrooms as a platform for evangelizing students against the follies of theism, Christianity, Catholic sexual ethics, and religious values. Then
the professors hire other A.C.L.U. attorneys to defend
themselves with a counter-suit on the grounds that
their academic freedom of speech has been prosecuted.

"Censorship!" cries the A.C.L.U. attorney for the
professors. "Remember the Freedom-of-Speech Amendment!"

"Indoctrination!" cries the A.C.L.U. attorney for
the students. "Remember the Separation-of-Church-
and-State Amendment!"

In the play, the two A.C.L.U. attorneys go at it, but
I'd leave it to Neil Simon to write an outcome. Maybe
he could work out Lewis Carroll's resolution of the fight
between the Gingham Dog and the Calico Cat in *Alice
in Wonderland*: They ate each other up! Sooner or
later, Charlie, the A.C.L.U. is going to be hoisted by its
own petard.

As a teacher in a public school, I would use the Socratic method, acting as God's advocate—not the devil's—to ask leading questions. I would conscientiously as a true-blue American not let my own values intrude to influence (i.e. "harm") the students in any way. You yourself, Charlie, indicate the difficulty of a teacher's being completely objective here. You say the teacher should be "neutral." I say, rather, that public school teachers have been neutered by the scalpel of libertarian activism in the teaching of values.

In a Catholic school or in any sectarian school situation, the English teacher need have no such restrictions. I need not wait indefinitely for a student to "discover" a certain value without my prompting. I can teach that value with no prejudice to my student's God-given freedom to discover and to grow in the truth, or to do the opposite. Neither Moses nor Jesus Christ hesitated to teach absolute values and to teach them absolutely. Neither of them thought it necessary to consult the multitudes, take opinion polls, submit amendments for approval, and then seek a two-thirds majority ratification. When I ask my students why we don't petition Congress to abolish or repeal the laws of gravity or thermodynamics for our occasional convenience, their laughter teaches them my object lesson. Are uprightness and integrity, fidelity and charity as absolute as the verities of physics and biology? Even more so!

This analogy between natural and moral law fails, alas, to instruct libertarians who will tolerate—in fact, they encourage—our teaching on the danger of violating exclusively physical laws. It seems to me that these libertarians think of ethical values, ultimately, only in terms of physical ramifications and results, whereas in my classroom, I speak of the dangers of violating both physical *and* metaphysical mandates. I like to use Jack London's gem of a story, "To Build a Fire," as an illustration.

In the story, the nameless protagonist is a brash young adventurer travelling with only a disinterested huskie to a destination in sub-zero weather somewhere in the Yukon. The man carelessly, even arrogantly, ignores precautions offered before the journey by authority figures, some old-timers who, the man thought, lacked self-confidence and daring. The reader gradually senses the horror of what happens when the know-it-all (a sovereign self) breaks the rules that somebody else had told him that he ought to obey. Refusing to be instructed by others, the foolhardy traveller ends up a frozen corpse. London's last lines are spare and superb. The dead man is sniffed by the dog, "howling under the stars that leaped and danced and shone brightly in the cold sky."

There is something of the natural-demonic in this celebration of Nature victorious over human hubris. Nature does not suffer fools. Mother Nature, I want my students to know, is far less kind than God, "the Father of mercies and God of all consolation" (2 Corinthians 1:3), who forgives the stupidity of man's (and woman's) hubris in the metaphysical order. Of this I can, and do, speak to my students. Of this I could *not* speak to students in a public school classroom. Demons of a different sort would bay and dance for my dismissal for having violated the metaphysics of proper pedagogical neutrality in the public school classroom of America.

Libertarianism, for all its glitz and glow and patriotic promise of individual liberties, does not uphold rights in the long run. It is not progressive, but regressive. It is not freeing, but repressive. I illustrate with an historical example: Ralph Waldo Emerson, evangelist for the Oversoul in the 1840s, was still going strong by 1860 when he spoke on personal and regional sovereignty:

> *...Washington aspires to become the centre of*
> *America.*
>
> *...the people are jealous of their rights and ready to*
> *resist the slightest encroachment under any circum-*
> *stances.*[1]

That kind of libertarian rhetoric must have been highly hailed south of the Mason-Dixon Line, where the Oversoul was beginning to vest its votaries in Rebel Gray. But hark! A few years later, with the eruption of the Civil War, the same Emerson was calling upon that same dastardly and intrusive central government to assume "in any crisis...the absolute powers of Dictator." Enter the Oversoul, now dressed in Yankee Blue.

Hark yet again! The best—or worst—is yet to come from this champion of personal sovereignty, this enemy of authoritarian intrusiveness that stifles creativity. In 1864, Emerson met with James Russell Lowell and Oliver Wendell Holmes to discuss establishing a national academy of letters, to be headquartered—where else?—in Washington, D.C. He reported to a friend that a special council of experts would act as a jury "to which questions of taste and fitness in literature might be carried":

> *...a jury to sit upon abnormal anomalous preten-*
> *sions to genius, such as trouble the public mind*
> *now and then. Custodians of sense and elegance—*
> *these colleagues are to be—in literature. They*
> *would be the college of experts, to which the Govern-*
> *ment might sometimes wish to refer questions touch-*
> *ing Education, or historic forms.*[2]

The bill to impanel a literary jury was introduced in Congress on July 2, 1864. Perhaps Civil War considerations took priority over concerns to protect the American public from those "abnormal anomalous pretensions to genius." Or maybe some of the gentlemen in Congress had bought too enthusiastically what Emer-

American public from those "abnormal anomalous pretensions to genius." Or maybe some of the gentlemen in Congress had bought too enthusiastically what Emerson had said so forcefully to the contrary in his earlier libertarian essays on "The American Scholar" and "Self-Reliance." For whatever reasons, fortunately for genuine intellectual freedom, the bill failed to pass.

Somewhere along the line, Emerson must have felt that liberty had been misread and translated into libertarianism. The irony, of course, is that a proclaimer of unlimited liberty turns out to be the very one who wants to curtail it. Isn't this true of so many libertarian movements in political and social history? The Russian Revolution of 1917 and the American Revolution of the 1960s, for two examples, are not so different as one might think.

The Bolsheviks shouted "Liberty!" to all the workers of the world, reminding them that the only thing they had to lose was their chains. But once the Revolution had been effected, the libertarians became the aristocrats in the oh-so-necessary dictatorship not *of* but *over* the proletariat—but only, they assured us, until things worked out so that this temporarily necessary and completely disinterested military aristocracy would gladly step aside and let a completely classless, a completely egalitarian, a completely free, a completely sovereign society rule itself! Absolutely every sovereign person in the world would then respect absolutely every other person's sovereignty, and everybody would live happily ever after in a citizen-workers' paradise. Brotherhood without God, and eventually without government, was the hollow promise to each sovereign member of the proletariat.

How very like the equally hollow promise of the new-age revolution of the American 1960s. "Do your own thing!" "Let it all hang out!" "Make love not war!"

Under the libertarian slogans of free love, free sex, and free dope, the revolutionaries of the '60s enslaved the minds of America's youth so that they could think no further than their feelings, their hormones, and their chemicals would permit.

How quickly, then as now, the libertarians become the new dictators: "Liberty, equality, fraternity for the masses, oh my brothers and sisters; but you must, of course, let *me* orchestrate those liberties for you." Thus spake Emerson and thus speak libertarians today.

Surely, Charlie, there is a place somewhere in Dante's *Purgatorio* for libertarians who will be tormented in dungeons where the horned and tailed wardens are rebellious youths enjoying their liberty to do whatever they please, including torturing libertarians. I imagine John Dewey and Jean Jacques Rousseau in the clutches of some of the teenage brats whom you and I both have known in schools over the years. If I were a cartoonist, I would have these teenagers tormenting their wards while reading "instructions" from their teachers' manuals, such as *Emile* and *Experience and Education*, those compendiums that urge teachers to be Deweyite progressives in education, and permit students to "express themselves" and to be "assertive."

Still thinking with Dante, I imagine an English teacher in the *purgatorio* of some public school in New York City trying to teach a lesson in values, when a student asks permission to go to the school dispensary for a free pack of condoms or a clean needle.

Recently, Charlie, my students and I read the "Vanity Fair" excerpt from John Bunyan's *Pilgrim's Progress* in our senior lit anthology. I asked them what Bunyan's protagonist, named "Christian," would have thought if, instead of visiting Vanity

Fair, he had visited our own Bourbon Street here in New Orleans during Mardi Gras.

My students felt that Christian would have been far more shocked. They imagined his being approached by someone who gives him a pack of condoms, gaily packaged and decorated in Mardi Gras hues of green, purple, and yellow. Some humanitarian group had actually chosen this way to help prevent communicating AIDS. The message of pragmatic values that my students knew better than to learn from this sort of "public service" is "Make the world safe for any kind of sex, sodomy included. The *only* ethic you have to consider is your physical health and that of others. The *only* moral health is the public's physical health." In my English classes, we are allowed to discuss these issues, and I, as teacher, am allowed to instruct my students according to a higher ethical standard. In the English classes that you are advocating, Charlie, I fear that I would have to remain deaf and dumb and hog-tied.

The same pragmatic message has been communicated about drug use. It was only after the devastating physical effects of drug use became manifest that secularists began to find fiber enough to tell kids, "Say no to drugs." Charlie, remember those deliriously libertarian days of the 1960s and '70s when every daring American adolescent was being told by peers to "turn on" with drugs? Imagine, just imagine, a "Say no to drugs" decal on cars or jackets at Woodstock! The message would have been hooted off the stage. Timothy O'Leary was a cult hero, and how large the cult was! Recall Johnny Carson making jokes on the *Tonight Show* about Colombian gold? No more. And why not? Now that the Surgeon General has finally established pragmatically what a better sense of ethics already knew: that drugs can destroy your physical, mental, and emotional health. We can talk about it publicly. But ethics, Charlie, is no longer to be factored in as a value in the public-school education of our democratic society, not according to your neutral stance.

Imagine an ethics-based bumper sticker that says: "Say no to illicit sex." Now wouldn't that get a grand guffaw and merciless satirizing by the crew of *Saturday Night Live!* Such a message would be construed as only one of two things: the work of either a wag or of a Puritan. But wait a minute! Change just one word in that ridiculous slogan: replace the word "illicit" with another, and voilà, not guffaws, but only approval for the sane and sober public-service announcement: "Say no to *unsafe* sex!"

True-story time: About ten or so years ago, a teacher at my school (a Catholic school, but not a Catholic teacher) told me that she had been approached by one of our graduates from a year or two before, asking for advice as to whether she should "have sex" with her boyfriend. This teacher told the young girl that in such a highly personal matter as this, she, the teacher, did not want to give any advice. It was solely for the young woman to make her own decision. The teacher thought that she was exercising supremely mature judgment by letting the girl rely exclusively on her own judgment.

Now, I ask you, suppose the girl had told the teacher that the boyfriend had an STD (sexually transmitted disease), a highly communicable and horribly life-threatening venereal disease—would that teacher have maintained her lofty reticence about values? No way! She would have said, "Are you crazy, kid? Where is your sense of values? Are you willing to risk your life for an hour (or less) of sexual pleasure?" Our libertarian ethos can see right and wrong only in pragmatic terms of physical, emotional, and social-economic well-being. Americans have their Bill of Rights, but the Constitution guarantees none to God. We maintain public silence about moral values, lest our arbitrary libertarian values-system be offended, and God's sovereignty threaten our "rights."

Yes, Charlie, I do believe that Secular Humanism is de-valuing morality in America, both directly and indirectly. Furthermore, *"j'accuse!"* It is my job—no, my calling—as an English teacher who knows something about humanity and values and literature and teaching to decry this seducer of ourselves and our youth, even if the task is difficult and risky. I put the same question to the libertarians that I put time and again to my students, whether in English class, history class, or homeroom: "What would the world be like if everybody lived by your values?" Call it the Golden Rule or call it Kant, it's the right question. The student who copies homework, who cheats, who lies chronically to parents and school authorities, who wants to "get by" with only minimal achievement, and then brags about how cool he is—this student confronted by my values question quickly realizes that he could not survive in a world full of dishonest parasites like himself. Some students pretend not to care a bit, considering themselves lucky to be the cleverer in a world full of suckers, but under my ethical guns, such a student has to face the truth about what he considers "good." If he were an evangelist preaching values for others to imitate, the converts would soon destroy the preacher. Macbeth had the basic honesty to realize his own moral poverty when he said, "We but teach bloody instructions, which being taught, return to plague the inventor."

That, Charlie, is what the libertarians have been doing. The "liberated" students, especially in our nation's public schools, have become in many places "King Mob." Egged on by the rhetoric and music of

what I have called the Sub-Humanists, the Secular
Humanists, and the Pseudo-Christian Humanists,
thousands and thousands of kids are now driven to be
rebellious. Unfortunately, it is not the civil libertarians
who feel the brunt of the rebellion, even though they
have occasioned so much of it, but rather we school
teachers, many of whom are being abused as never
before. Many of us are finding it increasingly difficult
to cope with kids who are in fact celebrating the "values" of selfishness, laziness, and arrogance, not only in
society at large but also right in the classrooms and
corridors of our schools.

I am reminded of how F. Scott Fitzgerald described two such selfish, lazy, arrogant *adult* children at the close of *The Great Gatsby*. How close it
comes to portraying so many of today's *adolescent*
children, or what they will be like in a few years.

> *It was all very careless and confused. They were
> careless people, Tom and Daisy—they smashed
> up things and creatures and then retreated back
> into their money or their vast carelessness, or
> whatever it was that kept them together, and let
> other people clean up the mess they had made.*[3]

Personal testimony time, Charlie, from a few people in the profession. (You, gentle reader, listening to
this argument between two brothers, probably could
tell stories like these of your own.)

- A former student of mine, a teacher for 25
  years, told me recently that the joy he knew in
  teaching evaporated about five years ago: too
  much laziness, selfishness, and arrogance from
  students.

- A public high school principal I have known
  since we began in the profession about 38 years
  ago said recently that he is retiring before age

65 because "I'm tired of fighting problem students and their parents."

- An English teacher and department chair in a large Midwestern public high school is quitting the profession because she is afraid for her safety in what was once a model high school.

- A former principal recalls a tour taken by participants at a principals' convention in a large city. A brand new high school, one year old, of model construction, and with excellent facilities, had been pathetically vandalized by its own students *during its first year of operation.*

- A former student of mine, an Education major in a university, changed her major when she and her class paid field visits to some grade schools. Her comment: "I don't think I could handle those brats, the way they act."

- The last and saddest case involves a male teacher in a Catholic high school who decided that he needed higher pay, and so made a switch to the public school system in a neighboring town. After a short while at his new school, he was dismayed to learn that the academic atmosphere of the big school was substandard because of the laziness, selfishness, and arrogance of many of the students.

Observing the faculty, he said he noticed there were three groups. The first were the still completely dedicated, who, like himself, were doing their darndest to be good teachers and help students to the utmost. The second group comprised teachers who had once shared this idealism and energy, but had largely given up in despair, lamenting: "It's like butting your head against a brick wall.

We feel so alone and unsupported." The third group were teachers who were virtually non-teachers. They put in their time, but hardly anything else. They no longer cared about much except their paycheck.

After a year of trying to work in this new situation, the teacher re-applied to his former Catholic school and, to his great relief, was accepted. The extra pay in the public system was just not worth it, he said.

At this point, Charlie, some really fine teachers in public schools may want to object that some of the problems in public schools are the problem students that Catholic schools (and other private schools) have "dumped" onto the public schools. I can appreciate this frustration. At the same time, I must point out that parents who send their children to Catholic schools (and not all of these parents are Catholics, either) are doubly taxed. They feel, and rightly so, that their double taxation entitles them to a school that has an excellent learning environment, where their own *values* as parents will be taught and upheld, and where short shrift will be given to those students who *persist* in being lazy, selfish, and arrogant.

On this point, I fear that some parents whose children are lazy, selfish, and arrogant need to be undeceived about what the proposed "voucher system" would do for them. The parent who thinks that his or her child will suddenly become a great student just by being admitted to a "better school" is mistaken. I could never favor a voucher system that would in effect compel private schools to accommodate their values to the lazy, selfish, arrogant propensities of any student who came in waving a voucher. The day that private schools are compelled by law to admit and *retain* students, no matter how troublesome and unproductive they are, King Mob will have its green light to complete the ruination of education in this country, while the retainers of King Mob wave their A.C.L.U. banners heroically.

American education has been pathetically wounded during the past three decades. It is ludicrous, stupid, inane—I grope for adjectives—to think that the problems of education are going to be solved by such expedients as "pumping more money into public education!" With far less money, many religious and private school systems, like my own, have fared far better with students. My own school's physical plant, our facilities, and our faculty are top-notch. Would tripling our budget solve our problems? Not at all. If our salaries, far below public school salaries, were doubled, or even tripled, would that double or triple my efficiency or my *dedication as a teacher?*

I'm not a mercenary who won't go to war until he's paid. I don't hold back in what I do in the classroom, in how I relate to my students, or in my willingness to lay it on the ethical line—until I get more money. Too many Americans, Charlie, are naive enough to believe that low salaries have driven away all the "good" teachers. Lack of money has not caused this crisis of values, and throwing money at the crisis will not win the war for public morality. Even so, I'm sure you will agree that if all of the "good" teachers who left the profession for financial reasons were to return *en masse*, they could do precious little, if anything, to turn back the tide of chaos now flooding American education.

"The problem, dear Brutus, is not in our stars, but in ourselves." The problem, dear Americans, is not with our finances, but with our values—or rather with the lack of them. The laziness, selfishness, and arrogance characterizing so much of adolescent America today is not going to disappear until we change the values with which we instruct our youth. Our kids are not going to become the enthusiastic, grinning little zealots for learning that we have seen for years in glossy ads from English textbook companies. ("See how your students will respond to this exciting, colorful new textbook!!!")

And, Charlie, laziness, selfishness, and arrogance are not the only factors that make our task frustrating. My guess is that many a beleaguered teacher over that past three decades, reading with considerable cynicism some of the articles in professional educational journals, has muttered something like, "If this teacher in his marvelous control situation, or that supervisor writing from her antiseptic office, or some college professor writing from a lofty tower about what *we* high school teachers should/could do with our students—if these people would only be compelled to come and try to teach in the *purgatorio* that is my daily existential milieu for even half a semester, they would change their tune! All ye armchair generals, all ye Monday-morning quarterbacks, come ye out into the field of battle, onto the field of play, at least once every five years! Show us *your* well-planned strategies in action in *our* milieux."

Those students whom I have labelled "lazy, selfish, and arrogant" are not only culprits but also victims in our values-absent society. When I step back to take a panoramic view of the 100 students I am teaching this year, viewing them with the increased perspective of an astronaut leaving

Earth, the higher I am lifted up the more I am able to see. Gradually I have a vision of all the students in all the high schools of America. This growing, sad panorama assaults my eyes the same way that the awful scene in *Gone With the Wind* shows the wounded and dying in the Atlanta train yard. Focused first on a small group of wounded soldiers, the camera backs off and the purview enlarges to take in dozens, then hundreds, then thousands of mangled soldiers in various stages of anguish, agony, and dying. (I remember the audience in the theater groaning.) This is my Ezekiel's vision of adolescent America, a generation horribly wounded and maimed by the ideology of libertarianism. Cry, the beloved country!

The innocent public goes mad with yellow ribbons about the nobility of our cause in the Middle East, our respect for even one human life, and the liberty that makes it worth living and dying; and ecology-conscious people knit their brows with concern over the pollution of the air from burning oil wells in Kuwait, but while the nation pipes these patriotic tunes, the majority blithely continues to ignore the pollution of our moral atmosphere in our educational system. We will fight a war to save the integrity of someone else's society while we sacrifice our own children's values and ethics to the pseudo-Constitutional demands of the libertines.

As an English teacher in a public high school, I would be free to administer the medicine of values to my wounded students to the extent that Confederate medics in that Civil War scene in GWTW were able to do, having been defeated, impoverished by war, and shorn of rations and supplies. As a public school English teacher, I would

Is all this a scenario for despair? God, I hope not! I love Mother Teresa of Calcutta's response to someone who once asked her how she kept from despairing when she looked at the millions of others who needed her ministering when she could reach so few. She responded by saying that when she goes outside her clinic in the morning (after having prayed for at least an hour), she sees the vast crowd outside, fixes her gaze on one person, and asks that poor wretch to come in. Then she does whatever she can. For Mother Teresa that, apparently, is peace-making. As she also says, "God does not ask for success; He asks only for our efforts." We English teachers, trying to teach values in spite of what the system is doing to inhibit us, can take courage from Mother Teresa. The demonic ideology of pseudo-humanism may seduce its thousands, promising freedom but delivering enslavement, yet we English teachers will go on teaching our hundreds the burden of values in our heritage of literature that sets the captives free.

Charlie, I gain confidence in another way, both as a teacher and as a Catholic. I remember something that Guy Lemieux, S.J., a beloved professor from Loyola University whom we both knew and respected, told me when I first began teaching. May I never forget what he said: "Bernie, as you look out over your students sitting in their desks, try from time to time to picture each one of them wearing a crown of thorns. Try to see the suffering Christ in each of them."

I opened my first argument in the discussion with you, Charlie, by quoting Gerard Manley Hopkins, who wrote at a time when, he said, his world was going bad. Nevertheless, any pessimism had to burn away "Because the Holy Ghost over the bent world broods with warm breast and with ah!

bright wings." How different, how salvifically different, Hopkins' response was from that of his contemporary Matthew Arnold, who in his poem "Dover
Beach" seems to have surrendered to despair:

The Sea of Faith
Was once, too, at the full, and round earth's
shore
Lay like the folds of a bright girdle furled.
But now I only hear
Its melancholy, long, withdrawing roar,
Retreating, to the breath
Of the night wind, down the vast edges drear
And naked shingles of the world.
...

For the world...
Hath really neither joy, nor love, nor light,
Nor certitude, nor peace, nor help for pain;
And we are here as on a darkling plain
Swept with confused alarms of struggle and
flight,
Where ignorant armies clash by night.

Charlie, it's all in two words of that last line, I
believe: "ignorant armies." Armies are ignorant because they lack vision, purpose, *values!* Technologi-
cally they may indeed be perfect in their capability to
destroy one another and themselves, but I do not buy
Arnold's sad vision for the students in my English
classes any more now than I did for myself when I
first studied Arnold in a graduate seminar at L.S.U.
back in the early '60s. I really must counter the
image of Arnold's tragic tide at Dover Beach with
another tidal-image, one by a medieval mystic, a
Fleming named Jan Ruysbroek:

God is like a sea, ebbing and flowing, cease-
lessly flowing into each person...according to
the needs...of each. And in His ebbing, He
draws back again all people to whom He has

given in heaven and on earth, with all they have
and with all of which they are capable....God de-
sires to be loved by us in accordance with His ex-
cellence.[4]

That is the ebb and flow I want to go on in my
English classroom. That is the ebb and flow the libertarians are determined shall *not* go on in public
school classrooms. Prevented by the anti-values system which you, Charlie, allege to be "neutral," English teachers in public schools are kept from
teaching God's values freely and openly through the
gift of God's values incarnate in human literature.
The American public-school system that you are defending forbids the study of any ebb and flow of God's
tide lapping against that god which is the student's
personal sovereignty. No, Charlie, I say **no** to that!

Not to teach the values of God and that supreme
value which *is* God, is to invite chaos. Not life and not
the world, Charlie, but American public education is
becoming that darkling plain where ignorant armies
of students and teachers clash without values, having
really "neither joy, nor love, nor light/nor certitude,
nor peace, nor help for pain." And after this deluge of
the neutrality of values, these confused alarms of
struggle and flight, comes what? The turbid and tor-
pid aftermath of the public school classroom battlefield strewn with laziness, selfishness, and
arrogance, to say nothing of ignorance, as well. And
after that, Charlie, what comes next? I have to
change poets to give answer. As Dostoyevsky said
most forcefully somewhere in one of his novels:

If there is no God, then everything is permissible.

change poets to give answer. As Dostoyevsky said most forcefully somewhere in one of his novels:

If there is no God, then everything is permissible.

NOTES

1. Quoted by Daniel Aaron in *The Unwritten War: American Writers and the Civil War* (New York: Oxford University Press, 1975): 35, 36; from *The Letters of Ralph Waldo Emerson*, R. L. Rusk, ed. (New York, 1939): V 395-6; and from *The Works of Charles Sumner* (Boston, 1875-83): XI 402-4.

2. *Ibid.*

3. Scribner's: (New York, 1925): 180, 181.

4. Jan van Ruysbroek, *Spiritual Espousals*, Eric Colledge, tr. (Westminster, Maryland: Christian Classics, 1983).

REFERENCES

Aaron, Daniel. *The Unwritten War: American Writers and the Civil War*. New York: Oxford University Press, 1975.

Van Ruysbroek, Jan. *Spiritual Espousals*, Eric Colledge, tr. Westminster, Maryland: Christian Classics, 1983.

Further Comment

Charles Suhor

I expected to find more areas of agreement between Ben's views and mine as our exchange proceeded, but instead I see increasing divergence. When staying within the limits of our topic, teaching values through literature, Ben intensifies his doctrinal stance and presents an inaccurate picture of what goes on in public school classrooms—the subject, alas, on which he is least knowledgeable.

Ben's strategy, more than his substantive arguments, makes it hard to get a handle on his response. He has turned up the volume, multiplied metaphors, introduced some non-sequiturs, and hauled in issues such as Congressional prayer, the Persian Gulf War, and Nativity scenes, issues that are at best peripheral to the subject at hand. Ben's targets are too many and too diverse, so I will not try to engage in a point-by-point rebuttal in this wrap-up. For example, I'll leave him to duke it out with Mr. Ingersoll on the proposal for a national Day of Prayer. I will also pass the opportunity to comment on Ben's critique of Emerson, except to say that if the analysis is also taken as a sample of pedagogy, it's a classic example of stacking the deck with selected snippets.

I focus my reactions mainly on Ben's most pertinent arguments, leaving many of his digressions, asides, and broadsides for discussion over *café au lait* when next we meet in New Orleans. In declaring part of my brother's text impertinent, I nevertheless acknowledge that the power of his arguments, the big ones as well as the one-liners, is largely derived from his contextualizing of them within his unifying vision of traditional Catholic theology. Public education can lay claim to core values, even to the democratic enterprise, but not to an interconnected system of beliefs that yield cosmological order.

However, an integrated vision can, and in Ben's case does, spin out as inflexibility on a grand scale. In the name of his world view, Ben measures—and often co-opts—all sorts of things, appropriating not only Dante and Mother Teresa but also Jack London, Robert Frost, F. Scott Fitzgerald, Matthew Arnold, Dostoyevsky, and *Gone with the Wind* in support of his points.

In terms of the focus of this debate, Ben's richly constructed myopia is not the problem. The real problem is that he seems ready to divert the public school classroom, not to mention public funds, to the service of his religious creed. When discussing public education, Ben strains to impose on us his particular kind of value system, *viz.*, an absolute, hierarchical system with fixed views on virtually all major metaphysical, moral, and socio-political issues that might arise in the discussion of literature and life. As a critic once said of G.K. Chesterton, another Catholic apologist and wit:

"He mistook his own borborygmus for the rumblings of the universe."

Public education is a joy and a wonder because it can accommodate in classroom discussion a multiplicity of belief systems so that many ideas—including the ideas of those who are as certain about *their* beliefs as Ben is about *his*—can become part of a vital dialogue about literary works and life experiences. Those whose beliefs are less fixed can also get into the fray, and they are often the most stimulating participants because they question those who profess to have all of the answers. Somehow, Ben translates this fertile ground of interaction into a place where matters of values, ethics, and religion are either suppressed or commandeered by "libertarian vigilantes" whose perspectives are exclusively "scientific, mathematical, or democratic."

Differences in Perception

Ben's response to my essay demonstrates that our differences go beyond educational philosophy. Our very perceptions of the world are sharply different. Like many other conservative religious leaders, Ben has constructed a world in which atheists and atheists' dupes have somehow won the day in our educational system; where most people "ignore the pollution of our moral atmosphere"; where "we sacrifice our own children's values and ethics to the pseudo-constitutional demands of libertines"; where English teachers either avoid discussing moral questions or simply audit students who "obey their own self-indulgent promptings."

That is not the world described in my essay, nor is it the world I have seen in three decades of work with English teachers. My view of public schools is derived from eight years as a high school teacher, from innumerable visits to urban classrooms, and in recent years from face-to-face contact with thousands of K-12 English and language-arts teachers throughout the country.

Regarding Ben's horror stories about public schools, I will grant that there are many schools where problems make teaching and learning virtually impossible. Thousands of students are being wretchedly neglected by the public, politicians, school boards, administrators, and often by teachers. But such situations are commonly tied in with larger social problems that are laid at the doorstep of the public school under the cruel assumption that the effects of mass poverty, racism, drugs, and inept social policy can be solved by teachers in underfunded schools.[1] I have been in those dreary schools, and I know that they need our help, not another poke in the eye.

Further, it is unfair and unreasonable to cite those heartbreaking situations, then leap to generalizations about "anarchy" and "the chaos in our public schools today." The overall picture of public education is by no means chaotic. The great American experiment in education for all, is chugging along despite its tormentors, as we try to educate populations of students who were ignored in previous generations on account of race or social class or other excluding factors. In 1920, only 10 percent of the American population was in school. In the 1940s and 1950s, when Ben and I were public-school kids at Washington Elementary and Nicholls High School, things were getting better, but less than half of all children were graduating from high school. Today some 83 percent of 19- and 20-year olds have graduated from high school.[2]

We need to do even better, both in quantity and quality, but are we pumping money recklessly into a failed system, as Ben suggests? If we take the long-term view, I respond, not at all; and even the immediate view is very revealing, seen in perspective. Among the seven most industrialized nations, the United States spends the least for education, devoting 4.1% of our Gross Domestic Product to education as compared to 7.0% for Sweden. (In between are Japan, Canada, West Germany, and France.) Our lack of support for preschool education is even more scandalous. In France, public preschools are in operation for 90% of 3-year-olds and 100% of 4- and 5-year olds. Public funds in the U.S. pay for a mere 16% of costs for 45% of 3- and 4-year-olds who are in nursery schools, day-care facilities, or preschools for part of the day. On this score, too, numerous other industrialized nations put us to shame.[3]

If Ben believes that public money for a voucher system or for other support of private and religious schools will transform American education, he needs to present persuasive data, not hair-raising anecdotes from a few of his colleagues. Chester Finn, Assistant Secretary of Education during the Reagan Administration, was not impressed with the non-public schools' performance on the 1986 NAEP (National Assessment of Educational Progress) tests of reading, history, and literature. He noted "a differential, but . . . a very small differential" between public and non-public school students. Albert Shanker of the American Federation of Teachers commented on the slight differences among private, parochial, and public schools on 1990 NAEP mathematics tests. Given the advantaged backgrounds of the majority of non-public school students, Shanker said, "private and parochial schools are doing a worse job."[4]

Ben ignores the fact that tens of thousands of teachers and millions of students in public schools are succeeding. Most do not have the top-notch physical plant and facilities that Ben claims for his school.

Most would find Ben's 100 students a significant reduction in workload, and many are teaching the students whom he describes repeatedly (and, it pains me to say, uncharitably) as "selfish, lazy, and arrogant"—students Ben would turn away if they appeared at his school's doorstep with a voucher. Somehow, the phrase "no room at the inn" comes to mind.

In Ben's response I saw continuing signs of perceptions shaped by an entrenched religious and metaphysical world view, with little consideration of alternative interpretations of experience. I saw little respect, indeed outright disrespect, for data. For example, responding to documented information about the pro-religious orientation of public school teachers and the American public at large, Ben allowed that Secular Humanism might not be at all widespread among school employees and the public, but he claimed that its "indirect" influence is "immense." He saw "a libertarian movement" encouraging a "horribly wounded and maimed" youth, who are the offspring of the "me-generation," who in turn were themselves victims when the "revolutionaries of the '60s enslaved the minds of America's youth."

Bless me, I just do not see things that way. I draw common-sense inferences from survey data, concluding that Secular Humanism has won the hearts and minds of very few people, and certainly not many elementary and high school teachers. Moreover, I lived through the '60s and '70s and '80s as a high school teacher, K-12 supervisor, and change agent in a national professional organization (not to mention as the father of 11 children, the youngest of whom recently turned 18). I can claim gut-level awareness of the wrenching problems of those decades, as well as of the present one. From where I stand, Ben's extreme statements about the ever-declining morality tell more about the fixity of his moral perspective than about the stuff that has been going on out there, both in the schools and in society at large.

Although I am reacting to particular comments in Ben's response, I am also challenging ideas about the decline and fall of America that many others have expressed. It seems to me that any doctrinal conservative who has observed social change and its effects on the teaching profession over the past 25 or 30 years must be looking at the world through some very dark bifocals.

First, there is the halcyon syndrome. Beginning with the teachers that Ben and I knew when we were growing up in the 1940s and '50s, I have never seen a generation in which many teachers in the fifty-something group did not sigh and say, "You know, Charlie, the students just aren't what they used to be."

Beyond that, certain doctrinal tenets that once enjoyed privileged legal status have not fared well in our life and times. Sectarian beliefs about a host of matters—from "blue laws" about working on Sundays, to dancing and drinking, to homosexuality—were once widely institutionalized in our local laws and school rules. Often these beliefs were not even considered subjects for public debate, much less discussion in the classroom. An absolutist—especially an absolutist who recalls the good old days when both the students and the social debate were more controllable—is likely to bemoan the increased separation between church and state, and to perceive the present social and educational climate in apocalyptic terms.

Ben holds that the wall of separation between church and state is analogous to Frost's "Mending

Wall," which symbolizes barriers that are maintained arbitrarily, through mindless habit. I disagree. Frost, you remember, described the mending wall as "just another kind of outdoor game,... / It comes to little more." The separation of church and state is no mere game, but a social institution purchased with the blood of our ancestors. "Before I built a wall," Frost says, "I'd ask to know / what I was walling in or walling out." To say it straight, Ben, we are walling in freedom of conscience, and walling out the double-edged sword of caesaropapism.

Although I have suggested that some veteran teachers idealize the schools and students of their past, I do not want to generalize. In my work with NCTE, I constantly meet teachers in my age category (I am 56), and younger teachers as well, who see the current generation not as self-centered brats but as young people who bring a different set of problems to the classroom. In fact, many adults are switching careers or returning to the workforce in order to teach, as evidenced by increasing enrollments in schools of education in recent years. Most education students have public school teaching careers in mind, and some of them want in particular to go into inner-city schools.

It frightens me anew to see Ben's penultimate paragraph, where he says that "English teachers in public schools are being prevented...from teaching God's values freely and openly through the gift of God's values incarnate in human literature." It should frighten Ben, too, upon reflection, because if one public school teacher were free to teach the values of Ben's God, then another would be free to teach the values of a god that Ben considers false, and others would be free to teach the values of secular humanism, atheism, and the A.C.L.U.

I suspect that in such a potentially explosive situation, all of these public school teachers who champion different doctrines would need to gather around a table and invent an idea like "pluralism" in which open discussion of moral and religious issues might be conducted in all of their classrooms, with the teacher trying to assure that a balanced, intelligent discussion goes on.

This group of teachers might also suggest that each teacher has the option of remaining neutral or frankly expressing his or her ideas as part of the open dialogue. They might develop guidelines, even "regulations," and then suggest that in fairness, teachers who persist in advancing a particular belief system should be cautioned about proselytizing, and ultimately fired if they persist in championing their creeds in their classrooms. If I were on the scene, that would strike me as a good idea. I would make a note to write it up some day.

The Nature of Teacher Neutrality

If this were one of those snotty exchanges we have all read in academic journals, at this point I would say, "It seems that Suhor the Elder has either not read my position carefully, or he has read it and failed to understand what I am saying, or he has read and understood it but chosen to distort its meaning for purposes of debate." Well, I will not put it quite that way, but let us look at Ben's characterization of my position on teacher neutrality in discussions of values in literature.

I find it strange that Ben, having read my text, can depict my viewpoint as an "anti-value system" in which the teacher is "deaf and dumb and hog-tied"; that he can characterize the neutral teacher as "neutered" or "gagged." And oddly, he has deduced that "ethics...is no longer to be factored in as a value in

the public-school education of our democratic soci-
ety.ʺ

First, I need to reiterate that the neutral stance
that I favor is not the only acceptable approach to the
teaching literature in public schools any more than
Ben's stance is the only Catholic one. Further, many
of my colleagues argue vehemently that teachers can
and should state their personal values as part of
classroom dialogue. They believe that their approach
is not inherently intimidating, and that students
need not be reluctant to challenge the teacher's opinion for fear of being downgraded, academically and
psychologically.

I find that argument weak. In practice I have
seen it abused. I will return later to the matter of
dialogical arm-twisting in connection with academic
freedom. Here I go on to clarify the nature of neutrality as I see it.

*Neutrality is not avoidance of controversy or re-
luctance to discuss values.* The wimp factor applies
only to those teachers, decreasing in number, who
limit discussion to retelling of plots and analysis of
form. Let me be as specific as possible on the matter
of inclusion of discussion of values in public-school
literature instruction. In the following list, I mention
again just a few of the complex, values-laden issues
that I noted in my two earlier statements or explored
in my extended examples of values instruction in the
appendix: paganism, anti-clericalism, racism, mercy-
killing, the American Dream, ambition, romantic
love, personal dedication to causes, war, definitions
of virtue, Christian and non-Christian ideals, lying,
gift-giving, anger, betrayal, personal responsibility,
the individual's rights and the state's rights, authority, self-assertion, loyalty, violence, and addiction.
We are not talking here about dodging tough moral

issues or shrinking from discussions of religious and philosophical belief systems.

Neutrality is not a strained attempt at "comprehensiveness." Clearly, one cannot discuss values in relation to a particular issue by covering *every* possible point of view. There is face-value absurdity in the idea of surveying the history of philosophy and religion so that every viewpoint on suicide and mercy-killing would be accounted for when studying Brian Clark's powerful play, *Whose Life Is It, Anyway?*

In dealing with complex and controversial works, it makes sense for the teacher to begin with open discussion by the class, which will have a finite repertoire of beliefs—some well-defined and some unformed—about the topic. Then, the teacher draws upon his or her knowledge of past and contemporary perspectives to select other reasoned, relevant ideas for discussion. The author's dramatization of the problem, the students' responses, and the teacher's professional judgments in expanding the discussion appropriately—these form the tripod of interaction about values in classroom study of literature.

Neutrality is not attacking the students' strongly held viewpoints. A skilled teacher asks students to develop and explain their ideas, calls on students to critique each other's statements of values, and asks key questions that prompt them to consider their unexamined assumptions. This is not the same as nailing a student against the wall until he or she either backs down or fully articulates the ideas and feelings that underlie a statement about values. The teacher is not an inquisitor, but a co-inquirer.

Our students' relative lack of sophistication makes them especially vulnerable to an approach that hacks away at their ideas under the guise of critical analysis. I have seen teachers "expose" the "flaws" in students' logic through relentless Socratic slugging. When students are humbled in this way, they learn the effective lesson of the exchange, *viz.*, to float no more ideas in the mined harbor of "open" classroom discussion.

I grant Ben's contention on a related point: University teachers are among the worst offenders in flagellating students who do not share the professor's opinions—and when criticized, our collegiate counterparts tend to raise the shield of academic freedom. That is deplorable, whether exercised by a militant Marxist at a public university or a neo-Thomist at a Catholic university. (I have been clobbered on occasion by both.)

During a recent debate on *Firing Line* about freedom of thought for students and faculty in higher education, liberals and conservatives alike agreed that the university is a unique intellectual community in which the flow of ideas must not be suppressed. This implies a broad academic freedom in which teachers can strongly advance personal beliefs. They teach under very few restrictions, unlike pre-collegiate teachers who work in a tempestuous fishbowl of local politics and parental concern.

K-12 teachers are assumed to be acting *in loco parentis.* They reach a much younger, more vulnerable, and broader student population, and they are committed by tradition and by law to recognize the wall of separation between church and state when dealing with matters of religious belief.

In some ways, the system is slightly crazy. It assumes that the twelfth-grade teacher is dealing with delicate and impressionable pysches, whereas the college teacher, a scant three months later, is working with tough young minds that can handle with equanimity a professor's triple *forte* challenge to their values.

Crazy as it is, I know of no better system. Happily, good K-12 public-school teachers have the judgment to look at students developmentally, moving them gradually into exploration of literature that deals with ever more complex moral issues. Most of these teachers accomplish this complex task without, in the phrase of poet Edward Field, spouting big, ripe absolutes.

By contrast, college teachers are free to build lectures and even entire courses around a particular belief system, and to take students deeply into relevant scholarship without highlighting competing ideas. Nevertheless, I trust that most college teachers truly see the university as a community dedicated to exploring ideas, and that they do not squelch intellectual dissent in their classrooms. Those who do are sometimes exposed, and when they are, they frequently plead academic freedom. That is abusive and cowardly, but to restrain them at the outset would be to frustrate the very idea of the university as a setting for advanced inquiry.

Neutrality is not compulsive self-monitoring. There are many ways of carrying neutrality to extremes. The dopiest is disclaiming any standards of value, as in the case of the counselor who did not wish to tell a student that a baldfaced theft was unethical. But surely, such stupidity must be exceptional. A more common and more complicated problem involves self-monitoring day-by-day to assure that one is keeping one's true beliefs in perspective.

As a teacher who was committed to the neutral approach, I tried to avoid showcasing my then-Catholic personal commitment, but I also tried to enjoy discussion without carrying neutrality scruples to excruciating extremes. The neutral stance involves striking a balance—gaining skill in self-monitoring without nervously censoring one's own discourse.

This goal of easefulness is not, I should add, a license for fudging. Ben asked whether a teacher might not advance a doctrinal view when "virtually everyone present" in a public school classroom or official event shares that view. I answer, certainly not. There is arrogance in the assumption that all of the students in a public-school setting are fully persuaded Catholics, Protestants, or what have you. In any such setting, the held beliefs of dissenting, minority believers, and the emerging beliefs of potential dissenters, must be respected as a matter of democratic principle.

The English teacher who exalted Christianity as the only life-path at the baccalaureate ceremony in East Texas may well have *assumed* that his audience was composed of 100% traditional Christians. Wrong. I was there, and the odds are powerful that other persons of different faiths were there, too. And even if no non-Christians were there, I believe that his sectarian stance was unethical in terms of the role of a public school teacher. His stance was surely un-Constitutional, in light of the Supreme Court's decision in *Lee v. Weisman* (1992) concerning prayer at a similar ceremony in Rhode Island.

In asking "What is it we are all striving for, ultimately?" and then saying, "God, of course," Amy Taggart might have been in tune with her times at Nicholls High School in the 1940s, but in my view she was not functioning as a public school teacher. A student who was an atheist at Nicholls—and there were some—would have a right to be indignant about being asked a loaded question and being given a theological response.

In a basic sense, Ms. Taggart's question was not posed in good faith because it was not an invitation to enter into a discussion about belief and nonbelief. A question bent towards the notion that we are all striving for God might be theologically adequate (though pedagogically suspect) in a sectarian school; but I do lament the tendency, implicit in many of Ben's discussions of literary works, to turn all literature of pain and quest into a disguised version of "The Hound of Heaven."

Neutrality on the teacher's part is not an endorsement of neutrality as the stance expected of students. I raised this point above, making a distinction between operational pluralism (i.e., the teacher's voluntary decision to conduct discussions without highlighting a particular religious or philosophical belief system) and officially sanctioned relativism. The latter would involve championing universal skepticism as a favored viewpoint, and it would in fact deny a commitment to pluralism. It is useful for the teacher to make this point explicitly, I believe, so that the students do not interpret the teacher's professional method as a nudge towards personal relativism.

So much for misconceptions about teacher neutrality. It follows from the above that I see neutrality as a desirable and important teaching skill. Pedagogical neutrality in discussions of values in literature involves evenhandedness, common sense, self-restraint, commitment to the classroom as a forum, and tolerance of multiple perspectives. In operation, it supports the values of common decency without appealing to any single belief system as normative.

In Retrospect

I do not know how Ben will view the evolution of our debate, but in summary, here is how I see the main areas of disagreement.

1. Both Ben and I acknowledge that there are valid differences in approaches to teaching values through literature in public and sectarian school settings, but we disagree on the benefits and hazards of the different approaches.

2. I see teacher neutrality—in dealing with belief systems, not in discussing core values like honesty, human dignity, and fairness—as the best stance for public school teachers as they conduct class discussions of values in literature. I admit that teachers can hypothetically bring in their personal views, stating them openly as part of the dialogue rather than as a privileged stance; nevertheless, I believe that this frequently results in students' being intimidated by the teacher's power as both persuader and evaluator.

3. Ben identifies teacher neutrality with pusillanimity, if not with relativism and nihilism. I deny this, offering numerous examples of vital teaching in which the teacher's belief system is not advanced. I distinguish the teacher's *practice* of neutrality from the idea that the teacher is *advocating* an agnostic stance on moral issues, the latter being an unacceptable retreat from pluralism.

4. I see Ben's absolutism as principled and philosophically defensible, but I argue that his doctrine drives his perceptions of society and schools, dimming his receptivity to alternative interpretations of literature and personal experience. Also, Ben seems to view empirical data about teachers' beliefs and school achievement as inadmissable evidence when unsympathetic to tenaciously held

creeds. I think that absolutists of any stripe, whether they are fully persuaded Muslim Fundamentalists, right-wing Christian activists, atheists like Paul Kurtz, or whatever, tend to process experience through a filter of non-negotiable givens. They become real inmates in imaginary prisons—hence, Ben's striking formulations of the triple terrors of sub-humanism, secular humanism, and pseudo-Christian humanism.

5. Ben sees schools as possible antidotes to various social poisons, and he views the study of values through literature as, among other things, a way of bringing important doctrinal truths to his students.

6. I do not believe that our monumental social problems can be solved by the schools alone, even by the best combined efforts of public, sectarian, and private schools. Nonetheless, I do see a vital moral mission in the teaching of English in public education. When we explore values through literature, we heighten each student's sense of moral reality. Further, we model the democratic process of exchanging ideas about values in ways that are rational, flexible, and sensitive to the views of others.

7. Methodologically, Ben sees the role of the English teacher in the religious school as that of the Socratic questioner who, when truly committed and intellectually honest, must ultimately come down on the side of doctrine. I acknowledge the internal consistency of his view, but I see a huge gap between the *intention* of conducting open discussion and the *effect*, even in the examples he cites. Ben gives short shrift to viewpoints that are out-

side of his belief system. Ultimately, Ben seems to admit only one position on most issues—the missionary position, one might say, with the teacher always on top.

8. Methodologically, I recommend large and small-group discussions of literature in which student response is respected. The student's reaction, however, is only the beginning point for productive thinking, talking, and writing about values and other aspects of literature in the English classroom. The teacher asks open-ended questions to start the exchange of ideas; encourages students to articulate their views clearly and to challenge each other fairly and tolerantly; uses Socratic questioning as needed, especially when probing the author's implied values, seeking consideration of viewpoints not expressed, and focusing attention on matters of literary structure.

I have never been fond of debates in which making points is the goal at the expense of seeking to clarify issues and find common ground. Reviewing the Suhor brothers' discussion of values in the teaching of literature, I find that the issues have become sharper in terms of our differences rather than our commonalities. That is better than pretending that the differences are insignificant, but I wish that our discovery had run in the direction of greater correspondence of viewpoints.

The rhetoric of the exchange became sharper-edged, possibly because each of us felt more challenged, intellectually and personally, as we read each other's elaborated positions. That, too, is all right. Few human beings can resist getting a bit scrappy in a debate. If we had stayed oh-so-civil in every line, our readers would have the right to suspect that we were playing medicine ball. Ben and I have always had discussions worthy of family members who disagree. I hope that our public exchange is worthy of the larger family of readers who are concerned about the teaching of values in all our schools.

NOTES

1. See, *e.g.*, Harold Hodgkinson's lucid documentation of this in "Reform Versus Reality," *Phi Delta Kappan* (September, 1991): 9-16.

2. "A Commitment to Quality." Brochure accompanying a film produced by the Education Commission of the States, n.d., p. 1; "Some progress seen toward educational goals," *News Gazette* (Champaign-Urbana, Illinois, September 30, 1991): A-12.

3. "It's Time for Action." Leaflet prepared by the National Education Association, 1991.

4. Julie Miller, "Wielding New NAEP Data, Shanker Assails Choice," *Education Week* (July 31, 1991): 36.

REFERENCES

Anonymous, "Some progress seen toward educational goals," *News Gazette* (Champaign-Urbana, Illinois, September 30, 1991): A-12.

Education Commission of the States. *A Commitment to Quality* (brochure and film). Washington, D.C., n.d.

Hodgkinson, Harold. "Reform Versus Reality," *Phi Delta Kappan* (September, 1991): 9-16.

Miller, Julie. "Wielding New NAEP Data, Shanker Assails Choice," *Education Week* (July 31, 1991): 36.

National Education Association. *It's Time for Action* (leaflet). Washington, D.C., 1991.

Further Comment

Bernard Suhor

"Ben, the kids just aren't getting values from their homes."

Charlie, that is what a good old colleague from years ago told me recently, since I wrote my response to you. His comment serves as a very good lead-in to my response to your critique.

This colleague is Jim, my friend, the recently retired high school principal whom I mentioned above (on page 126). I took him to lunch one day last summer for auld lang syne. Thirty-six years ago, he had been chiefly responsible for my applying to join the faculty of Redemptorist High School, where he was teaching and coaching at the time. Now, I had made my first professional move in all those years, and I wanted to tell him about my new job teaching English, Latin, and French at Archbishop Rummel High School in Metairie, a New Orleans suburb. (My new school is in the heart of David Duke country, the local politician with big ambitions and former connections to the Klan. Clarifying Christian and American values at school in my neighborhood, Charlie, is not purely an academic matter!)

Schools without Redeeming Social Values?

Jim, not I, introduced the subject of values. I said nothing about this debate of yours and mine till both Jim and I had said our pieces and compared notes. (Jim and I do not agree on everything any more than you and I do.) Jim cited a number of instances in schools where undisciplined students, and sometimes their parents, and sometimes their teachers, were disrupting the educational process. He spoke of dysfunctional adolescents.

I had to agree: A society without redeeming values (theological pun intended) is producing dysfunctional families, *and* vice versa. Either way, the kids are coming out dysfunctional also. Put enough of them into one school system, and voilá, you have a dysfunctional education system whether you like it or not.

This is the point at which we educators are supposed to work miracles and do during school hours what the society, the churches, and the families have failed over the years to do for the kids. We are told, often enough by experts outside the system, that we should succeed—that we *must* succeed, that we *shall* succeed—just as soon as enough money is pumped into public education.

Jim and I laughed at that one. Horsefeathers! Or horse something else. Jim and I agreed that what our students need, what their parents need, what we teachers and all America needs, is to have *values* pumped in. (Of course, we would be happy to have a fund pump, too.) To me, Jim is proof that those values can be communicated, both in public and private schools.

Assimilating those redeeming values has to start, Jim said, with a no-nonsense principal who has a clear vision of high values and correct priorities. He agreed that the libertarian philosophy in this country has run amok, has invaded the schools, and has forced an allegedly value-free approach on public-school teachers that is, in fact, value-laden.

I told him about my diagnosis of the three arch-heresies of Sub-Humanism, Secular Humanism, and Pseudo-Christian Humanism, the very sources of the corrosive values that teachers in the "value-free" classrooms claim not to have. Jim and I further agreed that preventing kids from bringing alcohol, drugs, and weapons onto our campuses (difficult as that is, in some places) is easier than keeping people from sneaking in the three lethal philosophies.

Jim cited a positive approach that he had used to get good values onto his campus. He always told teachers, parents, and students, that in this pervasively rights-conscious society of ours, he intended to uphold, protect, and foster in the school two fundamental rights: the right of the students to learn, and the right of the teacher to teach. The way Jim upheld, protected, and fostered those two basic intellectual rights for all concerned was by implementing the glorious principle of offering a democratic choice: Shape up or ship out! Of course, everyone was given due warning and time for values clarification and ultimate decision-making.

When he had started principaling at one school, Jim told me, the suspension-expulsion rate had been woefully high—too much shipping out. So he announced to everyone his intention to implement the two basic rights of learning and teaching. Within three years, the suspension/expulsion rate was reduced by 60%—not without howls from students who wanted to "do their own thing" following the sacred integrity of their churning hormones. Not without howls from parents who wanted their kids to have veto power over school policies. And not without occasional howls from some teachers who did not want to be bothered with enforcing high-minded and tough school policies.

On one occasion, Jim related, he had parents come to his office shouting abuse at him. First, he offered to discuss their grievances in a calm and courteous manner. When they persisted in their loud abuse, he told them that they would have to cease forthwith, or leave forthwith, or he would call the police forthwith to have them removed for disturbing the peace.

Jim said that his last year as principal was blissful compared with some of the previous years. What made the difference, he said, was reintroduction of values that once had been a part of both public and religious education systems, but which are now on the decline in America.

I find it ironic that Jim had done his undergraduate work at Loyola University in New Orleans, and then took his Master's degree at Columbia, that bastion of liberal thought and "progress," the citadel of the grand old man of American Pragmatism, John Dewey, of sacred—no, secular—memory. I wonder, if Dewey had gone through school situations like the ones that Jim faced, whether Dewey's pragmatist philosophy would have gotten him as far as Jim and his Judaeo-Christian values got. So many of the problems in education today—from guns and drugs to dysfunctionality—are, as I see it, the unintended products of Deweyesque laissez-faire Pragmatism. Similarly, I wonder how the sublime Sage of Transcendentalism, Ralph Waldo Emerson, would fare today, teaching sociology or civics in an inner-city high school facing guns and drugs and race riots and dysfunctionality, after he had spent the morning orienting his students to the importance of following the sacred integrity of their own minds and individual inclinations.

This brings me, Charlie, somewhat circuitously, to your critique of my first affirmative in this debate.

How to Be Wise as a Serpent and Harmless as a Dove

Charlie, my explicit, forceful reference to Christian values when teaching literature is an occasional thing, and—I hope—always an appropriate thing. I want my references to be forceful, when necessary, but never forced. I am trying to supply the salt that gives Christian savor to education. I am not trying to forcefeed the salt as if it were the entire meal. I think that you would have a difficult time finding students who claimed that I have been teaching religion rather than literature. I am too sold on my wares—literature and religious values—to risk having either of them despised.

Students whose values are Sub-human, Secular Humanistic, or Pseudo-Christian Humanistic are liable indeed to take exception to the values that I try to inculcate. Perhaps this indicates that I am really doing my job. Why should I "play fair," strike a neutral pose, and *not* try to influence my students? In your concern for neutral values, would you attempt to convince the propagators of what I call the three false gospels to be less forward, less vocal in making *their* pitches to my students? There is a war going on here, Charlie—yes, a war for the minds, hearts, and souls of my students. In this war, neutrality means that you are helping the powerfully destructive side.

You suggest that some of my examples actually lead to but one conclusion, the value that *I* want the students to accept. Well, yes. Isn't that what education and rhetoric are all about? In a democracy, one of our jobs as teachers is to help persuade our students with evident reasons of the superiority of democratic principles and institutions for our country. In a democracy founded on Judaeo-Christian values, should we do any less? Students are free to accept or reject the values. They are free to argue their objections.

Meanwhile, they are being bombarded by the media with an arsenal of phony and evil values. They come to school with questions, dilemmas, anxieties, and—yes—dysfunctionality over their family situations, their sexuality, and their futures. There I am, the English teacher, ready to open the tradition of literary excellence and beauty to them, and you want me to be neutral? They are fighting for their moral lives, and you want me, their teacher, to stand on the sidelines? Would you ask a high school football coach to do that—just stand on the sidelines and rarely "send in a play," especially when his boys are being battered and in danger of losing? The team *needs* their coach's values, his judgment, his expertise, his encouragement, his enthusiasm on the playing field. Those same kids need mine in English class. Non-directive teaching is worse than non-directive coaching. (Carl Rogers, eat your heart out!) In the American free marketplace of ideas, the values of Christianity deserve at least a hearing even in the public-school classroom, and especially in a Catholic classroom.

Charlie, if I believe a particular value to be absolute, why should I leave the impression in the minds of my students that somehow it is *not* an absolute value *in se,* that it is somehow up to them to change the very quality of its absoluteness to non-absoluteness? When I taught World History, I did not want to give my students the impression that it is all right for political powers to do anything they please in this world where we all think differently about values. Was it all right for Adolf Hitler to follow his superman philosophy to do whatever in his heart of hearts was sacred and right *for him?* An extreme example? Of course, it is. Heart-held values tend to extremes, both of evil and good. Was it all right for the United States to do any number of the things it has done? Were we Simon-pure in our war with Mexico? Or the way we "acquired" Hawaii? Or the way we grabbed the lands of Native Americans? Or the way we treated African-Americans? Should I have maintained in my classroom a values vacuum, remained neutral, and told my Social Studies students that they and I have no right to judge the actions of our Legislative and Executive officials because we must not judge anyone else's values by our own? Charlie, you would allow me the teacher's right to *teach* the *political* values that belong to democracy. Why, then, do you question my teaching the *spiritual* values that undergird those same political and democratic values?

Let us consider your objection to the way I teach a scene in the play *A Raisin in the Sun*, taking a forceful stand on the abortion issue. Although I have not yet used in class the bit about the NOW lady [see p. 62-64], I probably will use it pedagogically someday. I won't make the abortion issue a whole unit, or even a mini-unit; and I won't use the approach at all if I sense that it might be counter-productive with the group I'm teaching at the time. I will probably lead into it as casually as I can. Overkill is just plain dumb.

Yes, my rhetorical technique is on-purpose, but I wouldn't call it manipulative. I am only doing what I, as a Catholic and an American, believe democratically to be most protective of the basic right to "life"—especially life!—"liberty and the pursuit of happiness" of a defenseless and most vulnerable American citizen. Have you seen the bumper sticker that says "Equal Rights for Women—including Unborn Women!"? Abortion is the murder of unborn American citizens!

Why should I be gentle and polite in combatting a pernicious ideology? I suggest an uncomfortable parallel between America in the '80s and '90s and Germany in the '30s. What about Mother Germany's "right" in the '30s to abort her "less than human" offspring? Before Hitler committed Jews to the horrors of Holocaust, he had already told Mother Germany that she had a duty to herself to abort her hopelessly diseased, crippled, superannuated, insane, retarded, and homosexual children. If moral scruples had been loudly voiced in opposition, some highly articulate counterpart to the NOW lady would have spoken about the Motherland's need—her sacred duty—to sustain the *quality* of life in Germany, not merely life itself! Mother Germany *owed* it to herself to kill these less-than-human life forms consuming her vitals! And if a shocked world had known then what it knows now, that shocked world would have been told to mind its own damn business, that what went on inside Mother Germany's own body-politic was her choice, her right, and her business, and nobody else's!

No, I do not think the comparison is forced. I feel not only free, but in some way obligated, to combat the silent holocaust—and where better, more right, more reasonable a place to combat it than in the very class-room where the American public expects (and pays for) the inculcation of the political and moral principles of democracy in the minds of young citizens? Abortion is a front-and-center option being placed before America's adolescents. Considering their age, their hormones, and their social milieu, the *choice v. life* debate affects them in a most direct and personal way. Charlie, I make *no* judgment on people who advocate or permit abortion, but I do make a most terrible judgment on abortion itself, and I do it in a proper forum: my class-room. I want—*yes, I want*—my students to agree with Mrs. Lena Younger in the play: "We a people who loves children, not kills them." I cannot force my students to agree with her position. I cannot stop them from being parties to abortion later (or sooner) in life. But what I can and should do now, I will do. So thank you, Mrs. Lena Younger, and thank you, Lorraine Hansberry.

To Teach the Literature Is to Teach Its Values

Literature teachers are to literature what orches-tra conductors are to musical scores written by other composers: We did not write the novels that we teach, but if we "conduct" the literature expertly, we cannot help but communicate the symphony (or cacophony) of the values scored in its pages. If authors may influence their readers, and script-writers may move their viewing audiences into accepting their values, why may not teachers of literature do likewise? As a teacher in a Catholic school—just like teachers in any private school—I have as much right to use literature to promote the values of my school's religious creed as any writer has to promote whatever values he or she wants. The audience is captive in either case. My guess, Charlie, is that you do the same in your public school, whether you are aware of it or not; and that you, as a teacher whose students are dear to his heart, should be free to use your equal rights in the public school classroom to teach the religious, moral, and democratic values incarnate in the literature of the West, to the detriment, harm, or abuse of absolutely no one, and to the health of all.

Here is a quick run-through of some prominent literary works the authors of which, it seems to me, made no effort to conceal either their values or their desire to have the readership embrace them:

Inherit the Wind	*The Fountainhead*
Native Son	*The Gilded Age*
Paths of Glory	*All Quiet on the Western Front*
The Jungle	*Black Boy*
To Kill a Mockingbird	*Gentlemen's Agreement*
The Octopus	*Hard Times*
Uncle Tom's Cabin	*Oliver Twist*
Lord of the Flies	*The Chocolate War*
The Scarlet Letter	*The Crucible*
Vanity Fair	*The Pickwick Papers*

Huckleberry Finn   *Patterns*

Jane Eyre   *Twelve Angry Men*

Something of Value   *The Prime of*
                            Miss Jean Brodie

Just about every chapter in the first half of *Huckleberry Finn* is values-oriented, despite what Twain says to the contrary in his introduction. In fact, when Tom Sawyer re-enters the story, the novel begins to lose some of its momentum and greatness. Tom Sawyer created his own values-free society. After my students finish reading *The Great Gatsby*, I ask them which would have more likely pursued the path of Gatsby in later years, Huck Finn or Tom Sawyer. Invariably, their answer is Tom Sawyer; *they* tell *me* the reasons why.

Three more quick examples, Charlie, of how novels and films alike are directive of the audience in values-formation. Think of how contrived, but artistically contrived, are the three films *Citizen Kane, Hud,* and *Raging Bull.* Each is a modern morality play, a commentary on the biblical theme: "What doth it profit a man...?" Kane, Hud, and Bull have their feminine counterparts in three *femmes fatales* portrayed by Bette Davis in *Jezebel, The Little Foxes,* and *Mr. Skeffington.* The theme is biblical, and it begins to appear in secular literature most artistically, perhaps, in *The Pardoner's Tale* by Chaucer, in which three robbers get their comeuppance by destroying each other.

Let me also cite three other modern films of artistic merit with whose values, however, I *dis*agree: *The Graduate, Easy Rider,* and *Five Easy Pieces.* In these films, the message I pick up is that adult American society's values are almost totally wrong, and, for this reason, "no one over thirty is to be trusted." I do not propose to censor these films—certainly not. But I do want "equal time" to help my students examine the faulty, adolescent prejudice being put forth in them.

Why should I be faulted in my classroom either for helping my students see through nonsense or for promulgating the values which, I am convinced, have a firm foundation both in Natural Law and in that Revelation which is the very *raison d'etre* of my whole religious school system? Some praise producers and directors who make films like *The Last Temptation of Christ* for being "truly courageous," on the ground that such films challenge audiences to re-examine their traditional values. Why not, then, say that English teachers who challenge their students to evaluate literature by the standards of Christianity are also courageous, especially when those standards run sharply counter to the not-so-sacred traditions of secularism?

To Be "Neutral" Would Be to Compromise

If the master teachers of my own religious heritage promulgated specific values, why should I not also? Did not Jesus himself lead his listeners to preconceived "right" answers? Using a good rabbinic methodology in his parables and posing his questions carefully—the rabbinic-Socratic methodology, if you will—Jesus proved himself both "wise like a serpent," and "as simple as a dove" when he advocated moral values, concerning the verity of which he was already convinced. Read the Gospel, Charlie, and hear the Master Teacher of our religion advocate turning the other cheek, but without recommending compromise. No philosopher in search of values, Jesus "taught with authority," when he offered his one-and-only answer that he knew was the correct answer. Why should I not teach by that same authority and with the same sureness?

Nowhere, absolutely nowhere in Scripture did Jesus—or any of the great teachers of the Old Testament—ever say: "Now this is the way *I* see it, but let's discuss it. It is true for me, but I realize it may not necessarily be true for you. After all, each of us brings our own conditioning as we confront moral paradox. Let us listen and learn from one another, *but let's not get absolute about anything religious or moral.*"

Charlie, I feel no need, out of some misbegotten norm of fairness—imposed on us because we are in a school setting, whether religious or public—to become hyperconscious and feign gentility in combatting what we see as blatantly erroneous. No way! Two of my greatest personal role models in the sacred art of being both irenic and polemic are those two great Doctors of the Church, St. Anthony of Padua and St. Francis de Sales. Please God, I would be like those two giants, teacher of a pedagogy that is both tough and tender.

Anthony, the gentle Franciscan, whose statues portray him as carrying the infant Jesus, was a man of quiet demeanor who galvanized thousands when he preached about values. He was called the "Hammer of Heretics." No, he wasn't out to burn those who disagreed with him, but he did preach most vociferously against some of the Pseudo-Christian Humanists of his day. They were saying that once you got to be holy enough (as they claimed they were), then what you did with your body didn't really matter. The *body* was doing the sinning, you see, not the holy soul dwelling within the body! ("The devil made them do it!") Charlie, would even the A.C.L.U. accept that sort of poppycock from a rapist or pederast? Neither would Anthony.

Francis de Sales was similar. A gentleman and a bishop, known for his almost unflappable temperament, he nonetheless gave no quarter to what he and his church, since Apostolic times, considered doctrinally or morally wrong. Charlie, why should I be the one to observe the Marquess of Queensbury Rules in religious and ideological debate, while the libertarian opposition's rule is "Anything goes!?"

It is time to take aim at some of the weapons of this three-headed Goliath of Sub-Humanism, Secular Humanism, and Pseudo-Christian Humanism. Let me use my minuscule sling-shot strategically and prayerfully, but uncompromisingly and remorselessly. I am out to destroy no person or persons, but I would gladly knock down this pernicious ideology that is crippling and killing the kids I teach.

Look! Just look at the weapons this three-headed ideology is using! See what they have going for them, that I do not. *Sub-Humanism has Titillation. Secular Humanism has Obfuscation. Pseudo-Christian Humanism has Mitigation.* Let me illustrate these weapons and their use.

The Sub-Humanists are using titillation to evangelize my students.

They gear their titillation to sexual gratification and to violence. "If it feels good, do it!" scream their evangelists to my kids. The corollary-commandment is well epitomized in a bumper sticker I saw recently, in brash clashing colors on the car of a young American: *"SCREW GUILT!"*

"Welcome to the Jungle" is the title of an article in *Newsweek* (September 23, 1991). Reporter John Eland related one line from a current rock song: "So what about the bitch who got shot? F—her. You think I give a damn about a bitch? I ain't a sucker." The group that sings this lyric is known by its initials as N.W.A.; they cut an album that was "too raw to attract buyers through the radio play," but "became the No. 1 album in America within two weeks of release." Should I be more gentlemanly and restrained when communicating diametrically opposed values to the very students who are purchasing and listening to this garbage? Shall I be "neutral" and pull my punches? Shall I be silent when quasi-hero Magic Johnson preaches "Safe Sex!" to my adoring students? Or when Madonna orgies her way through "Truth or Dare" into their imaginations, minds and *values*? Let the Gospel of Titillation be anathema!

Sub-Humanism is a bit more cautious in winning us adults as converts. I recently received in the mail from a supposedly respectable publishing concern an invitation to join, as a discriminating reader, a book club for sophisticated adults with an appreciation for genuine erotic literature. Well, now, how is that for a sneaky snow job on my libido, boys and girls? The logo of this book club, by the way, is a bitten-into apple, with a snake coiled around it. ("Did God really tell you not to eat of the fruit?" Gen. 3:1) I can imagine Mrs. Murtagh telling me, "Young man, you will never be 'old' enough to be unchaste—whether in thought, word, or deed." She taught me that value, and I still thank her for it.

The Secular Humanists are using Obfuscation to evangelize my students.

Yes, they obfuscate. They hide. They try to eclipse God and/or His values. They want to replace the infinite with the finite. "*You* will be like gods." (Genesis 3:5)

It is interesting how atheistic communism tried obfuscation for over 70 years, and lo, the light shineth in the darkness.

Charlie, I can't agree with you that "If there is a Satan, and if he is wreaking havoc in our culture, the secular humanists have proved to be a weak phalanx."

First, whether weak or strong, there is an organization called the Council for Democratic and Secular Humanism waving the same banner that the founding fathers of Secular Humanism began waving some 60 years ago. They may be as impotent and as ridiculous as the Flat Earth Society, but they exist, nonetheless, and they are at work.

Second, and more formidably, the American Civil Liberties Union is one of the most powerful phalanxes—or tentacles—of the Secular Humanist movement in America today. In their apostolate to keep God out of American society, the A.C.L.U. has taken on even the Boy Scouts. The litigation being brought against the B.S.A. charges that it is un-American to require nine-year-old atheists to take the Boy Scout oath of loyalty to God and country.

The spirited McLaughlin Group on PBS (September 6, 1991) had a field day with these latest shenanigans of the A.C.L.U. Panelist Morton Kondracke, a *New Republic* Liberal, commented: "What the A.C.L.U. really wants to do is expunge religion from the face of American society. And it is a stupid endeavor politically. It also removes some of the basis for bourgeois behavior, which you're trying to inculcate into American kids." The more conservative Pat Buchanan added: "The A.C.L.U. is the Anti-Christian Liberty Union."

Third, and in support of Buchanan's charge, I quote from the *National Catholic Register* (September 22, 1991), referring to another group that is gnawing even more directly at the heart of the matter:

"On September 6, 'Stop the Church,' an anti-Catholic propaganda film, appeared on the local PBS station in Los Angeles. Produced by members of ACT-UP, an AIDS protest group which opposes Catholic teaching, *the film openly advocates disruption of religious services and crudely ridicules Catholic belief.*" (Emphasis added.)

Charlie, there are some very determined individuals and groups "out there" who are evangelizing Americans. They even include attorneys for nine-year-old atheists, and they are militantly intent on obfuscating, eclipsing, the existence of God and/or Natural law and/or the traditional religious and moral values of huge segments of American society. In effect, the most extreme are saying to my students, "*You* are the center of your own universe, your own values system. Be your own god, for there is no other, and there shall be no other in this country. So help me, First Amendment!"

The Pseudo-Christian Humanists are using Mitigation to evangelize my students

The basic message of the Gospel of Mitigation sounds a bit like this: "Re-think God as being as much in your own image and likeness as you are in God's. Stop trying to humanize by divinizing your life; divinize your life by humanizing it. Probe the depths of your own humanity. *Trust your instincts more*. Trust the Spirit speaking, first and last, in yourself—not through some supposed higher authority outside of, and alien to, your own spirit."

Charlie, one group of Christian feminists has actually prepared a ritual for "exorcising" passages in Sacred Scripture that they consider to be offensive to women. In this ritual, the offensive passage is read aloud, and the women respond in unison: "Out, demon, out!" I find that more scary than humorous, but it is happening.

Some of these evangelists of Pseudo-Christian Humanism are teaching in Catholic schools. They are conducting workshops and speaking at gatherings of Catholic catechists. They are speaking at Catholic education conventions, and some of them are bullying Catholic bishops, with some success.

Let me cite another instance of Pseudo-Christian evangelizing. It will help me respond to your problem with the way I dealt with values in Emily Dickinson's poem "Some Keep the Sabbath."

A Catholic nun was teaching some teenagers in a religion class her vision of the commandment: "Keep holy the sabbath day." In essence, this is what she said: "Just as a Catholic husband and wife should not have to make love 'by the calendar,' so also Catholic teenagers should not have to go to church specifically on Sunday, by the calendar, to show their love for God."

Notice how not-so-subtly the nun takes for granted that artificial birth control is "in," and natural family planning is "out." Moreover, the nun has a non-Roman Catholic attitude towards Sunday Mass attendance, which I can appreciate in an Emily Dickinson, but not in a nun who is evangelizing and catechizing in the name of Jesus Christ and the Church. This is Pseudo-Christian.

No, I do not quarrel with Emily Dickinson's moral right to worship God as she sees fit. Yes, I am willing to admit that her Sunday morning liturgy in her backyard might have been more genuine than that of many a "Sunday Catholic" who is in church with far less devotion and understanding of what liturgy is all about. Still, why shouldn't I take what has been called the "teachable moment" to illustrate for my students the differences in viewpoint, and to explore the *why* of compulsory Mass attendance for Catholics on Sunday? (Protestant parents have the same problems with Protestant kids.)

The kids drag out all the arguments that teenagers have dragged out for decades: "I have other things to do on Sunday. It's boring. My friends don't go. Too many Christians at church are hypocrites. The clergy is always asking for money. The weather is too bad to go to church. The weather is too good to go to church." And so on.

A homily à la Jonathan Edwards' *Sinners in the Hands of an Angry God* would definitely not be the thing to do; nevertheless, I have no form of titillation to win over students to what I know is the reliable and wholesome teaching of the Church on attendance at worship. It is far easier for that nun to make converts with her "good news" about not having to go to Mass on Sundays, than it is for me to convert them into wanting to go to church, to participate in the re-presentation of Jesus' sacrifice on Calvary.

Charlie, just as the Pseudo-Christian Humanists are busy about what they consider is their Father's business, so must I also be. The biggest difference, as I see it, is that they want to follow the will of God *without the mediation of any higher authority in the Church other than what they hear from themselves.*

Here's the Moral Point

Charlie and other dear readers, be forewarned: I am about to draw an analogy that will, I hope, guide you all, gently or otherwise, to a conclusion I want you to reach.

Assume that you are a parent who knows that there is an unknown pederast in the neighborhood of your child's school. His method is not to be violent, not to abduct, but to succeed by seduction; what's more, he is succeeding. His victims are willing, even eager, to be seduced. They do not consider themselves to be victims at all. They even think it's fun and exciting. Your child may be the next fervent convert he makes.

Question #1: If a teacher at your child's school could—by teaching or persuasion of any sort—convince your child and the others that being a party to pederasty is, like using cocaine or crack, extremely bad news, would you not be pleased with, and grateful to, that teacher?

Question #2: If a teacher at your child's school could—by teaching or persuasion of any sort—convince your child and the others that being a party to pederasty of the soul (by ideological bozos and bimbos) is extremely bad news (as bad as crack is for the body), would you not be pleased with, and grateful to, that teacher?

How you answer these two questions, and how you see their relationship to each other, is a mini-course in values clarification. Do you, as a parent, see your own negative attitude towards physical pederasty or spiritual pederasty as an unfair imposition of *your* values on your child? Is it not your duty as a parent to protect your child from all kinds of harm? Or, do you muddy your own moral waters by talking about the right of your child to choose for himself or herself to be a willing party to physical or spiritual abuse?

Why, then, is it that the teachers who do their best to safeguard the *physical* persons of their students from horrible abuse are regarded as heroes *in loco parentis*, whereas teachers who do their best to safeguard the *spiritual* persons of their students from similar horrible abuse are regarded as overzealous intruders upon their students' freedom of choice? *O tempora, O mores!*

Mea Culpa

Charlie, I do, nonetheless, take very much to heart your fraternal admonition: "I find Ben's text disturbing not because it is absolutist, Christian, and aglow with real belief, but because it too often falls prey to the genetic hazards of zealotry—*viz.*, an overweening certitude and an insensitivity to nonbelievers."

You are right, Charlie: I do need to be sensitive to those who do not share either my beliefs and/or my zeal for those beliefs. I do need to remember that as the salt of the earth, a Christian teacher is called to be a "preserver" and to "season" the daily fare of living. (Salt misused, salt abused, is like the killing chemical salts that abort the life of a child in its mother's womb.)

Truly, I need to write on the doorpost of my moral concern that rare command given by our divine Headmaster when he began by saying "Learn!" "Learn of me," he said, "that I am meek and humble of heart." (Matthew 11:29) I recall what Bishop Sheen once said when someone asked him his secret of making converts. He answered that he followed three very simple rules: "Be kind. Be kind. Be kind." So I am working on that, Charlie, although I am not as successful at being kind as I am at being morally outraged. (I take consolation in the comment of St. Francis de Sales, that paragon of manly gentleness, when he quipped that our passions die only a quarter of an hour after we do.)

"Catholic" Means "Universal"

Let me envision as catholic a vision of the future as I can.

Scene: the Pearly Gates.

Ben Suhor knocks, seeking entrance, after a lifetime of teaching (and evangelizing) in his English classes.

The door is opened by the NOW lady. She is lovingly attended by a dozen or so aborted infants, who like so many *putti* in Renaissance art, hang about her attentively. She embraces Ben and tells him that she has instructions to admit him on one condition: "No more proselytizing! That sort of thing is not needed—or tolerated—here."

Ben does a Jack Benny dead-pan routine: Hand on cheek, right arm supported by left arm across middle. Like Jack, Ben ponders, and says, "What's the alternative?" Then he shrugs his shoulders: "Oh, well."

Ben is admitted; he is greeted by a heavenly quartet of Francis de Sales, Anthony of Padua, Ralph Emerson, and John Dewey, singing in divine and human harmony. *Finis*, with subtitle: "May we all meet merrily in Heaven." (St. Sir Thomas More)

Years ago, Thomas Merton called theologian Rosemary Ruether to task. She was touting her "radical honesty." Merton countered that in so doing, she implicitly denied that those with whom she disagreed could be as "radically honest" as she was. To this day, Charlie, I am very uncomfortable listening to Christians impugn the sincerity of people with whom they disagree. Blaming either ignorance or bad will, Catholics take it out on the hierarchy in general and the Pope in particular. To me they are like some of the adolescents I meet every year, who, being at the heart and center of their own moral universes, regard virtually all authority as outdated and oppressive. Why do they do this? Because they hymn the tune of "the sacred integrity of their own minds." Instead of singing "*Veni Creator Spiritus*," they pray to the Oversoul speaking through the mouth of either a Secular Humanist or a Pseudo-Christian Humanist. Infallibility, for them, sits not on Peter's Chair, but proceeds from guts and glands.

"Overweening Certitude"

Charlie, do you think that my own certitude is any more overweening than is the smugness of the dogmatists whose values I am combatting? The same Headmaster who told me to be meek and humble of heart, also said: "I have come to set the earth on fire, and how I wish it were already blazing!...Do you think that I have come to establish peace on earth? No, I tell you, but rather division." (Luke 12:49, 51). What could the Prince of Peace have meant, if not that he had come to set a torch to our human values so that the wrong ones might be burned up, and the right ones might be purified?

My guess is that Secularists like John Dewey would have found great fault with both the message and the pedagogy in the ministry of Jesus the Christ, as well as Moses the Law-giver, centuries before him. Neither Moses nor Jesus would have bought into Dewey's Pragmatism. Charlie, I find both the message and pedagogy of Secular Humanism extremely overweening. Claiming to be democratically non-directive, members of the Church of Dewey are in effect "as harmless as serpents and as wise as doves" when they not only refuse to advocate but also smugly undermine the truths of God enshrined in the literature that you and I teach in our classrooms.

The world in which Jesus communicated his uncompromising values—especially through the medium of the literary form we call the "parable"—was not ready for what Jesus represented. Today's world—the world of today's teenagers—no less than Jesus' world, is not quite ready for the values he represents. And it never will be.

Listen to the uncompromising way that one writer has put it. You think I am zealous, overweening, and certain? How about this writer?

> *Do not love the world or the things of the world. If anyone loves the world, the love of the Father is not in him. For all that is in the world, sensual lust, enticement for the eyes, and the pretentious life, is not from the Father but is from the world. Yet the world and its enticements are passing away.*

That is not John Calvin, the reformer, speaking. It is not John Bunyan, the moralist. It is not John Brown, the abolitionist. It is John, the disciple, author of a little New Testament letter that carries his name. (1 John 2:15-17). He ends that letter on a highly practical note that I could echo against my three least favorite Humanisms: "Children, be on your guard against idols." (1 John 5:12).

Which idols? Which, indeed, if not those created for my students by Sub-Humanism, Secular Humanism, and Pseudo-Christian Humanism? The promulgators, the ever-active evangelists, of these false and lethal gospels that aim for the weak spots in the kids I teach—these evangelists would just love to see all Christian teachers turned into wimps and wusses, "meek and humble of heart" in a way Jesus never intended! Then they *could* mock our lack of conviction. No, Charlie, I will not be like some Christian teachers who hide their Christian lights under secular bushels, afraid to offend the secularist and humanist PC squads. Students in a Christian school, certainly, should never have to guess at the values of any of their teachers. Every teacher in a Christian school must in some way—I do it through literature in my English classes—be teaching them in the name of Christ "to observe all that I have commanded you." (Matthew 28:20). And Christians who teach in public schools, whether Catholic or Protestant, similarly know that our common Lord would have them ponder prayerfully how they can light a sacred candle on a darkling, secular plane.

Truth and Our Times Oblige Us to Teach Morality

Even if the three Humanist ideologies go the way of European Communism, and disappear, Christian schools will still have the obligation to teach values, and Christian teachers everywhere will still be called to their individual apostolates. We are, after all, in the saint-making business; if not, we had better close up shop. Charles Péguy said that the greatest tragedy is not to be a saint. Thomas Dubay in his remarkable *Fire Within* stated: "We can make sense of the saints only by recalling continuously that they are men and women entirely in love."[1] He shows that education geared towards loving is not a matter of learning skills, whether basic or advanced: "Christianity is no oriental exercise in which contemplation is the result of techniques. It is a love communion with a supreme Beloved and not a mere impersonal, neutral awareness of reality and of oneself at the center of it."[2] That, Charlie, is the root and ground of all Catholic, all Christian, education, within private schools and without. It's what gives us the edge (if we choose it), and it's what public school education lacks, unless Christian insiders refuse to be "neutral," preferring instead the wisdom of the serpent, the harmlessness of the dove, and the truth and love of the Lamb.

The kids we teach are having a rough time even being introduced to this kind of love precisely because the three false ideologies cause them to "place oneself at the center," in the words of Dubay's lament. The advertising agencies for these three isms are at it around the clock to make converts. Will anyone begrudge us English teachers in Christian schools, and us Christian teachers in public schools, the relatively few opportunities we have—in the English class—to show up these isms for the idols they are, and to try to topple them? Charlie, I recall a line from Bryant's "Thanatopsis," that poem you love to de-emphasize:

Each one as before will chase his favorite phantom.

In Bryant's day, the phantoms for adolescents to chase were fewer than they are today; now, their number is legion. Part of my job in a Catholic classroom is to show my maturing students that it is time to begin chasing a new phantom in their lives: the Infinite Ghost, the Holy Spirit. I find no reason to mitigate for my students the invitation-exhortation that St. Paul gave: "Let us also follow the Spirit." (Galatians 5:25). "Teaching" is listed in Scripture as one of the gifts of the Holy Spirit. To be a good facilitator in this marvelous spiritual cross-country pursuit, I take my roll book at the beginning and middle of the scholastic year and I go into church. Before the Blessed Sacrament in the tabernacle I ask the Lord to help me teach and love each of my students as he himself would do. There is no way I can do it alone. "Without me, you can do nothing." (John 15:5)

Charlie, in this debate I have been defending the morality and pedagogy that the majority of English teachers would have upheld throughout the 19th and into the 20th century. Would you have us, now, to be neutral and allow the immorality and pedagogy that have become fashionable towards the end of the 20th century in America? Will it actually go that way in the 21st century? Not if I, and other Christian English teachers, can be true citizens in the City of God first, and the City of Humanity second. Surely we can expect to feel the dynamic tension involved. Every Christian teacher is like St. Paul when he said to his spiritual children, "I am in labor pains until Christ is formed in you." (Galatians 4:19)

For the sheer mischief of it, I want to crisscross the morals of the centuries, spiking my discussion with you with a touch of holy derision. I want to put the values of the anti-heroine Lady Brett Ashley at the end of Ernest Hemingway's somewhat naturalistic, almost nihilistic novel, *The Sun Also Rises*, into the mouth of Hester Prynne at the end of Nathaniel Hawthorne's novel of high morality, *The Scarlet Letter*. The situations are similar in that both ladies are speaking to the men they loved: Lady Brett to her would-be (impotent) lover, Jake Barnes; and Hester Prynne to her former (one-encounter) lover, the Rev. Arthur Dimmesdale. It is the final scene, and Dimmesdale is dying of heart failure on a public platform in the town square, having just made his public confession of adultery to the Puritan populace of Boston. Hester, in the late 1600s, whispers into Arthur's ear the words of Brett Ashley to Jake in the 1920s:

> *You know, I feel rather damned good, Arthur....You*
> *know, it makes one feel rather good deciding not to be*
> *a bitch....It's sort of what we have instead of*
> *God....Oh, Arthur,...we could have had such a*
> *damned good time together.*

Charlie, sometimes I become discouraged on account of my failures when I behold, helplessly, the apparent successes of the three false ideologies in the lives of my students, but I am encouraged by the words of the Psalmist, "Those who sow in sadness someday will reap with joy." (Ps. 126:5). Joy at the end, not sorrow, is the Christian promise; so I ask John Donne to close my side of this exchange with a benediction on all of us involved in education, whether we are in public or private or religious schools. In keeping with Donne's valediction in *Holy Sonnet V* that forbids mourning, I want to exit with holy laughter.

Friend John Donne, please come forward. We recognize you as a past master at blending the sacred and the secular. We ask you to petition on behalf of all education in America. Those who object to praying in the school house may excuse themselves, if they wish, but, Master Donne, we shall include the absent in our petition, so please you:

Batter my heart, three-personed God; for you
As yet but knock, breathe, shine, and seek to mend;
That I may rise and stand, o'erthrow me, and bend
Your force to break, blow, burn, and make me new.
I, like an usurped town, to another due,
Labor to admit You, but O, to no end;...
Take me to You, imprison me, for I,
Except You enthrall me, never shall be free,
Nor ever chaste, except You ravish me.

NOTES

1. Thomas Dubay, S.M., *Fire Within: St. Teresa, St. John of the Cross, and the Gospel—on Prayer* (San Francisco: Ignatius, 1989): 122.

2. *Ibid.*, p. 108.

REFERENCES

Dubay, Thomas, S.M. *Fire Within: St. Teresa of Avila, St. John of the Cross, and the Gospel—on Prayer.* San Francisco: Ignatius, 1989.

Mott, Michael. *The Seven Mountains of Thomas Merton.* Boston: Houghton Mifflin, 1984.

Annotated Bibliography of Related Resources in the ERIC Database

Documents cited in this section provide additional ideas and activities for values clarification through teaching literature. The ED numbers for sources in *Resources In Education* are included to enable you to go directly to microfiche collections, or to order from the ERIC Document Reproduction Service (EDRS). If a citation has a CS number rather than an ED number, look in *RIE* or the ERIC database to find the corresponding ED numbers.

Atheism

"Christian Ethics. A Teacher Information Bulletin for Division IV." Regina, Saskatchewan Department of Education. 1984. 52 p. [ED 260 988]

Listed are print and audiovisual materials that support the "Curriculum Guide for Division IV: Christian Ethics" intended for use in grades 10, 11, and 12. The course is designed to help students articulate, reflect upon, and understand what they believe and practice. Cited in this resource manual are textbooks, teacher's guides, supplementary materials, reference materials, and audio-visual resources. The materials are organized under the headings of the themes found in the curriculum guide: (1) God and Man (Searching for God, Religions of the World, Faith and Atheism, and Life beyond Death); (2) The Christ in Scripture (Jesus of the Gospels; The Parables of Christ; The Beatitudes; God's People in the Old Testament; and Understanding the Bible); (3) The Contemporary Christian Community (The Church, Christian Worship and Sacraments, Prayer in Contemporary Spirituality, and Everyday Ecumenism); (4) The Christian (Christian Morality and Conscience, Moral Problems of Today, Marriage, and Social Justice). The publisher, date, and Canadian distributor are provided for each entry. A publisher/producer/ distributor directory is provided.

Schott, James C. "Holy Wars in Education," *Educational Leadership*, v47 n2 p61-66 Oct 1989.

According to Robert L. Simonds, president and
founder of the National Association of Christian
Educators, public education is a stronghold of the devil
that promulgates atheism and immorality. The key to
controlling education is to establish Christian Parents'
Committees in all 15,700 school districts across the U.S.
and elect members to local school boards. Includes 36
references.

Church and State

Connor, Eugene T. "Accommodating Religious Needs:
Policies and Procedures." *Religion & Public
Education*, v16 n2 p245-57 Spr-Sum 1989.
    Argues that the negative media attention focused on
public school boards as they struggle with issues of
religion and the public schools could be avoided if boards
would adopt policies on such issues. Discusses three
primary areas of policy concern: school personnel;
students' rights; and the school curricular and
extracurricular issues and activities.

Connors, Eugene T. "Religion and the Schools:
Significant Court Decisions in the 1980s."
Fastback No. 272. Publications, PDK Foundation,
8th Street and Union Avenue, Box 789,
Bloomington, IN 47402 1988. 42 p. [ED 296 472]
    This "fastback" examines the U.S. Supreme Court
decisions and a few lower court decisions concerning
religion and education rendered in the 1980s; for
background purposes, it also includes some decisions prior
to the 1980s. The first of four parts discusses cases
pertaining to prayer and religious activities in school.
Included in the discussion are cases concerning "moment
of silence," posting the Ten Commandments, school clubs
and the Equal Access Act, religious holidays and holiday
observances, Christmas pageants and other seasonal
observances, and prayers during school functions. The
second part discusses cases involving aid to parochial
schools. Litigation involving shared time programs and
Chapter I services is discussed, along with tax deductions
for education expenses. The third part addresses religion
in the curriculum, reviewing cases on religious objections
to compulsory school attendance, "creationism" and
evolution, using the Bible in the school curriculum,
teachers' rights to refuse to teach objectionable material,
and textbooks and "secular humanism." A list of cases is
appended.

Drovdahl, Robert R. "Religious Liberty in Schools: A
Search for 'Guiding Stars'," *Religion & Public
Education*, v16 n2 p233-44 Spr-Sum 1989.
Offers a perspective on the challenge that teachers
face with the question of religion's role in the public
schools. Discusses seven guidelines for curricular decision
making. Cautions against seeking absolute solutions to
the questions that will continue to surround the religious
liberty provisions of the First Amendment.

Gelfand, Gregory. "Of Monkeys and Men—An
Atheist's Heretical View of the Constitutionality of
Teaching the Disproof of a Religion in the Public
Schools," *Journal of Law and Education*, v16 n3
p271-338 Sum 1987.
Reviews court decisions on creationism, science, and
separation of church and state in relation to 1st and 14th
amendments, establishment clause, and free-exercise
clause. Discusses fundamentalist interpretation of
evolution and concept of "scientific neutrality." Proposes
that rights of religious minorities are best served if
teaching of evolution is excluded from elementary and
secondary public schools.

Gittins, Naomi E., ed. *Religion, Education and the
U.S. Constitution*. Publication Sales, National
School Boards Association, 1680 Duke Street,
Alexandria, VA 22314. 1990. 110 p. [ED 322 599]
Articles written primarily by practicing school
attorneys who represent public school clients are compiled
in this publication. Information about how the
establishment and free exercise clauses of the First and
the Fourteenth Amendments of the U.S. Constitution
affect curriculum, student programs and activities,
teacher employment, and school board administrative
decisions is presented. Articles are as follows: "Public Aid
to Parochial Schools," by Dennis G. O'Hara; "An Analysis
of the Expansion of Free Exercise and Establishment
Clause Challenges to Curriculum and Instructional
Practices in the Public Schools," by Jay Worona and
Margaret Chidester; "Unemployment Benefits and Free
Exercise Rights," by Jeffrey A. Davis; "Use of Facilities by
Outside Religious Groups," by John S. Aldridge; "Religious
Garb: May Public School Teachers Wear It?" by Fay
Hartog-Rapp, Gretchen Winter, and Michele Freedenthal;
"Home Schooling," by Perry Zirkel and David B. Rubin;
"Accommodation of Employees' Religious Observances," by

Fay Hartog-Rapp, Gretchen Winter, and Michele
Freedenthal; "Policies and Practices on Religious Expression
in the Schools," by Cynthia Lutz Kelly and Naomi E. Gittins;
and "The Equal Access Act and Student Groups," by Stephen
S. Russell. Membership and publication information about
the National School Boards Association Council of School
Attorneys is included.

Goldsmith, Kory. "The Equal Access Act: The
Supreme Court Upholds Its Constitutionality,"
School Law Bulletin, v21 n4 p9-15 Fall 1990.
    The Supreme Court affirmed in "Mergens" that the
Equal Access Act represents a legislative determination
that secondary school students are mature enough to be
exposed to an open forum. However, schools may either
recognize noncurriculum-related groups, restrict student
groups to curriculum-related activities, abolish student
clubs, or give up federal assistance. (46 references)

Graves, Michael P. "This Art of Straining Souls:
Incidental Faith/Learning Integration in the
Interpersonal Communication Classroom." Paper
presented at the Annual Meeting of the Speech
Communication Association, 1983. 1983. 16 p. [ED
240 641]
    Efforts by Christian colleges to integrate faith and
learning in communication courses through conscious and
direct planning are based on several questionable
assumptions: that faith must be learned through the
intellect, that all evangelical Christians share the same
theological roots, and that interpersonal communication
can be taught like any other subject. Faith can be viewed,
however, in two ways—as a series of propositions or as an
intuitive experience. The validity of both approaches is
substantiated by current research in cerebral dominance.
Injecting preplanned, conscious faith/learning integration
into courses might destroy the possibility for more
spontaneous, incidental learning. The Christian College
Consortium represents not a uniform view of faith, but a
variety of approaches reflecting different theological roots,
and although the cognitive/propositional approach appears
to dominate, Quaker writings offer support for incidental
faith/learning integration through their emphasis on
immediate revelation. While some teachers may prefer
preplanned and conscious approaches, other teachers are
by nature, personality, or philosophical commitment more
at ease with the incidental mode. The communication
classroom itself appears particularly suited for this mode.

A valid means of integrating faith and learning, the incidental method should not be eliminated from the interpersonal communication classroom.

Kealey, Robert J. *Everyday Issues Related to Justice and Other Gospel Values.* National Catholic Educational Association, Suite 100, 1077 30th St., N.W., Washington, DC 20007-3852. 1984. 82 p. [ED 259 981]

This manual presents situations that occur in the lives of most children and suggests to the teacher related activities which might cause students to reflect on the deeper meaning and significance of the situations. It seeks to make the teacher, and thus students, aware of the fact that peace, justice, and other value issues are part of daily living. There are 31 lessons included, all of which are designed to be used whenever the appropriate situation comes up rather than in a fixed order, as well as two chapters addressed to the teacher which focus on the importance of values education and how to use these lessons. The lesson situations include new students in class, culturally different students, the elderly, handicapped people, stealing, learning that a friend has stolen something, cheating in school, helping another student cheat, disagreement with a friend, unemployment, academic and athletic competition, the meaning of death, right to life, television commercials, destruction of property, the throw-away society, waste of food, assemblies, care of pets, loss of one's home through a disaster, embarrassing sickness, lack of volunteers, examination period, food drive, operation rice bowl, poking fun at other students, unkind nicknames, mimicking a physical handicap, school service project, Martin Luther King Day, and inaccurate language. Each activity includes the value to be taught, background, objective, and specific activities for primary and upper level students.

Kniker, Charles B. *Teaching about Religion in the Public Schools* (Fastback 224). Phi Delta Kappa Educational Foundation, Eighth and Union, Box 789, Bloomington, IN 47402. 1985. 49 p. [ED 256 688]

The purpose of this booklet is to clarify what can be taught about religion in public schools while remaining within constitutional guidelines and using teaching material that is pedagogically sound. The first section, "Religion is a Fact of Life," covers the historical

background, the current situation, and issues to resolve in
teaching about religion. "Preparing to Teach about Religion"
deals with the place of religion in the curriculum, teacher
preparation, and resources. "The Bible in Literature
Classes," discusses approaches to using the Bible and some
classroom problems. The next section, "Teaching about
Religion in the Social Studies," covers guidelines for this
area, a sample lesson, and curriculum resources.
"Community Relations and Teaching about Religion" deals
with the controversies surrounding this topic, involvement of
the community in developing policy guidelines,
implementation of such guidelines, and resources. Two pages
of additional references are also provided.

Kniker, Charles R. "A Survey of State Laws and
    Regulations Regarding Religion and Moral
    Education," *Religion & Public Education*, v16 n3
    p433-57 Fall 1989.
        Summarizes findings of a 50-state survey of state
    laws, regulations, and guidelines concerning religion and
    moral education. Describes legislation affecting the
    curriculum, student and teacher behavior, and nonpublic
    schools in 30 topic areas. Reports the need for further
    verification and clarification. Finds minimal regional
    differences. Correlates amount of legislation to enrollment
    size. Includes tables showing results.

Mahon, J. Patrick. "*Mergens*: Is the Equal Access
    Issue Settled?" *Journal of Law and Education*, v19
    n4 p543-47 Fall 1990.
        The United States Supreme Court ruling in "Mergens"
    gives school districts the following options: (1) require all
    student groups to have a direct relationship to curriculum;
    (2) have a "limited public forum," therefore allowing
    noncurriculum-related groups to use school facilities; or
    (3) choose to ignore the law and forego all federal funds.

McCarthy, Martha M. "Read This Review of Case Law
    before Religious Controversy Hits Your Schools,"
    American School Board Journal, v169 n1 p33-34
    Jan 1982.
        Reviews court cases in which parents challenged
    school practices on religious grounds. Puts particular
    emphasis on recent attempts to make the curriculum
    conform to religious views.

McCarthy, Martha M. *A Delicate Balance: Church,
    State, and the Schools.* Publications, Phi Delta

Kappa, Eighth and Union, Box 789, Bloomington, IN 47402. 1983. 186 p. [ED 236 780]

Focusing on current legal issues in church, state, and school relations, this book examines four critical areas in the controversies surrounding the respective rights of public education and religious education; it then addresses the issues of state aid to, and governmental regulation of, parochial schools. Court opinions about religious observances and activities in public schools include decisions regarding Bible reading and prayer, the uses of religious holidays and symbols, the religious content of graduation exercises, and the distribution of religious literature in public schools. The author further examines the judicial balancing between the constitutional protections of religious exercise and the government's requirements for compulsory schooling and mandated areas of curriculum. The legal challenges offered to public school curricula are also analyzed, including efforts to introduce the teaching of creationism and to censor instructional materials in public schools. Finally, the book addresses the problems in the relationship of the states and parochial schools by noting the judicial interpretations (both federal and state) regarding the various forms of aid to parochial schools—transportation aid, loans for services, tax relief for parents of parochial school students—and discusses the lawsuits and decisions relevant to the question of the state's authority to regulate parochial schools and home education programs.

McCarthy, Martha M. "Student Religious Expression: Mixed Messages from the Supreme Court," *West's Education Law Reporter*, v64 n1 p1-13 Jan 17 1991.

Although the Supreme Court's "Mergens" decision settled the controversy over the constitutionality of the Equal Access Act, the ruling seems to make more ambiguous the definition of a limited open forum for student expression and the legal status of devotional activities. (55 references)

Morris, J. B. "Guidelines and Compatible Components on Religion in the Public Schools," *Religion & Public Education*, v16 n1 p131-33 Win 1989.

Suggests specific ways of bringing the academic study of religion into a secular curriculum. Presents general guidelines and procedures for administrators, in working with school boards, to design and implement the teaching of religion. Argues that state boards of education are

instrumental in making the academic study of religion a
vital part of public school curriculum.

Nord, Warren A. "Religious Literacy, Textbooks, and
Religious Neutrality," *Religion & Public
Education*, v16 n1 p111-21 Win 1989.
> Describes religious illiteracy among undergraduate
> students. Examines high school textbooks in United
> States and world history, economics, home economics, and
> biology. Finds religion almost completely ignored. Argues
> that the religious neutrality mandated by the Supreme
> Court effectively eradicates religion from the
> curriculum. Suggests a new test of neutrality.

Nord, Warren A. "Taking Religion Seriously," *Social
Education*, v54 n5 p287-90 Sep 1990.
> The National PTA holds the position that religion
> should be dealt with in public schools in an academic, not
> a devotional, way. Discusses the implications of Supreme
> Court decisions on religion in the schools and appropriate
> ways of including religion in the school curriculum.

Nuger, Kenneth Paul. "The U.S. Supreme Court
Applied the 'Lemon' Test to Louisiana's Balanced
Treatment Act," *West's Education Law Reporter*,
v46 n1 p1-15 Jun 23 1988.
> Reviews antievolution curriculum legislation in the
> courts and the background of the Supreme Court's ruling
> that Louisiana's Balanced Treatment for Creation-Science
> and Evolution-Science Act unconstitutionally advanced
> particular fundamentalist religious views.

Park, J. Charles. "The Religious Right and Public
Education," *Educational Leadership*, v44 n8 p5-10
May 1987.
> The growth of groups on the religious right has
> resulted in a major ideological division in the United
> States. Outlines the strength of these groups, the
> particulars of the secular humanism debate, and the
> ability such groups have to coordinate issues and join
> together in campaigns influencing public education.

Quay, Richard H. *The New Right and American
Education: A Bibliography. Public Administration
Series Bibliography P-1508*. Vance Bibliographies,
P.O. Box 229, Monticello, IL 61856. 1984. 10 p.
[ED 248 817]

A bibliography of approximately 88 materials on the New Right and education in the United States is presented. Although some of the publications are from the 1970s, most cover the 1980-1983 period. Specific topics include the following: school politics and the influence of interest groups and social movements; secular humanism and the schools; textbook and curriculum censorship in public schools; taking the moral majority seriously; the New Right movement and its impact; conservative pressures on the curriculum; censorship and creationism; the effect of conservatism on teacher education; morality, ethics, and the New Right; the resurgence of conservative Christianity (the Fundamentalist phenomenon); the new Christian right as a social and political force; the question of whether political ideologies influence education in the United States; the future of education's liberal consensus; the effect of new conservatism on women in education; the case for tuition tax credits; and the balance between church, state, and the schools.

"Religion in the Public Schools." Publication Sales, American Association of School Administrators, 1801 North Moore Street, Arlington, VA 22209-9988. 1986. 68 p. [ED 274 061]

This booklet offers school administrators guidance on the constitutional foundation of religious freedom and the relationship between church and state in the United States. Most of the recent Supreme Court cases dealing with religion in the schools and many current issues in the field are discussed. Questions that administrators may wish to address before considering specific policies are also raised. The booklet's first chapter introduces the basic issues affecting the relationship between religion and public education. Chapter 2 outlines the law and its constitutional basis, focusing on religious freedom, the "Free Exercise" and "Establishment" clauses of the First Amendment, religious activities within schools, aid to religious schools, and freedom of speech. The third chapter reviews the place of religion in the public school curriculum, addressing religious instruction by religious leaders, instruction about religion, and the inclusion of religiously sensitive material in the curriculum. Chapter 4 examines the noncurricular policies of public schools involving religion; it covers religious holidays, religious observances, meetings of extracurricular religious groups or clubs, school district aid to religious schools, and partnerships between schools or districts and religious institutions. Examples, suggestions, guidelines, and policy

recommendations related to religion and the schools are
interspersed throughout the text.

Sendor, Benjamin B. "The Role of Religion in the
Public School Curriculum," *School Law Bulletin,*
v15 n3 p1-9 Jul 1984.

The establishment clause of the First Amendment
permits public school instruction that serves secular
educational goals, but it forbids instruction that instills
religious beliefs in children. Although the free exercise
clause protects those who oppose such secular courses,
their sole remedy is partial or total exemption from the
courses.

Sendor, Benjamin B. *A Legal Guide to Religion and
Public Education.* Publication Sales, NOLPE,
Southwest Plaza, Suite 223, 3601 SW 29th,
Topeka, KS 66614. 1988. 64 p. [ED 298 665]

This book is designed to give readers a basic grasp of
the general legal principles controlling the role of religion
in public education, to apply those principles to typical
church-state issues in the schools, and to equip readers to
address other related issues as they arise. The book covers
the following topics: (1) general legal principles; (2)
noncurricular religious activity by students (school prayer,
extracurricular student relgious clubs, prayers at special
occasions, display of religious symbols, holiday
observances, and Bible distribution); (3) religious
objections to secular, noncurricular student activities; (4)
religion and the curriculum (courses, religious objections
to secular courses, and religious objections to secular
instructional materials and methods); (5) religious activity
by personnel (prayer, discussion of religion with students,
wearing religious apparel or religious symbols, and leave
for religious reasons); and (6) other religious activities on
school grounds (prayer at school board meetings and the
use of school facilities by outside groups).

Sherman, Edward F. "The Role of Religion in School
Curriculum and Textbooks," *Academe,* v74 n1
p17-22 Jan-Feb 1988.

Three significant federal court cases addressing the
issue of the role of religion in public school curriculum and
textbooks are described. The claims of the Christian
fundamentalists were rejected in all three cases, reflecting
continued judicial adherence to strict separation of church
and state in public education.

Sinensky, Jeffery P.; Kahn, Jill L. "Church-State
Separation: Recent Trends and Developments,"
ADL Law Report, v6 n3 p1-30 Fall 1984. [ED 250
417]
    This report analyzes recent cases and legislation in
the area of church-state separation. A brief introduction
asserts that the Supreme Court's method of evaluating
establishment clause controversies is undergoing
pervasive changes that have permitted incursions on
establishment principles. The rest of the paper, providing
support for this interpretation, discusses particular
developments within these areas of concern: (1) religious
practices in public schools (prayer, student religion clubs,
and curriculum); (2) government aid to parochial schools;
(3) display of religious symbols on public property; (4)
religious discrimination and accomodation (religious
discrimination in the military and in public schools,
sabbath observer rights, and the Arab boycott of Israel);
and (5) public sponsorship of religion (tax exemption for
racially discriminatory private schools, church veto power
over liquor licenses, and state-employed legislative
chaplains). Argues that government's aid to and
sponsorship of religious activities is proliferating. Asserts
that the free exercise clause does not alter government's
obligation to treat all religions neutrally; rather, it
mandates only government respect for each individual's
religious beliefs.

The Williamsburg Charter: A National Celebration
and Reaffirmation of the First Amendment
Religious Liberty Clauses. Williamsburg Charter
Foundation, Washington, DC. 1988. 24 p. [ED 310
042]
    The religious liberty clauses of the First Amendment
to the Constitution of the United States are the most
important political decisions for religious liberty and
public justice in history. Two hundred years after their
enactment, they stand out boldly in a century darkened by
state repression and sectarian conflict. The controversy
now surrounding the clauses is a reminder that their
advocacy and defense are tasks for each succeeding
generation. While acknowledging their deep and
continuing differences over religious beliefs, political
policies, and constitutional interpretations, the signers of
this charter agree that the following principles are in the
shared interest of all U.S. citizens: (1) Religious liberty is
a precious, fundamental, and inalienable right founded on

the inviolable dignity of the person and undergirding all
other rights and freedoms secured by the Bill of Rights. (2)
The two religious liberty clauses address distinct concerns,
but serve the same end, freedom of conscience for citizens of
all faiths or none. (3) The 'no establishment' clause separates
church from state but not religion from public life. (4) The
'free exercise' clause guarantees the right to reach, hold,
exercise, or change beliefs freely. (5) While conflict and
debate are vital to democracy, how citizens debate is more
critical than what they debate. (6) Citizens must develop, out
of their differences, a common vision for the common good.
(7) Each person and group must guard for others those
rights they wish guarded for themselves. These principles
require a fresh consideration in order to sustain a free people
that would remain free.

Tilley, James G. "Argumentation and Controversy:
The Separation of Church and State in
Education." Paper presented at the Annual
Meeting of the Southern States Communication
Association, 1989. 16 p. [ED 305 681]
      The two religion clauses of the First Amendment of the
Constitution clearly declared the objectives of the framers,
toleration and separation, but the means whereby these
objectives were to be achieved were left to be decided
through the dynamic processes of the courts. The history
of these two clauses reveals that Americans are still
seeking to secure these objectives. For example,
Americans are still wrestling with these objectives in the
schools, where there is much conflict revolving around the
issues of "separation" and "tolerance." There have been
three well-known recent attempts to censor the public
school curriculum: the creationist-evolutionist dispute; the
secular humanism controversy; and the debate regarding
using the schools to establish "traditional values" or to
censor materials which do not maintain these "traditional
values." These challenges are also an outgrowth of forces
at work in the wider society and represent the evolution of
society. Some issues of this connection are basically legal
questions, such as the creationist controversy. Other
issues are more philosophical, such as the humanist
controversy. The question of values is a psychological and
moral one. Each of these challenges, however, represents
points of friction between often widely different views of
the past, present, and future and is to be expected in a
society that is both free and diverse.

Zakariya, Sally Banks, ed. *Religion in the Curriculum: A Report from the ASCD Panel on Religion in the Curriculum.* Association for Supervision and Curriculum Development, 125 N. West Street, Alexandria, VA 22314-2798. 1987. 33 p. [ED 288 776]

Religion's place in the curriculum, and how school administrators can avoid litigation while discharging the obligation to educate, are discussed in this report, designed to give school policymakers guidance in arriving at informed decisions about religion's place in the curriculum. Chapter one examines the dilemma of adequately educating students who lack an understanding of religion's influence in history. Chapter two analyzes how classroom practices are based on a series of defacto policies that encourage educators to avoid explicit reference to religion. Chapter three is an examination of the religious, historical, sociological, educational, legal, and political assumptions that undergird present curricular policies. Chapter four explores the legal basis for teaching about religion. Chapter five describes how public protest has hindered thoughtful treatment of religion in textbooks. Chapter six emphasizes that the proper role of religion in the school is the study of religion for its educational value and presents suggestions for proper inclusion of religion in schools. Chapter seven points out that commonly stated educational goals cannot be achieved without proper integration of religion into the curriculum. The concluding chapter contains a list of recommendations for ending public education's silence on religion.

Financial Support

Birch, I. K. F. "Nonpublic Education in the United States of America and Australia: The Courts in Educational Policymaking." 1981. 37 p. [ED 225 298]

Examined here is the role of the courts as educational policy makers regarding church-state separation in the United States and Australia. The first part examines the relationship of the public schools to religion, both regarding the teaching of religion in the schools and compulsory education. It is noted that in spite of challenges, the courts have upheld "general" (rather than sectarian) religious teaching in Australian schools. The second part of the paper examines litigation concerning private schools in both countries, especially regarding government aid. It was found that in the United States, private school aid is tightly judicially policed, though very limited aid is allowed. In Australia, however, state aid to private schools is mandated by the legislature and unchallenged by the courts. Policy implications of the laws on church-state relationships are discussed, especially regarding the future of government aid to private schools in both countries. It is concluded that in the United States, legislation benefitting mainly the nonpublic sector is unlikely to withstand judicial challenge, though aid might validly flow to the nonpublic sector when benefitting a broad class of beneficiaries and promoting public welfare. In Australia, private school aid, entrenched in the platforms of all major political parties, is likely to continue to have considerable public support.

"Church and State," *National Forum: Phi Kappa Phi Journal*, v68 n1 p2-15 Win 1988.
Church and state is discussed in four articles: "Religion, Separation, and Accommodation: A Recipe of Perfection?" (Delos B. McKown, Clifton B. Perry, pp. 2-7); "Public Religion: The Republican Banquet" (Martin E. Marty, pp. 8-9); "Religion in the 1980s" (Ernest van den Haag, pp. 10-11); and "Education in Religious Schools: The Conflict over Funding" (John M. Swomley, pp. 12-15).

"Church and State," *National Forum: Phi Kappa Phi Journal*, v68 n1 p34-43 Win 1988.
Church and state is discussed in four articles: "Religiously Inspired Censorship in Public Schools" (John H. Buchanan, 34-35); "Public Funding of Education in Religious Schools" (Eugene W. Hickok, Jr., 36-38); "Neutrality in Teaching Moral Principles in Public Schools" (Francis William O'Brien, 39-40); and "The Most Wonderful Instrument Ever Drawn by the Hand of Man" (Michael Kammen, 41-43).

Splitt, David A. "School Law," *Executive Educator*, v9 n5 p12 May 1987.
Summarizes a variety of religious issues before United States courts, including two religion-in-the-schools cases in New Jersey and Georgia and two New York cases involving public assistance of private schools. Discusses a wrongful death lawsuit in Connecticut concerning a teenage suicide.

Vergon, Charles B., ed. "The Church, the State, and the Schools: Contemporary Issues in Law and Policy." Publication Sales, Office of Professional

Development, University of Michigan School of
Education, Ann Arbor, MI 48109-1259. 1986. 163 p.
[ED 276 112]

Analyzes contemporary legal controversies concerning
religion, the states, and the schools, and the interface
between law and education. The introduction provides an
overview of issues treated in the following seven chapters
and includes a series of tables that place recent
controversies in the historical context of prior U.S.
Supreme Court precedent. Part 1, "Remedial Education
Programs for Private School Children: Judicial
Developments and Future Prospects" (Michael W.
McConnell) and "Shared Time Programs on Public School
Premises: Private Rights and Public Responsibilities"
(Linda L. Bruin). Part 2, "Policy Communication and
Implementation: The Remedial Services and Shared Time
Rulings," contains three chapters: "Intergovernmental
Communications and Interpretations"; "Impact and
Implications at the Local Level: A Public School Point of
View" (Elmer Vruggink); and "Implementation Problems
and Prospects: A Private School Perspective" (Donald
Cook). Part 3, "Religious and Governmental Influences on
Education: The Continuing Conflict," presents two
chapters: "Religious Influences in the Public Schools"
(Gail Paulus Sorenson) and "The Constitution and State
Regulation of Private Schooling" (Tyll van Geel). Part 4,
"References and Resources," provides a bibliography,
Supreme Court summaries, constitutional and statutory
references, and information about the monograph's
contributors.

Humanism

Bjorklun, Eugene C. *Secular Humanism: Implications
of Court Decisions, Educational Forum,* v52 n3
p211-21 Spr 1988.

The author reviews various court decisions that have
had an impact on the inclusion or exclusion of secular
humanism in the public school curriculum. Particular
attention is paid to one decision stating that secular
humanism is a religious belief system for the purposes of
the first amendment.

Brandt, Ron. "Defending Public Education from the
Neo-Puritans," *Educational Leadership,* v44 n8 p3
May 1987.

Recent court decisions in Tennessee and Alabama
requiring the teaching of "creationism" and the banning of

"secular humanism" challenge educators to listen to the
critics and present a wider curriculum including the role of
religion in human affairs while protecting our heritage of
intellectual freedom.

Kaasa, Harris; and others. "Humanism: A Christian Perspective." 1981. 80 p. [ED 213 275]

As part of a four-college project to integrate the
religious tradition with humanities teaching, humanism is
discussed from a Christian perspective. Definitions of the
terms humanism, religion, Christianity, and Christian
humanism are provided. The latter is viewed as the issues
surrounding the Christian approach to the dichotomy of
good and evil and the condition of being human. An
introductory historical survey of Christian humanism
traces this ideology from its origins in Protestantism and
Catholicism, through conflict with secularization, and into
the context of education, specifically modern higher
education. Losses and gains of Christian humanism in the
twentieth century are outlined, looking at the varied
American religious scene, changes within each group, and
academic *versus* grassroots theology. It is concluded that
at the heart of the current dilemma faced by Christian
humanists are the separation between Christianity and
culture, or secular life, and a related ignorance of the
tradition of Christian humanism. Specialization in
higher education curriculum is seen as a prime example
of this separation. Literature appropriate to the academic
study of this tradition is suggested. In addition to this
literature, a new approach to the teaching of Christian
history is recommended to bridge the existing gap between
secular and religious history instruction and to emphasize
the continuity of the tradition of Christian humanism
from early times to the present. Appended is an article by
R. W. Franklin, "The NEH Christian Humanism Project at
Saint John's, Collegeville."

McCarthy, Martha M. *Religious Challenges to the Public School Curriculum.* Policy Memo Series No. 3. Consortium on Educational Policy Studies, Bloomington, Indiana. 1988. 30 p. [ED 295 315]

Focuses on religious challenges to the public school
curriculum, specifically those involving claims that public
schools are prompting "secular humanism"—an allegedly
antitheistic creed that places human reason above divine
guidance. While some courts have recognized that "secular
humanism" may be considered a "religion" for First
Amendment purposes, the judiciary has repeatedly

rejected charges that specific courses and materials
unconstitutionally promote this "creed" in public schools.
Nonetheless, there are mounting efforts to secure judicial
and legislative prohibitions against the promotion of "secular
humanism" in public education. Courts have been receptive
to requests for curriculum exemptions and religious
accommodations unless they impede students' academic
progress or the management of the school. The Supreme
Court has also distinguished the permissible academic study
of religion from unconstitutional religious indoctrination. Yet
several recent studies have indicated that the historical role
of religion in western civilization is given insufficient
attention in the public school curriculum. Correcting such
distortions might avert some of the claims that public
schools are advancing "secular humanism." These religious
challenges raise two troublesome issues for educational
policymakers: (1) balancing governmental interests and
parental interests in educating children; and (2)
guaranteeing religious neutrality, rather than advancement
or hostility, in the public school curriculum.

Strazicich, Mirko, ed. *Moral and Civic Education and
Teaching about Religion. Handbook on the Legal
Rights and Responsibilities of School Personnel
and Students.* Bureau of Publications Sales,
California State Department of Education, P.O.
Box 271, Sacramento, CA 95802-0271. 1988. 63 p.
[ED 313 285]

Adopted by the California State Board of Education on
June 10, 1988, this handbook outlines the legal rights and
responsibilities that school personnel have and their
educational responsibilities in such areas as morality,
democratic values, and religion in the schools. Section I,
"Moral Values and Public Education," addresses the issues
of morality, truth, justice, patriotism, self-esteem, and
values. Section II, "Instruction on the Rights and
Responsibilities of Citizenship," includes the code of ethics
for the teaching profession, a discussion of democratic
values and principles, the rules for student conduct, and
the important elements of a constitutional democracy.
Section III, "Teaching about Religion in the Public
Schools," cites the legal rights and responsibilities that
school personnel have for teaching about religion and
offers suggestions for subject matter content and
guidelines. Section IV, "Morals, Values, and Teaching
about Religion in Recently Adopted Curriculum
Frameworks," opens with suggested guidelines for
including ethical issues in the curriculum. It includes a

description about how the "California History-Social Science Framework" and the "English-Language Arts Framework" address moral and civic education and teaching about religion. A list of 59 publications from the California State Department of Education concludes the document.

Multicultural Education

Banks, James A., Banks, Cherry A. McGee, eds. *Multicultural Education: Issues and Perspectives.* Simon & Schuster, 160 Gould Street, Needham Heights, MA 02194-2310. 1989. 337 p. [ED 311 102]

The purpose of this six-part curriculum of articles was to provide future teachers and in-service teachers with the knowledge, insight, and understanding needed to work effectively with both male and female students, with exceptional students, and with students from various social classes and religious, ethnic, and cultural groups. A major assumption is that substantial reforms must be made in schools to give each student an equal chance to succeed academically. These reforms are conceptualized as an institutional process that involves changing the total school environment through multicultural education. Part I, "Issues and Concepts," concerns the implications of culture for teaching in a pluralistic society, and comprises the following chapters: (1) "Multicultural Education: Characteristics and Goals" (J. A. Banks); (2) "Culture: Its Nature and Meaning for Educators" (B. M. Bullivant); and (3) "Race, Class, Gender, Exceptionality, and Educational Reform" (C. A. Grant and C. E. Sleeter). Part II, "Social Class and Religion," concerns the effect of these two variables on student behavior and the educational process, and comprises the following chapters: (4) "Social Class and Educational Equity" (C. H. Persell); and (5) "Religious Diversity and Education" (J. K. Uphoff). Part III, "Gender," takes up the questions of how educational opportunity differs for female and male students and how schools can foster gender equity, and comprises the following chapters: (6) "Gender and Educational Equality" (M. Sadker *et al.*); (7) "Integrating Content about Women and Gender into the Curriculum" (M. K. T. Tetreault); and (8) "Transforming the Curriculum: Teaching about Women of Color" (J. E. Butler). Part IV, "Ethnicity and Language," treats the problems of and opportunities for educating racial, ethnic, and language minorities, and comprises the following chapters: (9) "Ethnic Minorities and Educational Equality" (G. Gay); (10) "Integrating the Curriculum with Ethnic

Content: Approaches and Guidelines" (J. A. Banks); and (11) "Language Diversity and Education" (C. J. Ovando). Part V, "Exceptionality," describes the issues involved in creating equal educational opportunity for handicapped and gifted students, and comprises the following chapters: (12) "Educational Equality for Exceptional Students" (W. L. Heward and M. D. Orlansky); (13) "Teaching Handicapped Students in the Regular Classroom" (J. B. Schulz); and (14) "Teaching Gifted Students" (R. F. Subotnik). Part VI, "School Reform," focuses on multicultural education as a process of school reform, and comprises the following chapters: (15) "Alternative Paradigms for Assessment in a Pluralistic Society" (J. R. Mercer); and (16) "Parents and Teachers: Partners in Multicultural Education" (C. A. M. Banks). Each chapter includes a summary, a list of questions and activities, and a list of references. Some chapters include illustrations and statistical data on tables and graphs. A glossary, a list of contributors, and an index are included. A bibliography of 113 multicultural resources is appended.

Banks, James A. "Multicultural Literacy and Curriculum Reform," *Educational Horizons*, v69 n3 p135-40 Spr 1991.

A major goal of a curriculum that fosters multicultural literacy should be to help students know, care, and act in ways that will develop a democratic and just society where all groups experience cultural democracy and empowerment.

Carr, Jean Ferguson. "Cultural Studies and Curricular Change," *Academe*, v76 n6 p25-28 Dec 1990.

The renaming of literature appreciation as cultural studies marks a rethinking of what is experienced as cultural materials, going beyond reading and writing to media, popular culture, newspapers, advertising, textbooks, and advice manuals. It also marks the movement away from the study of an object to the study of criticism.

Chace, William M. "The Real Challenge of Multiculturalism (Is Yet to Come)," *Academe*, v76 n6 p20-23 Dec 1990.

There are two approaches to multiculturalism in the college curriculum, the formally academic and the political. Few proponents of either have defined with precision what their multiculturalism would be in practice. The challenge is to describe the common culture while preserving integrity of cultures not yet part of traditional conformity.

"Facets: Literature–Common Background vs. Cultural Diversity," *English Journal*, v75 n6 p18-21 Oct 1986.

Four educators offer their opinions on whether a core curriculum should promote the study of traditional literature or introduce a varied selection of minority literature to promote cultural diversity.

Gay, Geneva. "Achieving Educational Equality through Curriculum Desegregation," *Phi Delta Kappan*, v72 n1 p56-62 Sep 1990.

Desegregation generally has not produced equal educational opportunities and outcomes for culturally diverse students. A dual system of access to knowledge and accountability has emerged. Third-generation curriculum reform should support second-phase ideological principles embedded in multiculturalism, pluralism with equality, and school restructuring. Includes 21 references.

Greenberg, Douglas. "Reforming History Curricula: Some Thoughts on Democracy and Western Civilization," *OAH Magazine of History*, v4 n1 p5-8 Win 1989.

Urges that the changes in the ethnic, religious, and cultural pluralism in the United States, as well as those in politics of the educational system, be taken into account when designing history curricula. Argues that world history should replace the western civilization course.

Hayford, Elizabeth R.; and others. "The Liberal Arts in New International Perspective," *Liberal Education*, v71 n2 p93-140 Sum 1985.

Wingspread Conference (October 1984) presentations are given: "Pilgrims and Immigrants: Liberal Learning in Today's World" (Frank F. Wong); "How Can One Know America, Who Only America Knows?" (Robert L. Nichols); "Internationalizing the Curriculum in the Natural Sciences" (Jack L. Carter); "International Perspectives on Campus" (Franklin M. Doeringer). Summary is by Francis X. Sutton.

Hollins, Etta Ruth. "Debunking the Myth of a Monolithic White American Culture; or, Moving toward Cultural Inclusion," *American Behavioral Scientist*, v34 n2 p201-09 Nov-Dec 1990.

Presents teaching strategies used in an educational foundations course that helps preservice teachers view themselves as part of a culturally diverse society. Describes an assignment that involves students' researching their family history to heighten sensitivity to the cultural struggle of all ethnic groups.

Metzger, Devon J. "The Challenges Facing Global Education," *Louisiana Social Studies Journal*, v15 n1 p13-16 Fall 1988.

Analyzes seven barriers to teaching global education, focusing on teacher education, teaching methods, textbook bias, curricular rigidity, and student attitudes. Stresses the importance of understanding global interdependence as a part of citizenship education and the social studies curriculum. Suggests that understanding the barriers to global education can help overcome them.

Montero-Sieburth, Martha. "Conceptualizing Multicultural Education: From Theoretical Approaches to Classroom Practice," *Equity and Choice*, v4 n3 p3-12 Spr 1988.

Multicultural education, a complex, organic process, needs to be re-examined and redefined by teachers. Multicultural education is a reality today. How to define it, teach it, and use it to increase achievement are important issues to address. Approaches to multicultural education are discussed.

Passow, A. Harry. "Designing a Global Curriculum," *Gifted Child Today* (GCT), v12 n3 p24-25 May-Jun 1989.

Provides a rationale for providing gifted students with a global curriculum with such components as peace education, cross cultural studies, thinking skills, human problems, ethics, emerging concepts, future studies, networking with students from other nations, and active problem solving.

Rabitoy, Neil. *Cross-Cultural Perspectives in the Curriculum. Academic Challenges.* Academic Program Improvement, Office of the Chancellor, The California State University, 400 Golden Shore, Long Beach, CA 90802-4275. 1990. 28 p. [ED 329 170]

This booklet evaluates 13 cross-cultural education projects that were initiated at California State University campuses. The projects all strived to incorporate into the curriculum and educational environment more scholarship on ethnic studies and a greater sensitivity to the values and needs of minority cultural groups. Among the findings of the evaluation were the following: (1) the kind of curricular reform required in order to establish a cross-cultural emphasis in the college curriculum requires substantial time to implement; (2) projects of this type require strong yet sensitive leadership and genuine administrative support; (3) the most effective curricular reform was that aimed specifically at the disciplines as opposed to introducing reform into the entire university curriculum; and (4) to be truly effective, curricular reform efforts must meet the needs of the faculty, and the faculty must be given the tools with which to implement changes. Contains 5 references.

Rasinski, Timothy V.; Padak, Nancy D. "Multicultural Learning through Children's Literature," *Language Arts*, v67 n6 p576-80 Oct 1990.

Presents a theoretical framework for using children's literature in dealing with cultural differences. Suggests classroom approaches that capitalize on the power of literature to promote intercultural and multicultural appreciation.

"Redefining Multicultural Education: A Roundtable Discussion," *Equity and Choice*, v4 n3 p19-23 Spr 1988.

Presents the transcript of a roundtable discussion among three bilingual teachers on defining multicultural education, and developing teachers' understanding of multiculturalism, assimilation, and integration. Aspects of a successful multicultural program are discussed.

Sellen, Robert W. "How to Internationalize a Parochial Curriculum," *Social Studies*, v78 n2 p80-84 Mar-Apr 1987.

Shows how the lack of education about foreign countries leaves Americans ignorant of international issues. Proposes that changes be made in traditional curricula to include international information. Provides a sample lesson to demonstrate how a U.S. history class could fulfill this need.

Solomon, Irvin D. "Strategies for Implementing a Pluralistic Curriculum in the Social Studies," *Social Studies*, v79 n6 p256-59 Nov-Dec 1988.

Examines the pedagogic concept of cultural pluralism and outlines specific methods for implementing the concept in the social-studies curriculum. Identifies and analyzes various forms of cultural biases, reviewing means for identifying such biases, and presenting remedies for eliminating them from the instructional setting.

Steinberger, Elizabeth. "Multicultural Curriculum Uncovers Common Bonds, Individual Strengths, and Fiery Debate," *School Administrator*, v48 n4 p8-13 Apr 1991.

By 2020, demographers predict that minorities will comprise nearly half the school-age population. Court-ordered segregation, the push for bilingual education legislation, and recent demands for massive education reforms have brought multiculturalism to the fore. The Eurocentric perspective dominating American schooling must yield to curricula reflecting the nation's true cultural diversity.

Theel, Ronald K., Ed. *Planning for Multicultural Education at the Elementary and Middle School Levels*. Syracuse City School District, N.Y. 1990. 14 p. [ED 330 762]

The Syracuse City School District recognizes that infusing the curriculum with multicultural education is essential to equal educational outcomes. The following recommendations for the elementary level are made: (1) every curriculum area should be taught with a multicultural perspective; (2) field trips should be organized to expose students to culturally diverse experiences; (3) assemblies should be organized around multicultural themes; (4) multicultural classroom materials should be designed focusing on cognitive and affective domains; (5) cooperative learning should be used; (6) literature should represent multicultural perspectives and experiences; and (7) self-directed free play and structured games should be encouraged. The following recommendations for the middle schools are made: (1) multicultural education should be integrated into the total school program through an interdisciplinary approach; (2) curricular focuses should include the development of critical-thinking skills; (3) multicultural classroom materials should be designed focusing on cognitive and affective domains; (4) materials, activities, and experiences should be varied; (5) cooperative learning groups and peer tutoring should be used; (6) a home-based guidance program should provide positive role models; (7) a mentor program should use community members with culturally diverse backgrounds; and (8) teaching strategies should reflect the learning styles of

students from diverse cultures. Statistical data in four
graphs are appended.

"Value and Virtue: Moral Education in the Public
Schools," *Religion & Public Education*, v16 n3
p337-40 Fall 1989.
Reprints the 1987 statement of the Administrative
Board of the U. S. Catholic Conference concerning the public
schools' responsibility to provide students with a basic value
system. Links youth problems to the lack of moral education.
Stresses the need for national discussion to examine how
schools may best teach moral values.

Whittier, Charles H. *Religion in the Public Schools:
Pluralism and Teaching about Religions.* CRS
Report for Congress. Library of Congress,
Washington, D.C. Congressional Research Service.
1989. 17 p. [ED 330 589]
The growing movement for teaching about religion in the
public schools, as distinguished from religious instruction or
devotional exercises, reflects widespread concern regarding
the phenomenon of religious illiteracy and the lack of
knowledge or understanding of the significant role played by
religion in U.S. life, past and present, and in world history
generally. Such teaching, recognized as constitutional and in
accord with separation of church and state, acknowledges
the formative influence of religions in culture. A principal
concern of those who would implement such programs is how
to deal fairly with the religious and cultural diversity of U.S.
life without fostering indifference to questions of truth and
related values. Some who oppose teaching about religions
believe its effect might be to further relativism. One
approach distinguishes pluralism from relativism by
defining the first as a way of living with authentic
differences that can coexist in the body politic when it is
informed by freedom of conscience, religious liberty, and
traditions of civility. Teaching about religions, as
distinguished from values education, civil religion, and
similar movements, is intended to be disinterested,
comprehensive, and sensitive to the complexities of faith,
careful to avoid even the appearance of advocacy in belief or
practice. Defining religion for teaching programs presents
another difficulty, requiring that students discriminate
between narrow and broad categories and that teachers
avoid both religious and secularist bias. A descriptive
approach can help students perceive the relationship
between religion and culture by examining world faiths. The
report lists proposed general goals for such programs, typical

problems that hinder their implementation, and guidelines for attaining them. Finally, specific curricular materials and programs are cited as exemplary models for emulation and further development.

Wiley, Ed, III. "Scholars Push for Cultural Diversity in Curriculum," *Black Issues in Higher Education*, v6 n15 p1,10 Oct 12 1989.

Reports on a conference, "Race, Ethnicity and Gender in Higher Education," held in Philadelphia during which academicians discussed infusing cultural diversity into college curricula. Briefly describes programs at Mary Washington College, Indiana State University, and Bloomfield College.

Religion and Schools

Anthrop, Mary E. "The Controversy over School Prayer," *OAH Magazine of History*, v5 n1 p40-47 Sum 1990.

Outlines a lesson for high school students covering religious controversies in New York City schools in the 1840s. Issues pertain to Irish-Catholic immigrants' objections to public school religious instruction and attempts to obtain public support for parochial schools. Includes handouts concerning religious freedom, Bishop John Hughes' opinion, political cartoons, and the conflict's resolution.

Beach, Waldo, ed. *Church, State and Education. [Volume IV.] Church, State and the First Amendment: A North Carolina Dialogue.* 209 Abernethy Hall, University of North Carolina at Chapel Hill, Chapel Hill, NC 27514. 1985. 85 p. [ED 316 492]

This anthology is one of four collections of background readings on church/state issues that comprise "Church, State and the First Amendment: A North Carolina Dialogue." These anthologies are designed to provide primary materials through which North Carolinians can better understand the religion clause of the First Amendment. Volume 4 of the series includes readings on the school prayer controversy, the creationism- evolution debate, the "humanism"-in-the-schools dispute, and government regulation of religious schools. There are seven chapters, each with an introduction and a number of readings, followed by questions for discussion. A 14-item bibliography is included.

Bjorklun, Eugene C. "Prayers and Extracurricular Activities in Public Schools," *Religion & Public Education*, v16 n3 p459-70 Fall 1989.

Examines the constitutionality of public school personnel organizing prayers at extracurricular events, and of using ceremonial prayers, invocations, and benedictions at school activities. Reviews court litigation and Supreme Court decisions that use the Establishment Clause and Lemon test to determine legality. Finds, in most cases, that prayer at extracurricular activities is unconstitutional.

Bjorklun, Eugene C. "School District Liability for Team Prayers," *West's Education Law Reporter*, v59 n1 p7-14 May 10 1990.

An examination of the constitutionality of team prayer shows that pregame prayers violate the First Amendment's Establishment Clause, and their use can lead to liability problems for both coaches and school boards. Advises school boards to adopt policies specifically prohibiting team prayers.

Bjorklun, Eugene C. "The Rites of Spring: Prayers at High School Graduation," *West's Education Law Reporter*, v61 n1 p1-9 Aug 30 1990.

Because of the lack of a definitive United States Supreme Court decision on prayers at graduation, school officials are left without clear direction. Analyzes two decisions that illustrate the differences in judicial opinion on the legality of prayers at graduation ceremonies.

Boles, Donald E. "Religion and Education at the End of a Decade," *Religion & Public Education*, v16 n1 p35-37 Win 1989.

Reviews current Supreme Court doctrine as tested in lower federal and state courts in three areas in which public schools are involved. Examines Court decisions on silent meditation, equal access, and baccalaureate and commencement services. Finds the issues have not been fully resolved.

Constitutional Amendment Relating to School Prayer. Hearing on S.J. Res. 2: A Joint Resolution Proposing an Amendment to the Constitution of the United States Relating to Voluntary Silent Prayer or Reflection, before the Subcommittee on the Constitution of the Committee on the Judiciary, United States Senate, Ninety-Ninth Congress, First

Session (June 19, 1985). Congress of the U.S., Washington, D.C. Senate Committee on the Judiciary. 1986. 268 p. [ED 310 006]

Senate Joint Resolution 2 calls for an amendment to the U.S. Constitution to allow voluntary silent prayer or reflection in public schools. The hearing report consists of testimony on the proposed legislation by expert witnesses, prepared statements by various individuals and organizations, and newspaper article reprints and Supreme Court opinions regarding the case of Wallace v. Jaffree, in which the Court struck down an Alabama statute that provided for a daily period of silence in all public schools for meditation or silent prayer. The individuals who participated in these hearings debated several issues, including these: (1) What were Thomas Jefferson's positions on the role of religion in the United States and prayer in school? (2) Does freedom of speech include the right to pray in school? (3) Would allowing silent prayer or reflection in the school be seen as encouraging religion by providing time for silent prayer or as protecting students from the encouragement of religion by allowing them the option to engage in silent reflection (or non-prayer)? (4) Are some "moments of silence" statutes constitutional while others are not? (5) What controls on implementation can be guaranteed so that teachers do not go beyond the letter of the proposed legislation? Main witnesses testifying before the committee were these: Congressman Joe Barton, Georgia; Reverend Dean Kelly, National Council of the Churches of Christ in the U.S.A.; Congressman Thomas Kindness, Ohio; Dr. Michael Malbin, American Enterprise Institute; Thomas Parker, Attorney for Alabama in *Wallace v. Jaffree*; and Dean Norman Redlich, College of Law, New York University.

Ehrhardt, Cathryn. "Religion in Public Schools: Free Exercise, Information, and Neutrality," *Updating School Board Policies*, v21 n1 p1-3 Jan 1990. 5 p. [ED 313 813]

Politics and sex are regular entrées on the school curriculum menu, but since the Supreme Court's 1960s revival of the "wall of separation" between church and state, religion has been censored from the curriculum as well as from the school routine. The free exercise of religion, guaranteed by the First Amendment, is accommodated in U.S. school systems; however, the prohibition against establishment of religion in schools (also guaranteed by the First Amendment), while theoretically simple, is difficult in practice. The exclusion of the role of religion in society's past and present in school textbooks, courses, libraries, and class

discussions has resulted in "ethically illiterate" students.
Policy development in religious studies should follow the
same processes chosen for other new initiatives. A public
information program as well as teacher training should be
included in religion curriculum planning.

Furst, Lyndon G. "Bible Reading and Prayer in the
Public Schools: Clearing Up the Misconceptions."
Paper presented at the Annual Meeting of the
American Educational Research Association, 1989.
17 p. [ED 306 665]
    The purpose of the research was to provide practitioners
in the public schools with an empirical basis for their efforts
to find the proper place of religious ritual and instruction in
the school setting. This paper analyzes two Supreme Court
decisions regarding prayer and Bible reading in the public
schools: (1) "Engel v. Vitale"; and (2) "School District of
Abington Township, Pennsylvania v. Schempp." The
headnotes of each case, as supplied by the editors of the
"Supreme Court Reporter" are listed in a table. These
headnotes denote the legal principles expressed in the actual
text of the Court's decision. Beside each headnote is placed
the words that limit the legal restrictions in the note. The
analysis indicated that the activity banned by the Supreme
Court in "Engel v. Vitale" was the imposition of the religious
activity of prayer by government and not the actual act of
prayer itself. Prayer by students or teachers is not forbidden.
Prayer imposed by the government or one of its agents is
forbidden. The analysis also indicated in the "Schempp"
decision that reading the Bible in a public school was not
forbidden; what was banned was the required reading of the
Bible as a religious exercise.

Kahn, Ann P. "Religion and Values," *PTA Today*, v14 n4
p12-14 Feb 1989.
    The National PTA holds the position that religion should
be dealt with in public schools in an academic, not a
devotional, way. This article discusses the implications of
Supreme Court decisions on religion in the schools and
appropriate ways of including religion in the school
curriculum.

Kathan, Boardman W. "Prayer and the Public Schools:
The Issue in Historical Perspective and Implications
for Religious Education Today," *Religious
Education*, v84 n2 p232-48 Spr 1989.
    Explains the persistence of the issue of school prayer
and provides historical background for understanding the

ways in which the issue has changed over time. Shows that school prayer is not as long-standing a custom or as widespread as commonly assumed. Lists the implications that this information has for religious education.

McMillan, Richard. "School Prayer: A Problem of Questions and Answers," *Religion and Public Education,* v15 n2 p200-03 Spr 1988.

Uses responses to the 1987 "Phi Delta Kappan/Gallup Poll of the Public's Attitudes toward the Public Schools" to point out the possibility that proponents of school prayer may not be interested in religious devotion, but may be seeking the establishment of sectarian religion in public schools.

Rossow, Lawrence F; Rossow, Nancy D. "High School Prayer Clubs: Can Students Perceive Religious Neutrality?" *West's Education Law Reporter,* v45 n2 p475-83 May 26 1987.

Two distinctive populations, 262 high school students and 137 college students, were administered questionnaires to determine whether public high school students could perceive neutrality if school authorities permitted prayer clubs to meet on school premises before or after school. The data indicate that high school students cannot perceive religious neutrality.

Rossow, Lawrence F. "Equal Access Act: Garnett v Renton School District No. 403," *West's Education Law Reporter,* v54 n2 p391-98 Aug 31 1989.

Contends that a circuit court ruling prohibiting a student religious group from holding meetings in a public secondary school erodes the intent of the Equal Access Act to provide access for students wishing to exercise religious speech.

Rossow, Lawrence F. "Limits on Discretion in Applying the Equal Access Act: Mergens v. Board of Education of Westside Community Schools," *West's Education Law Reporter,* v56 n1 p1-8 Nov 23 1989.

Conflicting opinions between two circuit court decisions set the stage for another consideration of school officials' discretion in deciding whether the Equal Access Act would apply to their schools based on the presence or absence of a limited open forum.

Rossow, Lawrence F.; Rossow, Nancy D. "Student Initiated Religious Activity: Constitutional Argument or Psychological Inquiry," *Journal of Law and Education*, v19 n2 p207-17 Spr 1990.
Traces the legal history of prayer clubs and related religious activities in schools. Cites psychological arguments that high school students are generally independent and capable of critical thinking; contends that research is needed in determining whether high school students can specifically perceive religious neutrality.

Schamel, Wynell Burroughs; Mueller, Jean West. "Abington v. Schempp: A Study in the Establishment Clause," *Social Education,* v53 n1 p61-66 Jan 1989.
Reviews a series of First Amendment court cases related to school prayer and Bible reading, including the 1963 decision (Abington v. Schempp) against a Pennsylvania law requiring Bible reading and prayer recitation. Provides suggestions for teaching this case using a portion of Justice Tom C. Clark's opinion. Reproducible copies of the document are included.

Religious Education

Blair, Andrew G., comp. *The Policy and Practice of Religious Education in Publicly Funded Elementary and Secondary Schools in Canada and Elsewhere. A Search of the Literature.* Ontario Dept. of Education, Toronto. 1986. 56 p. [ED 273 551]
This study is a compendium of information regarding the policy and practice of religious education in publicly funded schools in each of the provinces and territories of Canada, in England, the United States, Australia, and with less detail, in several countries of Western Europe. Most information was acquired from published sources, but letters and telephone calls provided supplemental material. An account of the laws, policies, and regulations dealing with the prohibition of, permission for, or requirement of religious education is set within a brief description of the types of publicly funded school systems in each jurisdiction. Included is information with regard to who may teach religious education and what provisions are made for those who dissent. Also included is information on interpretations of "religious education," the role of the school in the religious education of students, and some mention of the controversies surrounding that role. References to curriculum materials

are provided. Summarizes the information, compares jurisdictions, makes some pertinent classifications, draws attention to some important patterns in policy, and provides the reader with an introductory guide for further reading in the study. Extensive references within the text and a three-page bibliography are provided.

Carey, Loretta; and others. *Dimensions of Justice and Peace in Religious Education.* National Catholic Educational Association, 1077 30th Street, NW, Suite 100, Washington, DC 20007-3852. 1989. 62 p. [ED 310 953]

In addressing the process of religious education, the constraints of time, space, and materials often force choices on religious educators. The purpose of this booklet is to propose the dimension of justice and peace education to what already exists in most religious education programs. It is suggested that educators change their perspective from a personal/ interpersonal level to a structural level in an attempt to analyze the political, economic, social, and cultural structures of human activity and to see that change can be effected in those structures that deny or inhibit human life. Empowering the poor to make decisions and to act for change has been added to the requirement of the Judeo-Christian religious tradition of service to the poor. Conflict-resolution skills should be introduced as a practical alternative to violent response to help convince students that alternatives to violence are available and workable both on the interpersonal and political levels. Because culture is a powerful force in transmitting values, students must understand the nature of cultural messages so that they can celebrate what is good, and resist and transform that which is bad. Lastly, a sense of global community and hope must be fostered among youth so that changes for justice and peace can be made. Each section is followed by short bibliographies for background reading and resources for programs and curriculum. Four appendices contain additional resources, ideas for evaluation of instructional materials, and a list of resource distributors.

Cheney, Lynne V. "Catholic Schools: A Gift to the Nation." Address to the Convention, Exposition, and Religious Education Congress of the National Catholic Educational Association, 1989. 15 p. [ED 308 608]

Raises awareness of the accomplishments of Catholic schools and discusses the model of high-quality education that Catholic schools represent. First, a picture of American public education as a whole is presented, followed by a description of three areas in which the Catholic schools serve as a model for the reforms happening in American public school systems. The first area is curriculum, which is humanities-based and aimed at ethical as well as cultural literacy. The second area deals with teacher education and that Catholic teachers are not required to train in colleges of education. The third area is the administrative structure and the recognition that the larger the administrative bureaucracy, the lower the quality of education. Other issues discussed are inner-city Catholic schools and school choice.

Greer, J. E. "Religious and Moral Education: An Exploration of Some Relevant Issues," *Journal of Moral Education*, v12 n2 p92-99 May 1983.

Religious and moral education have a close relationship; they should be planned together and not conceived as separate subjects in the school curriculum. Religious education cannot avoid a moral dimension, and moral education must be based on some kind of an ideology, religious commitment, or naturalistic stance for living.

Griggs, Donald L. "The Bible: From Neglected Book to Primary Text," *Religious Education*, v85 n2 p240-54 Spr 1990.

Presents a proposal of what is possible and necessary for teaching, studying, and learning the Bible with children, youth, and adults of religious congregations. Looks to scripture to gain clues regarding its important role in the spiritual formation of believers of all ages. Offers examples of ways to implement effective strategies for teaching the Bible.

Hawkins-Shepard, Charlotte. "Bridging the Gap between Religious Education and Special Education." Paper presented at the Annual Convention of the Council for Exceptional Children, 1984). 29 p. [ED 245 499]

The need for religious instruction for handicapped children is addressed, and lists of curriculum guides and materials for religious education are offered. The sparseness of literature on special religious education is pointed out, and the Episcopal Awareness Center on Handicaps, which helps make the church accessible to the disabled, is mentioned. Titles and publisher information is given for materials designed for mentally handicapped and hearing impaired students.

Kay, William K. "Philosophical and Cultural Bearings
on the Curriculum and Religious Studies,"
Educational Studies, v8 n2 p123-29 1982
Discusses how religious studies can be integrated into
various approaches to curriculum design. Examines ways
that religious studies can be included in knowledge-based,
skills-based, and culture-based curricula.

Miller, Ralph M. "Should There Be Religious
Alternative Schools within the Public School
System?" *Canadian-Journal-of-Education*, v11 n3
p278-92 Sum 1986.
Denominational instruction within public schools is
inadequate for parents whose religious convictions are not
satisfied by secular education. Fears of division in society,
narrow curriculum, shortage of pupils, and shortage of
funding have set legal and practical limits for establishing
alternatives.

"Religious Studies Guidelines." Wisconsin State Dept. of
Public Instruction, Madison. Division of
Instructional Services. 1982. 31 p. [ED 218 188]
In addition to providing important factual information,
these guidelines are designed to encourage, facilitate, and
help improve the academic study of religion(s) in public
primary and secondary schools in Wisconsin within
Constitutional bounds. The guidelines may also be used by
educators in other states. A basic rationale for religious
studies in public schools is first presented. A basic rationale
is that religion has been a major influence in human affairs,
and that the academic study of religion(s) is, thus, essential
to a complete education. The legal basis and requirements of
public education religious studies in Wisconsin are
examined. The remainder of the guidelines focus on the
curriculum and other particular aspects of teaching about
religion in the context of the legal boundaries, the rationale,
and goals. The best way to include religion in the curriculum
is discussed; guidelines for inclusion are presented; special
units and separate courses are discussed; and standards for
teacher certification in religious studies are presented. The
guidelines conclude with a selected list of printed sources,
references, and guides.

Welch, Mary Leanne. *A Beginning: Resource Book for
Incorporating Values and Church Teachings in the
Catholic School Curriculum*. National Catholic
Educational Association, 1077 30th Street, NW,

Suite 100, Washington, DC 20007-3852. 1990. 146 p.
[ED 330 606]

The permeation of gospel values into the entire curriculum is a mandate for the Catholic school. Permeation involves viewing, articulation, and evaluating content, methods, structures, and relationships through the eyes of faith. This guide provides methods, background, and resources to use in value permeation of classroom content. There are four chapters in the guide: (1) Methodology (2) Resources for Social Studies (3) Resources for Science (4) Resources for Literature. A summary of topics and a bibliographic list of references also is included.

Sex Education

AIDS Education Curriculum Guide. Horry County Board of Education, Conway, S.C. 1989. 86 p. [ED 313 570]

Based on sound principles of human growth and development, this curriculum guide was developed to present the most recently available information on AIDS (Acquired Immune Deficiency Syndrome). The curriculum presents information on the known facts about AIDS and the AIDS virus infection; addresses the potential for adolescents and adults to contract the AIDS virus, explaining the extent to which promiscuity and drug abuse contribute to the potential spread of AIDS; emphasizes the decision-making process; and affirms clear moral standards for AIDS education and provides information on how to help people resist social pressures that contribute to dangerous behavior. The curriculum guide contains 11 lesson plans for units on AIDS. Each lesson plan includes unit topic, suggested teaching time, key teaching resources, objective, teaching activities, suggested resources, and evaluation methods. Tests and answer keys are provided. Transparency masters are also included.

Bennett, William J. "Sex and the Education of Our Children." Transcript of an address delivered at the National School Boards Association Meeting, 1987. 15 p. [ED 284 148]

Schools, teachers, and principals must help develop good character by putting children in the presence of adults of good character who live the difference between right and wrong. Sex education is about character; in a sex education course, issues of right and wrong should occupy center stage. In too may cases, however, sex education in American classrooms is a destructive experience. Statistics such as the number of teenage pregnancies illustrate how boys and girls are mistreating one another sexually. Many sex education courses offer the illusion of action, relaying only technical information, and possible outcomes are devoid of moral content. This kind of teaching displays a conscious aversion to making moral distinctions; it encourages students to make not the "right" decision but the "comfortable" decision. Most American parents value postponing sex and raising children in the context of marriage. Despite this fact, some say that teenage sex is such a pervasive reality that there is nothing to be done but to make sure that students are supplied with contraceptives. But schools are supposed to point to a better way. Research has shown sexual behavior to be connected to self-perception, and experience has shown that values are teachable. Students must learn that sexual activity involves men and women in all their complexity; in fact, sex may be among the most value-loaded of human activities. Sex education courses should do the following: (1) teach children sexual restraint; (2) teach that sex is not simply a physical act; (3) speak of sex within marriage; and (4) welcome parents and other adults as allies. Finally, it is crucial that sex-education teachers offer examples of good character by the way they act and by the ideals and convictions they must be willing to articulate to students.

Bennett, William J. "Sex and the Education of Our Children," *Curriculum Review*, v27 n3 p7-12 Jan-Feb 1988.

Discusses the form and content of sex education courses in the classroom. Topics covered include contraception, decision making, morality, values, character formation, self-image, the role of teachers, and the role of parents.

Bertocci, Peter A. "The Search for Meaning in Adolescent Sexuality and Love," *Teachers College Record*, v84 n2 p379-90 Win 1982.

Sex education should articulate values as well as provide sexual information. A biomorphic explanation that stresses organic needs alone is insufficient for adolescents trying to cope with mature needs and emotions; instead, a psycho-organic- ethical foundation dealing with love and commitment is needed.

Evans, Abigail Rian. "Bearing One Another's Burdens," *Religious Education*, v83 n2 p170-89 Spr 1988.

Stating that educational campaigns are mandatory, prudent behavior required, and limited screening and quarantine recommended, Evans addresses two questions:

(1) Will a religiously based sexual ethic help prevent AIDS?
(2) How should we respond to the person with AIDS?
Concludes that religious education must replace fear of AIDS
with compassion.

Howe, Kenneth R. "AIDS Education in the Public
  Schools: Old Wine in New Bottles?" *Journal of
  Moral Education,* v19 n2 p114-23 May 1990.
    Investigates Acquired Immune Deficiency Syndrome
(AIDS) education in public schools, arguing that
preoccupation with sex education masks several problems
associated with AIDS education. Contends that
moral-political educational issues are renewed by the AIDS
problem. Identifies liberal and conservative positions on
AIDS education, showing their basis in explicit values.
Suggests procedures for curriculum development.

Klein, Daniel. "Sex Education: A Historical
  Perspective." 1983. 31 p. [ED 231 797]
    A review of literature on sex education in the schools
traces the changing opinions and attitudes on the subject
over the past century. Early sex education efforts (1880s to
1920s) in the schools focused upon the repression of sexual
activity, the prevention of immorality, hygiene, and
prevention of venereal diseases. A gradual movement (1940s
to 1950s) away from heavy emphasis on morality brought
new insights into the value of using sex education to
contribute to the long-term sexual adjustment of individuals
and a positive, rather than negative, approach toward
attitudes about sex. While the purely biological approach
toward sex education remained during the 1960s and 1970s,
opinions evolved on the role of the school in helping students
to make sound and responsible judgments, to deal with
sexual issues objectively, and to guide students in matters of
sexual morality as an integral dimension of their character
development. Present approaches to sex education indicate
that it is still in a period of growth and change. While
opposition remains to sex education in the schools, the
opposition, for the most part, represents a minority view.
Sex education programs need to continue to attempt to meet
the needs of society.

Sockett, Hugh; Alston, Kal. "Courage, Friendship and
  Character Education." Paper presented at the
  Annual Meeting of the American Educational
  Research Association, 1989. 26 p. [ED 307 692]
    This document explores the way in which courage, as a
central virtue, and friendship, as a valued human state,

have a significant place within the view of the education of character. Education of character is determined to bridge the gap between moral judgment and moral action. This paper has five sections. First, the need for character education is examined using the example of the failure of sex education. Second, the need for character education is approached from the academic context using the weakness-of-will issue to substantiate the need. The two contemporary perspectives on moral education (espoused by Lawrence Kohlberg and Barry Chazan) are discussed. Third, it is argued that friendship and courage are necessary elements of character education. Fourth and fifth, the development of courage and friendship is discussed. Appended are 20 references.

Stafford, J. Martin. "In Defense of Gay Lessons," *Journal of Moral Education*, v17 n1 p11-20 Jan 1988.

States that unwarranted negative attitudes toward homosexuality need to be countered by dissemination of correct information and constructive discussion. Urges moral educators to guide people toward, and foster respect for, caring and committed relationships whether they be homosexual or heterosexual.

Stronck, David R., Comp. *Discussing Sex in the Classroom: Readings for Teachers.* National Science Teachers Association, 1742 Connecticut Ave., NW, Washington, DC 20009. 1982. 98 p. [ED 243 681]

This reader provides teachers with background material on a range of sex-related subjects likely to surface in any classroom at every level, but particulary in middle or high-school science classrooms. The first section presents statements of the National Science Teachers Association supporting the right and responsibility of teachers to provide sex education. The second section provides articles which focus on the debate between advocates of sex education and its opponents as well as on the past and future role of sex education in schools. The third section develops the concept that an adequate sex education program can help students to clarify their values and to recognize personally as well as socially acceptable moral and ethical principles. At the same time, this section is designed to present practical examples of both content and technique to assist in the sensitive teaching task that sex education presents. Each article in this section stresses that adequate sex education consists of more than strictly biological information. The fourth section reinforces the need for teaching specific topics which sometimes are eliminated by censorship. Articles in this section focus on such topics as venereal disease, birth control, premarital sex, abortion, and homosexuality.

Went, Dilys J. "Sex Education and the School Curriculum: Some Issues For Discussion," *Westminster Studies in Education*, v11 p47-58 Nov 1988.

Identifies issues arising from the inclusion of sex education in the school curriculum. Issues range from the questions of content and organization to those concerning teaching based upon moral considerations. Examines the primary school and the secondary school's curriculum. Calls for a program that is realistically tailored to the needs of pupils.

Teaching *about* the World's Religions

Bergen, Timothy J., Jr.; Mi, Han Fu. "Teaching Islam to American High School Students," *Georgia Social Science Journal*, v19 n1 p11-20 Win 1988.

Presents a flexible two-week lesson unit for teaching high school students about Islam. Provides learning objectives and activities, as well as a bibliography of resources. Includes seven study guides which cover such topics as Islamic prophets, the Koran, Islamic morality, and Jihad.

Dilzer, Robert J., Jr. "Including the Study about Religions in the Social Studies Curriculum: A Position Statement and Guidelines." Paper presented at the Annual Meeting of the National Council for the Social Studies, 1984. 12 p. [ED 251 350]

Based on a National Council for the Social Studies position statement on the essentials of social studies, a rationale for teaching about religions in the social studies is presented. The author's rationale includes the following points: (1) that knowledge about religion is not only characteristic of an educated person but also necessary for understanding and living in a world of diversity, (2) that knowledge of religious differences and the role of religion in the contemporary world can help promote understanding and alleviate prejudice, (3) that omitting study about religions gives students the impression that religion has not been, and is not now, a significant part of the human experience, and (4) that knowledge of the religious dimension of human history and culture is needed for a balanced and comprehensive education. Following the rationale, supporting statements by Supreme Court Justice Tom Clark in the case of "Abington *versus* Schempp" and the concurring opinion of Justice William Brennan are quoted. Fourteen guidelines for the study of religion, nine course objectives for a semester-length course entitled "Religions of Man," and a course outline are presented. Course topics include: introduction to religious studies, Judaism, Zoroastrianism, Christianity, Islam, Hinduism, Buddhism, Jainism and Sikhism, Confucianism and Taoism, and Shinto. A bibliography listing over 50 books, periodicals, filmstrips, slide presentations, and organizations dealing with religious studies concludes the paper.

Dilzer, Robert J., Jr.; and others. *World Religions: A Curriculum Guide*. Newton Public Schools, CT. 1987. 45 p. [ED 299 184]

This curriculum guide is for a semester length elective course on the world's major religions designed to be used at the 10th-grade level in the Newtown Public Schools, Newton, Connecticut. It reviews each religion's origins, historical developments, sacred literature, beliefs, values, and practices while emphasizing the impact of religion on history, culture, contemporary issues and affairs, and the arts. The course units concern primitive religions, Judaism, Zoroastrianism, Christianity, Islam, Hinduism, Buddhism, Jainism, Sikhism, Taoism, Confucianism, and Shintoism. Outlined for each unit are objectives, content, text materials, audiovisual materials, and suggested activities. The document also contains a National Council for the Social Studies paper entitled "Including the Study about Religions in the Social Studies Curriculum: A Position Statement and Guidelines" ("Social Education," May 1985) and the following front matter: (1) a description of the Newton Public Schools Social Studies philosophy and goals; (2) Bloom's Taxonomy chart; (3) an outline of the components of the writing process; (4) a speaking, listening, and viewing skills position statement; (5) a list of speaking skills objectives; (6) a list of listening /viewing objectives; and (7) the K-12 Social Studies Scope and Sequence.

Galloway, Louis J. "Hinduism: A Unit for Junior High and Middle School Social Studies Classes." 1989. 12 p. [ED 322 075]

As an introduction and explanation of the historical development, major concepts, beliefs, practices, and traditions of Hinduism, this teaching unit provides a course outline for class discussion and activities for reading the classic epic, "The Ramayana." The unit requires 10 class sessions and uses slides, historical readings, class discussions, and filmstrips. Worksheets accompany the reading of this epic which serves as an introduction to Hinduism and some of its major concepts including (1) karma, (2) dharma, and (3) reincarnation.

Haynes, Charles C. "Resources for Teaching about Religion," *Educational Leadership*, v47 n3 p27 Nov 1989.

As more states mandate study about religions, educators now have support for including religion in the curriculum. To address religion's role in American history and culture, three new curriculum publications from the Wiliamsburg Charter Foundation, the National Council on Religious and Public Education, and the World Curriculum Development Center are described.

Johnson, Donald J.; Johnson, Jean E. *The Wheel of Life: Through Indian Eyes, Volume 1.* Revised Edition. Center for International Training and Education, 777 United Nations Plaza, Suite 9-H, New York, NY 10017. 1981. 154 p. [ED 210 241]

This book, which can be used in secondary and college courses, is the first of two volumes that present an Indian view of India and the world. The reality of everyday life as experienced by the Indian people is recreated in the series. Almost all of the material in both volumes has been written by Indians and has been taken from a variety of sources: autobiographies, fiction, poetry, newspaper and magazine articles, and historical documents. Volume one focuses on the most personal aspects of Indian life: family relations, marriage, caste membership, and religious beliefs. Each primary source selection is preceded by an editor's introduction that provides background information and a few questions for class discussion. Examples of selections include the following: Indian family life is compared with American family life. Ravi Shankar (the world famous sitar player) describes the ideal relationship between the student and his guru. One selection tells how an upper-class, well-educated family arranges the marriage of their eldest daughter. Dowries are the topic of one reading. In another, an Indian journalist analyzes the concept of woman power in India showing that the expectations for men and women are quite different. An Indian girl describes to her brother how their mother used stories to educate her. An imaginary conversation between an American teacher and an Indian businessman will help students understand the caste

system. Several readings attempt to clarify some of the
religious concepts of the Hindu way of life.

King, Ursula. "World Religions, Women and Education,"
Comparative Education, v23 n1 p35-49 1987.
Examines religious traditions—Hinduism, Buddhism,
Judaism, Islam, and Western Christianity—to see how
women were taught and what knowledge was transmitted to
them. Notes that women have always had some access to
religious knowledge in informal ways but were excluded
from formal education once sacred knowledge became
transmitted in an institutional manner.

Pellicano, Grace; Pellicano, Roy R. "A Mini Teaching
Sequence on the Totality of Islam," *Social Science
Record*, v24 n1 p29-31 Spr 1987.
Provides a secondary teaching unit on the Islamic
religious faith and government. Maintains that students
must understand the totality of Islam in order to make sense
of recent events in Egypt, Morocco, Tunisia, Nigeria, and the
Sudan. Included are complete teaching instructions and
necessary handouts.

Ring, Diane M. "Hindu Mythology: Gods, Goddesses and
Values." 1990. 24 p. [ED 329 506]
This unit on Hindu mythology is designed to help
secondary students see beyond the exotic elements of
another culture to the things its people have in common with
people in the West: a continuous effort to find a purpose in
existence, to explain the unknown, and to define good and
bad, right and wrong. Students are asked to analyze Hindu
religious stories in order to understand the Hindu worldview
and moral ideals, and then to compare them with their own
and those of the West. Five lessons are presented: (1) The
Hindu Triad (2) The Ramayana (3) The Image of Women (4)
Hindu Worship and (5) Religion: A Comparative Essay. For
each lesson a number of objectives are identified, several
activities are suggested, and the materials needed to
complete the lesson are listed. A 15-item bibliography also is
included in the document.

Sanneh, Lamin. *Source and Influence: A Comparative
Approach to African Religion and Culture*. Harvard
Univ., Cambridge, Mass. Graduate School of
Education. 1984. 29 p. [ED 254 479]
The importance of studying the primary context of the
relationship between "source" and "influence" in a
comparative science of religion and culture is emphasized

throughout this article. Focusing primarily on the situation in Muslim and Christian Africa, the article distinguishes between in-coming "sources" and indigenous "influences." Although it seems reasonable to consider how Christianity and Islam changed Africa, it is more consistent and critical to consider the effects Africa has had on the two religions. The issue of vernacular languages is seen as the key to the process of the transformation of Christianity and Islam in Africa. Comparisons between reactions to the language of the missionary as unsuitable for the expression of religion in African culture and reactions to the intrinsic untranslatability of the Islamic Koran are made. Specific examples drawn from the Akan and Hausa cultures and the Ibo (Nigeria), Wolof (Senegal), Mandika (Mali), and Swahili (Kenya) languages are presented. The paper concludes that (1) if borrowing takes place at all, it is on the basis of an original mutual attraction, (2) depending on the level of such mutual attraction, indigenous criteria act on the incoming materials by domesticating them, and (3) once assimilated, the new materials may act both to judge and justify the earlier materials. A passage from the travels of Sir Richard Burton is used as a concluding example of what African culture can do to foreign cultural materials.

Sefein, Naim A. "Islamic Beliefs and Practices," *Social Studies*, v72 n4 p158-64 Jul-Aug 1981.

To help social studies classroom teachers present a realistic picture of the Middle Eastern religion of Islam, this article presents an overview of major beliefs and religious practices of Muslims. Information is presented on religious fundamentals, Islam's relationship to Judaism and Christianity, the development of Islam, the role of women, and acts of worship.

Wires, Richard. "Islam: Basic Terms and Concepts," *Indiana Social Studies Quarterly*, v36 n1 p51-61 Spr 1983.

The news media constantly uses words and references that require specific knowledge and understanding if the public is to grasp the substance and implications of events and developments concerning the Islamic religion. Most frequently encountered Islamic terms and ideas are explained.

Values Curriculum

Bell, Darnell. *Winners: A Culturally-Based, Values Clarification-Oriented, Creative Writing Primary Prevention Workbook for the Black Child. Volume I.*

Darnell Bell, 1576 East King Jr. Blvd., Los Angeles, CA 90011. 1987. 153 p. [ED 296 783]

Providing a substance-abuse prevention curriculum that is designed to be culturally relevant to black youth, this workbook provides 102 creative writing activities promoting self-esteem, values clarification, feelings validation, cultural awareness, and decision-making skills. Each of the 11 sections of the workbook are organized around positive qualities of role models for black youth: (1) the assertiveness of Maxine Waters; (2) the blues of B. B. King; (3) the creativity of William "Count" Basie; (4) the devotion of Frederick Douglass; (5) the eloquence of Jesse Jackson; (6) the fearlessness of Bishop Desmond Tutu; (7) the glamor of Queen Cleopatra; (8) the humor of Bill Cosby; (9) the inventiveness of Benjamin Bannecker; (10) the judgment of Thurgood Marshall; and (11) the kingliness of Dr. Martin Luther King. Each section provides a brief biographical sketch and worksheets for writing exercises.

Beller, Edward. "Education for Character: An Alternative to Values Clarification and Cognitive Moral Development Curricula," *Journal of Educational Thought,* v20 n2 p67-76 Aug 1986.

Discusses the weaknesses inherent in Sidney Simon's values clarification method and Lawrence Kohlberg's cognitive moral development method, suggesting that single-class, isolated instruction overlooks the affective, unconscious elements of character formation. Recommends an alternative, holistic approach based on John Locke's concept of all education as education for character development.

Burton, Grace M. "Values Clarification for Pre-Service Teachers: A Basic," *Contemporary Education,* v53 n1 p39-42 Fall 1981.

Values clarification activities help preservice teachers understand their own values while developing activities which might be used in their own classrooms. Exercises are described which serve to orient the students to the teaching profession while presenting the philosophical, historical, and sociological foundations of education.

Dunbar, Louise H. "The Utilization of Values Clarification in Multicultural Education as a Strategy to Reduce Prejudicial Attitudes of Eighth Grade Students." Ed.D. Dissertation, Northern Arizona University. 1980. 129 p. [ED 221 643]

This study investigated the impact of values clarification in multicultural education as a teaching strategy to reduce racial and ethnic bias and prejudices against older people, women, and the handicapped among eighth graders at the Meadowbrook Middle School, Poway Unified School District, California. The study also examined students' general attitudes toward school. Before the workshop, social-science teachers participated in a workshop on developing and implementinq multicultural education units and teaching strategies. An assessment survey of students' multicultural attitudes was administered to the Meadowbrook subjects and to a control group, before and after the values clarification program. Results indicated that the values clarification strategy, as the experimental "treatment," did not significantly reduce students' racial/ethnic prejudices or alter their attitudes toward school, although it improved students' ability to clarify their own attitudes and perceptions toward other ethnic groups. Initially positive attitudes toward the elderly, women, and the handicapped remained unchanged after the treatment. Male and female differences in attitudes and values were attributed to differences that existed before the treatment. No differences in attitude changes were found among the ethnic groups in the sample.

Howell, Joe A.; Eidson, Donald. *A New Agenda: Building Colleges with Values*. A New Agenda, Central Methodist College, Fayette, Missouri 65248. 1990. 149 p. [ED 327 087]

The argument is made that the institutional mission of colleges and universities can be used as the agent for social progress and a vehicle for bettering the human condition. The development, implementation, and benefits of institutional missions in which faculty members and students grapple in a sustained way with what it means, personally, educationally, and professionally, to teach and learn at an institution where its mission is taken seriously are explored. Two themes run throughout the discussion: (1) Institutions of higher learning must have a clear and definitive mission, must insure that the mission is pervasive, and must have specific, well-funded programs to insure its success (2) There must be a planned program to put a consideration of values into the curriculum and student life of an institution. It is suggested that governing boards mandate that a mission core exist, that there be a core of experiences for all students both in and out of the classroom, and that students understand the context in which they are studying. It is further noted that once the policy is in place, the faculty must implement it under the direction and leadership of the president.

Leach, Mary S.; Page, Ralph C. "Why Home Economics Should Be Morally Biased," *Illinois Teacher of Home Economics*, v30 n5 p169-74 May-Jun 1987.

The authors argue that the home-economics curriculum should be designed to help students deal with the conflicting values of family and career, which the authors see as a major force behind gender discrimination and inequality of the sexes.

Leming, James S. "School Curriculum and Social Development in Early Adolescence," *Childhood Education*, v61 n4 p257-63 Mar-Apr 1985.

Reviews research on the effect of school climate on the social development of early adolescents and on three curricular programs (values clarification, moral development, and cooperative learning). Concludes that schools can positively influence socio-moral development through non-traditional schooling, i.e., open and democratic environments, discussions of moral dilemmas, and cooperative learning activities.

Morrow, S. Rex. "Values and Moral Education: Revisited," *Southern Social Studies Quarterly*, v14 n1 p31-36 Fall 1988.

Examines changes in social-studies education from the late 1960s into 1980s, stating that it is important to teach about social issues using some form of values clarification. Advocates the use of these methods so that students may effectively confront challenges such as Acquired Immune Deficiency Syndrome, drug abuse, alcoholism, sex education/safe sex, and other major social issues.

Moy, Caryl T. "From Divergent Lifestyles to Professional Issues: Fifteen Years with a University Sexuality Course," *Teaching Sociology*, v15 n3 p263-67 Jul 1987.

Describes a college course on human sexuality, its goals and evolution. Includes a section on student enrollment, student reasons for taking the course, and a discussion of goals and techniques for human sexuality instruction.

Odom, John G. "The Status of Ethics Instruction in the Health Education Curriculum," *Health Education*, v19 n4 p9-12 Aug-Sep 1988.

A survey on the preparation that preservice health educators receive in the ethics of health education, revealed that required courses involving ethics, morals, or values were offered infrequently. Suggestions are made for incorporating ethics instruction in the health-education curriculum.

Pratte, Richard. *The Civic Imperative: Examining the Need for Civic Education. Advances in Contemporary Educational Thought Series, Volume 3.* Teachers College Press, 1234 Amsterdam Ave., New York, New York 10027. 1988. 198 p. [ED 303 412]

Students should be taught civic competence, values, and dispositions; and skills needed for a democratic society should be acquired through formal education. U.S. schools must teach moral and civic values consciously, yet these values should be taught beyond civics and values clarification courses. The narrow focus of this type of course is to make good citizens, not develop good people; but the idea behind civic education should be that good people will make good citizens. The ideal values to be learned include respect for all people, belief in human dignity, concern for others, justice, fairness, tolerance, caring, and commitment to reflective reasoning, while the good citizen lives an ethic of obligation and service to others. This concept of citizenship and democracy reflects the thought of John Dewey and other contemporary theorists. The chapter titles are (1) "The State of Civic Education Today" (2) "Two Democratic Philosophical Traditions" (3) "The Moral Dimensions of Philosophical Civic Republicanism" (4) "Democracy, Citizenship, and Community Service" (5) "Social Heterogeneity and E Pluribus Unum" (6) "Civic Competence." A 104-item bibliography concludes the document.

Stradling, Bob. "Controversial Issues in the Curriculum," *Bulletin of Environmental Education*, n170 p9-13 Jul 1985.

Reviews the problems and benefits associated with instruction of controversial issues, questioning the effectiveness of a neutral and objective position in the discussion of controversial topics. Also assesses prevalent teacher tendencies in instructional approaches and offers suggestions for classroom adoption.

Values in the English Classroom

Alfonsa, Regina. "Modules for Teaching about Young People's Literature—Module 3: Values Children Can Learn from Picture Books," *Journal of Reading*, v30 n4 p299-301 Jan 1987.

Offers a teaching method to help teachers focus on important values embodied in a children's book, and the ability of children to grasp the book's lesson either independently or with assistance. Lists children's picture books expressing values.

Bogdan, Deanne. "A Case Study of the Selection/Censorship Problem and the Educational Value of Literature," *Journal of Education*, v170 n2 p39-57 1988.

A rebellion against a given work of literature in a course on women's literature and feminist criticism appeared to function as censorship. Raised the following questions: (1) Censorship and the selection of literature; (2) The literary *versus* the stock response; and (3) Humanistic assumptions underlying the educational value of literature.

Christenbury, Leila. "Teaching Poetry/Exploring Values," *English Journal*, v73 n8 p60-61 Dec 1984.

Reviews new publications dealing with the teaching of poetry and the consideration of values in the language-arts classroom.

"Facets: The Role of the English Teacher in the Development of Moral Values," *English Journal*, v74 n8 p14-17 Dec 1985.

Four teachers offer definitions, experiences, and opinions relating to the teaching of moral values in the classroom.

Fuchs, Lucy. "Religion as a Source of Strength or Weakness in Young Adult Literature." Paper presented at the Annual Meeting of the National Council of Teachers of English, 1990. 10 p. [ED 326 869]

A survey of books for young people reveals that some of the best (and even award-winning) novels deal with the controversial issue of religion. Although most of these books deal with religion only in the background, some clearly present this issue in the forefront. One book, Cynthia Rylant's "A Fine White Dust" (1986), traces a religious quest. In this story the reader sees a young man, at the end of the seventh grade, making a revival which will change his life.

The pattern is a rather common one—when religion is portrayed as a sincere faith or relationship with God, it is usually seen as a positive benefit. When churches or religious leaders are portrayed, their image is often negative, as seen in *Is That You, Miss Blue?* by M. E. Kerr. Organized religion as experienced in a religious school is a sham compared to the true religious experience of the heroine. *Beyond the Chocolate War* (1985) by Robert Cormier and *Tree by Leaf* (1988) by Cynthia Voight are representative of novels that depict the suffering of religious people in their quest for personal meaning. These and other books show the hunger for God and the search for spiritual meaning in life present in young people, and, as such, are worthy of study. (A list of 10 religious books for adolescents is attached.)

Gambell, Trevor J. "Choosing the Literature We Teach," *English Quarterly*, v19 n2 p99-107 Sum 1986.

Discusses the teachers' and the students' roles in the selection of literature to be taught, developing a selection policy, the place of the classics in literature curriculum, and the connection between literature and values education.

Garver, Eugene. "Teaching Writing and Teaching Virtue," *Journal of Business Communication*, v22 n1 p51-73 Win 1985.

Explores the analogy between teaching writing and teaching virtue, and concludes that teaching writing with its focus on practical reasoning and prudence is bound up in similar ways with teaching moral goodness.

Greenlaw, M. Jean. "Science Fiction as Moral Literature," *Educational Horizons*, v65 n4 p165-66 Sum 1987.

The author discusses the use of science fiction as a catalyst for values education for adolescents.

Haddon, John. "Finding Value in Shakespeare," *Use of English*, v41 n3 p13-21 Sum 1990.

Calls for a curriculum that uses the plays of Shakespeare to teach human values. Suggests that attention to certain moments within Shakespeare's plays may enhance or refine the understanding of moral qualities. Acknowledges that some critics would deny that those values are universal or eternal.

Hickey, M. Gail. "Folk Literature as a Vehicle for Values Education," *Social Studies and the Young Learner*, v2 n3 p6-8 Jan-Feb 1990.

Recognizes the necessity to develop a values curriculum. Advocates using folktales (myths, legends, fables) to teach values to elementary students in a manner nonthreatening to parents. Provides examples of appropriate fables and folktales and their morals. Cites two sources to help teachers guide children in their moral development through folk literature.

Hollingworth, Brian. "Crisis in English Teaching," *Use of English*, v34 n2 p3-8 Spr 1983.

Suggests that structuralist arguments in the teaching of English question the ideology that has traditionally informed the study of literature—the very idea that such a study is a "humane" activity.

Kazemek, Frances E. "Literature and Moral Development from a Feminine Perspective," *Language Arts*, v63 n3 p264-72 Mar 1986.

Explores the relationships between children's literature and moral development. Discusses characteristics of a "female morality" and why such a perspective is important. Describes some children's books that exemplify this perspective; offers suggestions for their use to help children develop morally as well as cognitively and socially.

Knafle, June D.; and others. "Assessing Values in Children's Books," *Reading Improvement*, v25 n1 p71-81 Spr 1988.

Reports the development of a scale to assess values in children's books. Applies the scale to Caldecott winners from 1938 to 1986. Concludes that the scale could be useful for research purposes or teacher training classroom exercises.

Knafle, June D.; and others. "Values in American and Hispanic Children's Readers." 1989. 27 p. [ED 311 406]

A study was conducted to assess the values presented in American and Hispanic-American children's readers. The categories of primary interest on the values scale used include positive behavior, positive feelings, negative behavior, negative feelings, traditional values, Judeo-Christian religious values, other religious values, and neutral values. The values scale was applied to two widely used basal reader series, Scott Foresman and Houghton Mifflin, grades one-four, and to seven Hispanic basal reader series of variable grade levels through grade four presently used in the Chicago area. An examination of the findings revealed noticeable differences between the two American series in the categories of neutral values, positive feelings, positive behavior, and negative feelings. The stories found in the Hispanic basal readers included values that have religious and traditional moralistic overtones along with very idealistic family values and roles. On the other hand, negative behavior was also presented, such as being drunk, fighting, and treating people cruelly. The Hispanic series examined were very much in accord with Hispanic culture, especially concerning Judeo-Christian religious values and traditional values, so these values are much more prescriptive in the Hispanic series than in the American series. While it seems that the American publishers have gone to a great deal of trouble not to be offensive to any group in a pluralistic society, such is not the case with the Hispanic basal readers. (Five tables of data are included and 18 references are attached.)

Leonard, Lana S. "Storytelling as Experiential Education," *Journal of Experiential Education*, v13 n2 p12-17 Aug 1990.

The American Indian teaching tale "Jumping Mouse" is used to illustrate how storytelling can provide a learning experience—the listener's active participation in the storytelling process through emotional engagement and creative imagination, and the resulting change in perspective and clarification of values.

Lepman-Logan, Claudia. "Moral Choices in Literature (Books in the Classroom)," *Horn Book Magazine*, v65 n1 p108-11 Jan-Feb 1989.

Describes several books for junior-high-school students that focus on moral choices. Asserts that books with moral choices that have no clear-cut solutions will stimulate classroom discussion.

Mackey, Gerald. "Teaching Values and Values Clarification in the English Classroom," *Exercise Exchange*, v32 n2 p39-41 Spr 1987.

Presents a rationale and framework for teaching values using high-quality works of literature.

Moline, Jon. "The Moral of the Story," *American Educator: The Professional Journal of the American Federation of Teachers*, v7 n1 p25-30 Spr 1983.

Reviews "The Moral of the Story: Literature, Values, and American Education," by Susan Resneck Parr. Discusses the problem that teachers face when dealing with moral themes in literature taught in the classroom.

Pradl, Gordon. "Games of Chance, Games of Choice," *English in Australia*, n81 p16-25 Sep 1987.
Suggests that while teachers may wish to guide students in their reading of literature—to give them only "good" literature and to help them see the "right" interpretations of it—such guidance leaves students' understanding to chance, and does not help them choose to think and construct values of their own.

Prothero, James. "Fantasy, Science Fiction, and the Teaching of Values," *English Journal*, v79 n3 p32-34 Mar 1990.
Addresses two misunderstandings about science fiction and fantasy: that fantastic literature is not serious; that modern scientific civilization neither has nor needs mythology. Argues that values can be transmitted through science fiction and fantasy, which are modern-day forms of mythology.

Storey, Dee C. "A Legacy of Values: War in Literature for Adolescents," *Social Studies*, v76 n2 p85-88 Mar-Apr 1985.
By reading literature about wars, secondary students can learn about the values of different cultures and societies. Teaching approaches are suggested, and specific titles are discussed.

Sullivan, Emilie P.; Yandell, Carol. "What Are the Religious/Spiritual Values in Children's Books? Do Children Get the Values Messages?" Paper presented at the Annual Meeting of the American Reading Forum, 1990. 34 p. [ED 328 884]
A study investigated the religious and spiritual values in selected children's books. A second study investigated children's comprehension of the values messages. Thirty realistic fiction books which won, or were honor books for, the John Newbery Medals for 1974-1988 were selected. A modified version of the Values Category Scale was developed, including five categories: negative religious, non-religious, humanistic, Christian-Judeo religious, and other religious. A panel of 5 experts in children's literature, 3 educational library media specialists, and 2 children's literature professors read and independently evaluated all 30 books. Results indicated that 24 of the books had non-religious content while only 7 of the books had Christian-Judeo content exceeding 25%. Results also indicted that historical fiction works were more likely to

contain religious values than contemporary fiction works. In the second study, 8 children's librarians in northwest Arkansas selected a total of 29 Newbery Award books and identified specific spiritual values in those books. Thirty-five third- through sixth-grade students voluntarily read a total of 21 of the titles chosen by the librarians. The students were then interviewed to discover what spiritual values they recognized, and whether they identified the same values as the librarians. Results indicated that (1) the librarians and the children were able to identify a wide range of spiritual values in the books; (2) librarians chose stories emphasizing family relationships, love of parents, family unity, or the need for children to experience a loving and supportive, traditional or non-traditional, family unit; and (3) in those books conveying spiritual values that adults interpret as having religious significance, child readers focused only on the value in a non-religious connotation. (Eight tables of data are included; 37 references are attached.)

Taylor, Anne. "What Shall We Tell the Children?" *Emergency Librarian*, v.15 n3 p9-15 Jan-Feb 1988.

Discusses the use of adolescent literature in the English curriculum as an appropriate forum for exploring the moral and social values of sexuality. Several books that deal with sexuality and homosexuality are reviewed; criteria for reading material selection are discussed. A reading list is provided. (8 references)

Teplitsky, Alan. "Life, Literature, and Character: Some Cornerstone Principles." Paper presented at the Annual Meeting of the National Council of Teachers of English, Spring Conference, 1987. 86 p. [ED 312 643)

There is a widely felt need to do something in education about the moral wasteland of contemporary American society. It is appropriate for English teachers to posit some usable dimensions of moral education. Seven cornerstone principles appear to be universally involved both in the lives of literary characters and in the kind of heart-deep character development which educators try to nurture in students through the English curriculum. The seven principles are design, authority, conscience, love, power, destiny, and wisdom. The principles suggest a possible thematic scope and sequence for a complete literature curriculum, both within and between grade levels. Within each grade level the central theme could be examined in the light of each of the other principles. Presented in this way, the cornerstone principles would generate a kind of spiral curriculum of morally educative units, each year adding to the students' understanding of important social and ethical values. Year after year, they can be engaged in a vital and personal experiencing of literature, be asked questions that require them to come to grips with some universal principles of character, and be motivated towards an active involvement in solving personal and community problems. A series of exercises revolving around Shakespeare's *Hamlet* illustrate how the cornerstone principles can be applied. Educators must recognize that character development is a lifelong process, and that there are more key factors outside the classroom than in it. (One figure is included; two extensive appendices containing a character- development ladder and a detailed examination of the cornerstone principles; and 82 endnotes are attached.)

"The Literature Center: Using Good Books to Explore Children's Concerns," *Learning*, v19 n3 p71-73 Oct 1990.

Stories can help teachers give children models and mores for reflection and growth. Suggests specific books that deal with lying; provides guidelines for class discussion.

"The Round Table," *English Journal*, v76 n8 p55-58 Dec 1987.

Nine secondary English teachers articulate their teaching philosophy as they answer the question: "Should English teachers be involved in the teaching of values in the classroom? If so, how?"

Tyack, David B.; James, Thomas. "Moral Majorities and the School Curriculum: Historical Perspectives on the Legalization of Virtue," *Teachers College Record*, v86 n4 p513-37 Sum 1985.

As the United States became urban, industrialized, and heterogeneous a century ago, politically powerful groups decided that state laws must mandate their values in public schools. This article describes three crusades: for temperance instruction, for compulsory Bible reading and the banning of Darwin, and for patriotic rituals and Americanization.

Wade, Barrie; Sheppard, John. "Marx in Narnia," *Use of English*, v40 n3 p51-58 Sum 1989.

Argues that teachers must understand the different values found in children's literature. Examines four aspects of values present in C. S. Lewis's "Chronicles of Narnia." Asserts that teachers must take responsibility for how such texts are received by young readers in the current multicultural, sexually equal society.

Warshaw, Thayer S. "The Bible as Textbook in Public Schools," *Religion & Public Education*, v17 n1 p127-38 Win 1990.

Offers approaches for using the Bible as a textbook in literature, social studies, history, and humanities classes, based on the author's "Handbook for Teaching the Bible in English Classes." Recommends that creationism not be included in the science curriculum, and that teachers be trained for sensitivity to student pluralism. Comments on relevant U.S. Supreme Court opinions.

Wicks, Robert S. *Morality and the Schools*. Occasional Paper 32. Council for Basic Education, 725 15th Street, NW, Washington, DC 20005. 1981. 27 p. [ED 210 246]

Moral contradictions and cross purposes in society make formal moral training in the schools difficult, if not impossible. Values clarification and school-wide programs of moral education are of questionable merit. Nevertheless, effective moral education is implicit in teaching the subjects that comprise good basic education. A mathematics teacher, for example, might encourage students to think of the ways data are gathered and organized. She might have a student discuss the moral implications of gathering information through computers. Science teachers might make students aware of the values that determine the way science is done—its openness to new formulations of reality, or the rigorous testing of theories before they are accepted. English teachers have a wealth of material that provides models of human conduct, writing about conduct good and bad, and reflections on how people change as they gain insight, or suffer, or discover how their behavior affects the lives of others. History and social studies teachers might fill some of the gaps and omissions in the customary accounts of our past. They need to remind their students that what is chosen to be studied reflects a point of view that screens out more than it admits. The arts are one of the best vehicles for the transmission of values. For example, Golden Age sculpture and architecture provide a chance to teach the ancient Greek's moral vision of balance and proportion. It is morally imperative to bring young people and adults together in cooperative association outside the classroom.

Willinsky, John. "Recalling the Moral Force of Literature in Education," *Journal of Educational Thought*, v22 n2 p118-32 Aug 1988.
Reviews the arguments of Matthew Arnold, F. R. Leavis, and Louise Rosenblatt for making literature a mainstay of education. Defends the moral and educational value of literature in both its aesthetic and testimonial aspects.

Yeazell, Mary I.; Cole, Robyn R. "The Adolescent Novel and Moral Development: A Demurrer," *Journal of Reading*, v29 n4 p292-98 Jan 1986.
Argues that carefully selected, adolescent novels can foster young people's moral development and describes the four essential characteristics that such books should display: a moral dilemma, identified alternatives, moral reasoning, and a moral decision.

Do You Have An Idea to Share?

Research to Report?

A Cause to Champion?

This excellent book was copublished by the ERIC Clearinghouse on Reading and the Communication Skills, a unit within the U.S. Department of Education's farflung network of information processing for everyone interested in education, and by the National Council of Teachers of English.

At ERIC/RCS, we are always looking for high-quality manuscripts having to do with teaching English, the language arts, reading, writing, speech, theater, mass communication, the media, personal communication, thinking, literature, and literacy. We publish original research and scholarship, teaching guides and practical applications for educators and others who work with youth. In conjunction with EDINFO Press and our other partners in education information, such as the National Council of Teachers of English, we publish books of all kinds within the field of education.

Do you have a novel understanding of some timely issue, an innovative approach to a troubling problem, or an especially effective method of teaching? Does one of your colleagues have something burning to say on curriculum development, professionalism in education, excellence in teaching, or some other aspect of schooling? If so, let us know. We'd like to hear from you. Tell us that reading this book gave you an incentive to get in touch.

Contact:

Warren Lewis
Assistant Director, Publications
ERIC/RCS
Smith Research Center, Suite 150
Bloomington, IN 47408-2698
812/855-5847
800/759-4723
BITNET% WWLEWIS@IUBACS

Values Clarification through Teaching Literature

Values Clarification through Teaching Literature, by Margaret Dodson, was designed specifically as a companion volume to accompany the discussion between Charles and Bernard Suhor, *Teaching Values in the Literature Classroom: A Debate in Print.* The ERIC database was searched for teaching strategies, particularly about the pieces of literature that the Suhors touched upon in their exchanges, including, among others, *The Catcher in the Rye, Hamlet, Huckleberry Finn, The Odyssey, The Bible,* and *1984.*

Beyond these, Dodson included many other kinds of writing to offer an extensive range of possibilities from which teachers may build their own courses for teaching values by reading and discussing literature: among these, folk literature, student autobiography, Native American and other ethnic literature, poetry, and a special section on the mentally retarded in literature and in fact. All reading levels, from beginners to sophisticates, are represented, but because "good literature is universal," the values discussed in reference to each piece of literature are valid for any reader who can understand the literature. These lesson suggestions can be tailored to most students' reading levels in any grade in middle or secondary school.

An introductory section "especially for teachers" gives directions on setting up a program in values clarification through literature, offers advice from a Kohlbergian perspective on teaching values in sensitivity to students' respective "stages of moral reasoning," and supplies the teacher with all kinds of starters, activities, and ideas. For writing classes as well as reading and literature classes, several lessons involve students in exploring values through "writing to learn"—by writing about their own values as a way of finding out what they think and feel and believe.

Values Clarification through Teaching Literature, by Margaret Dodson (T13) $16.95.

In *A High School Student's Bill of Rights*, by Stephen S. Gottlieb, an Indiana prosecuting attorney puts into perspective the liberties and limitations under the law of high-school students and other legal minors. Students, like grown-ups, are citizens with rights, but students' rights are limited so long as they are "underaged" and under the care of their parents and school authorities. They have freedom of speech in school assembly, but not completely; their lockers are protected from search and seizure, but not entirely; they have the right to publish their opinions in the school newspaper, but not if the principal says no.

Gottlieb draws on three major documents in testimony to our basic rights: The U.S. Constitution and its "Bill of Rights," the Northwest Ordinance of 1787, and the U.N. Declaration of Universal Human Rights. He interprets these basic statements according to the process of judicial refinement that has arisen in the courts through lawsuits and other contests over civil rights.

❖ Must students be "Mirandized?"
❖ May students be frisked in the hall?
❖ May a student speaker talk dirty in the school assembly?
❖ Do teachers have the right to paddle school kids?
❖ Who controls which books go into the school library?
❖ Is religion really outlawed in schools?
❖ May the principal abridge freedom of the school press?
❖ What are the rights of a student who has been suspended?
❖ What is the legal status of Black v. White at school?
❖ Do we really *have* to go to school?

Gottlieb structures his approach to the history, law, and concern for rights and freedoms in terms of critical reading, critical thinking, and critical writing--an across-the-curriculum workbook for English teachers and reading-and-writing specialists, history, social-studies, and civics teachers.

A High School Student's Bill of Rights, by Stephen S. Gottlieb (T09) $14.95; foreword by John J. Patrick, Director, ERIC/ChESS.

Ship to:

Name _____

Address _____

_____

City_____State_____ ZIP _____

Phone (_____) _____

Item No.	Quantity	Abbreviated Title	Price	Total Cost
			$	
			$	
			$	
			$	
			$	
			$	
Minimum money order or check			Subtotal	
order $5.00			Plus Postage and Handling	
Minimum credit card order $10.00			TOTAL Purchase	

Method of Payment

❏ check ❏ money order

❏ P.O. # _____

❏ MasterCard ❏ VISA

cardholder _____

card no. _____

expiration date_____

Make checks payable to ERIC/RCS.

Order Subtotal	Postage/Handling
$5.00 - $10.00	$2.00
$10.01 - $25.00	$3.00
$25.01 - $50.00	$4.00
$50.01 - $75.00	$5.00
$75.01 - $100.00	$6.00
$100.01 - $125.00	$7.00
$125.01 - $150.00	$8.00
over $150.00	$9.00

Send order form to:
ERIC/RCS
Indiana University
2805 E. 10th Street, Suite 150
Bloomington, IN 47408-2698
(800) 759-4723
FAX (812) 855-4220